D0489026

RESEARCH
CLASSICS

Information – A Prescription
against Pain

Prescription for Recovery

RESEARCH
CLASSICS

FROM
THE ROYAL COLLEGE OF NURSING

Information –
A Prescription
against Pain

JACK HAYWARD

Prescription
for Recovery

JENNIFER R.P. BOORE

Scutari Press • London

Scutari Press

Viking House, 17–19 Peterborough Road,
Harrow, Middlesex HA1 2AX, England

A subsidiary of Scutari Projects, the publishing company of the Royal College of Nursing

First published 1994

British Library Cataloguing in Publication Data:

Hayward, Jack
  RCN Research Classics. – (RCN Research
  Series)
  I. Title   II. Boore, Jennifer R. P.
  III. Series
  610.73072

ISBN 1–873853–03–3

Reprinted by Intype, London

Information —
A Prescription
Against Pain

JACK HAYWARD

Ph.D., B.Sc., S.R.N., R.M.N., R.N.T.

Dip. Nursing

List of Contents

SECTION I – THEORETICAL CONSIDERATIONS

SECTION II – THE PILOT STUDY

SECTION III – THE MAIN STUDY

APPENDICES

List of Tables and Figures

4

Acknowledgements

The author would like to thank all those concerned with the Study of Nursing Care project for their help and support whilst this study was being carried out.

In particular, thanks are due to Professor D. E. G. Plowman of the London School of Economics and Political Science, who acted as Academic Supervisor for the study on which this report is based.

Thanks are due also to the staff of the hospitals concerned for their unfailing patience and generosity.

J. C. Hayward

Preface

This study is one of 12 undertaken as part of the research project "The Study of Nursing Care" sponsored by the Department of Health and Social Security, and administered by the Royal College of Nursing and National Council of Nurses of the United Kingdom.

The main objective of the Project was to develop techniques of measuring the effectiveness of nursing care in general hospitals. Earlier work and some of the conceptual and practical problems faced by the team are discussed in *The Proper Study of the Nurse*, McFarlane, J. K., 1970, Rcn, London.

Nurses appointed to work with the Project as Research Assistants each selected one aspect of nursing care and used a variety of methods to study their topic in depth. Some of these methods are now being refined with a view to being incorporated in a scale of effective nursing care.

The individual studies in isolation, therefore, do not achieve the main objective of the Project. Though laying the foundations of more extensive work, individual studies were not designed to stand alone. They all, however, contribute factual information about the practice of nursing as observed by the authors, and their discussion by nurses in hospitals and units could stimulate improvement in nursing care. It is for this reason that the individual studies are being published.

Dr. Hayward's study proves that relevant information given to patients expecting an operation substantially reduces their post-operative pain and anxiety. General friendliness, although desirable, is no substitute for factual information and the author's information schedule might well be adapted to other aspects of nursing care.

The experimental design of the study is unique in the present series and should prove of outstanding interest to nurse researchers.

U. Inman
December, 1974

Introduction

Until very recently professional judgement was undisputed in deciding standards of nursing care. This compares very unfavourably with the example set by Florence Nightingale who was scathing in her condemnation of lack of sound evidence, and who was, as Knopf (1961) indicates, a considerable statistician. Such was her influence in nursing circles, and so devoted her followers that a type of "prestige model" of nursing practice evolved which influenced thoughts and policy within the profession long after the situations which Florence Nightingale faced had disappeared, and which she herself would have deplored. This rigidity is clearly brought out in the following extract:

> Obedience came to be regarded as a virtue in itself. It was retained as part of the nursing ethic long after the individual and social circumstance which had determined its importance had disappeared. The nurse had learned never to ask "why" and as rarely as possible "how". The spirit of enquiry had been effectively checked. Simpson (1971).

Professional judgements still play a major role in the determination of nursing standards, and they may play an important part in defining target areas. In the final analysis however, they lack direct indices of quality in what is perhaps the ultimate criterion, namely patient welfare.

It was following the fairly recent interest in objective indices of nursing care that the "Study of Nursing Care" project was set up, with the important aim of producing research findings which will lead to improvements in patient care.

There are other reasons why research into nursing is important, not the least of these being the effects on the nursing profession itself. With increased public awareness and expectations of the National Health Service, any steps which lead to improvements in hospital care will reflect upon a wide range of factors appertaining to nursing.

There is also evidence of changing public attitudes to health care (Cartwright, 1964; Wieland and Leigh, 1971). It is now 27 years since the National Health Service was formed, and the proportion of the population who remember the "charity bed" days continues to fall. The rise in patient welfare associations, and official recognition that patients have a right to complain (Carstairs, 1970), imply that no longer is the patient "seen, but not heard" but is tending to develop a consumer attitude to health care.

For many years nursing has been a "service oriented" career, admirably following tradition and with little attention being paid to individual aims and aspirations. Greater attention to personal needs in the industrial situation has led to increased job-satisfaction and productivity in almost all sectors of industry (Brown, 1954), but there is little evidence of a similar change in attitudes by leaders of the nursing profession (Hubert, 1967). Some of these factors have been documented by MacGuire (1966) in a study of nurse recruitment and selection. It is logical to expect that the findings from other areas would apply equally to nurses and that greater attention to the individual needs of nurses would be favourably reflected in higher standards of patient care. Research which could identify a body of specifically "nursing" knowledge and expertise would therefore help to foster this desirable state.

A major aim in any research is to see findings reflected in the relevant educational system. This is especially so in nurse education where, at present a minimal amount of source-based material is taught. Nursing is also unlike other professions in that, in the main, nursing research is performed outside and independent of the teaching situation. This can result in serious long-term delays in feeding-back research findings into the education of nurses.

A key question for the intending researcher is to define the area of investigation within feasible limits. Several authors, after reviewing large-scale organizational studies (e.g. Wieland and Leigh, 1971) have stressed the need for small-scale detailed investigations of specific areas. With reference to nursing:

> There would appear to be a value in studies of individual phenomena of nursing, particularly in the clinical care area. These could help to isolate factors of quality in small, perhaps critical areas. McFarlane (1970).

The purpose of the present study is to examine the effects of giving information to patients about events leading up to, and following, a surgical operation, and to attempt an evaluation of this procedure in terms of appropriate dependent variables associated with patient welfare.

As few precedents exist for this type of experimental research in British hospitals there was little background experience to draw upon. The literature review is necessarily selective as three major areas are involved, i.e. pain, anxiety and information, not to mention the complex interrelations between them.

It is hoped that this study will make a contribution to the total body of nursing research in that it will examine the nature and sources of patients' pain, fears and anxieties. It will look at some of the relationships between pain and anxiety, and the effects of information on both of these. It is hoped to gain some further insight into underlying processes which affect patients' welfare, and to make a contribution towards evolving a patient care policy which will allow the most rapid recovery to take place under optimal conditions.

SECTION I

Theoretical Considerations

CHAPTER 1

The Concept of Pain

Problems abound in any attempt to define the pain experience. The well-known statement of Lewis (1942) that pain is:

> Known to us by experience and described by illustration

cogently summarizes the situation facing the would-be definer.

The problem of finding an appropriated terminology is inherent in any discussion of behavioural phenomena which involve both sensory and feeling states; pain forms no exception as many philosphers have admitted.

> Joy and pain like other simple ideas cannot be described or their names defined. Like other sensory ideas we can get to know them only by experience (John Locke, *Essays Concerning Human Understanding*).

With the rare exceptions of individuals who seem unable to feel pain everyone knows what pain is but no one can adequately describe it, and, when this problem is extended to experimental investigation, the difficulties become abundantly clear.

Such a phenomenon, involving both physical sensations and feeling states, raises the issue common to all experiences of this type, namely, the relationship between physical processes and conscious awareness. If pain has a physical component which operates via the central nervous system (and few would deny this), then where, how, and when does this physical input become translated into consciousness? This problem is familiar to students of human behaviour as the *body/mind relationship*. It is beyond the scope of this work to examine these issues extensively but a brief mention is not amiss.

The position adopted by medical authors on the body/mind problem varies with the nature of the speciality and the topic under scrutiny, but in general they have tended to describe two categories, physical pain and mental pain. This type of division into mental and physical components is usually known as *dualism*.

Although the majority of medical writers on pain accept dualism, this acceptance is by no means general among philosophers and psychologists, and indeed may well be a minority view. The opposing doctrine of *epiphenomenalism* also has vigorous adherents. Epiphenomenalism holds that all mental phenomena such as ideas, values, opinions and emotions are a product of specific underlying physiological processes, i.e. that a particular physiological activity will produce a certain thought in consciousness.

In recent years the philosophical discussion of pain has been overshadowed by a more empirical approach, which, via the medium of research, seeks to understand pain in terms of the actual behaviour exhibited by people, and looks for practical methods by which pain can be reduced. The majority of workers who have carried out field research into pain suggest that its separation into "mental" and "physical" components is no longer justified and that pain is more appropriately seen as unitary.

Early writers referred to pain as a feeling state or "quale" but, as part of the generally increased scientific efforts of the nineteenth century, its general physiological properties were examined by researchers such as Helmholtz, Weber and von Frey. Additionally, psychologists such as Wundt and Galton examined individual differences in pain responses, the main objectives of these early researches being the establishment of physiological and psychological constants in much the same way as had already been achieved for the physical sciences. What is perhaps the earliest of "modern" approaches, the "specificity" theory derived its origins from nineteenth century research. This, together with two subsequent theories is now discussed.

Three theories of pain

1. Specificity

This assumes that specific pain receptors exist in the skin as free nerve endings, that special pain fibres called A-delta and C fibres are activated, and that these impulses are carried to specific pain centres such as the thalamic nuclei by the lateral spino-thalamic tracts. If these pathways are stimulated into activity, then, states the specificity theory, pain will be felt.

This approach met with considerable support from the medical and scientific fraternity, particularly as it was to a great extent based on research findings and because it fitted the scientific ethos of the time. Also, in one sense, this view of pain is correct, for actual tissue damage does transmit impulses along these pathways. It cannot, however, be the entire answer as the specificity theory assumes that activity in these systems always produces pain (which it does not), and that feelings of pain inevitably follow such activity (which they do not).

Some of the phenomena which cast doubts as to the ability of the specificity theory to explain all pain satisfactorily are mentioned by Sternbach (1968):

> It is because of this (specificity) model that a great number of "paradoxes" exist. Phenomena such as the failure of surgical intervention to relieve

14

pain, and "phantom limb" pains are "paradoxes" to a model which assumes a direct relationship between stimulus intensity and perceived pain. ... Although it is possible to retain the view of specialization of receptors and fibres for pain stimuli, this may be done without assuming that the specialization implies as a necessary consequence specificity of pain responses (page 40).

2. Pattern theories

In attempts to overcome objections to the strictly "specific" type of theory, students of pain have looked for explanations which take into account the known facts of neurological function, but which also allow the necessary flexibility. In general, pattern theories suggest that subjective pain is effected by patterns of impulses which may travel the same routes as ordinary sensory stimuli rather than along specially designed pain tracts. The theories of Weddell (1962) and Noordenbos (1959) are examples of this approach.

3. Gate theory

This theory, proposed by Melzack and Wall (1965) focuses attention firstly on the cells of the dorsal spinal cord which are said to control the intensity of sensory input from the peripheral nerves. The authors suggest that these cells act as a "gate" by modulating the membrane potentials of the terminals for incoming fibres. By controlling these potentials, control of intensity is achieved, the actual degree of control being determined by central mechanisms.

The main advantage of this theory is that unlike the specificity theories it allows for pain perception to be influenced by the psychological state of the individual.

Can pain be defined?

Returning to Locke's *Essays*:

Joy and pain like other simple ideas cannot be described or their names defined. Like other sensory ideas we can get to know them only by experience.

This rather dismissive approach may be philosophically accurate but it gives little encouragement to the would-be researcher who needs his terms operationally defined without ambiguity. Strictly speaking Locke may be right, but it may be possible to obtain a useful definition based upon observations of people in pain and by verbal reports of their subjective experiences so as to establish a working basis for research. Hence Merskey (1964) offers the following definition of pain:

An unpleasant experience which we primarily associate with tissue damage or describe in terms of tissue damage, or both.

15

Closely associated with some definitions of pain are those bodily response mechanisms which operate when pain is experienced. Some of these response measures have been eagerly seized upon by researchers, as they appear to offer the chance of an objective measure of pain with all the implications for exactness that this offers. Physiological and behavioural changes associated with pain include: alterations in the galvanic skin response, changes in heart rate, respiration, pupil size, and palmar sweat index. Changes in behaviour are less easy to measure, but manifestation of pain such as restlessness, sweating, moaning and crying, and variations in facial expressions have all been used as indices.

Perhaps the major problem in identifying an objective pain measure is that there seems no accurate way of deciding whether or not variations in response are due to pain alone. It may be true that all of the responses mentioned accompany pain, but they also accompany other states such as anxiety or fear. Therefore, although the apparent objectivity of physiological recordings may seem attractive at first sight, it must be remembered that they always need supplementing by verbal report.

Analysis of pain behaviour

During the late nineteenth and early part of the twentieth century considerable progress was made in the understanding of perception by the approach now generally called psychophysics. This attempts to investigate scientifically and define closely the limits of perceptual processes and asks the following basic questions:

1. How intense must a stimulus be to be subjectively perceived?
2. What is the relationship between the physical stimuli and the corresponding conscious sensation?

The first question concerns what has been termed the "absolute threshold", which is the minimum amount of energy of a particular type which allows the subject to perceive a stimulus. Although feasible when considering visual or auditory perception, the absolute threshold approach is less successful in the measurement of pain, as other sensations may precede or accompany the pain stimulus. For example, in those methods which utilize increasing pressure such as the algometer (Keele, 1954) a sensation of touch precedes pain. The determination of an "absolute" threshold is therefore difficult so this is usually replaced by a "pain perception threshold" or similar term. It has also been customary to investigate the upper threshold limits of pain by asking the subject to tolerate as much pain as he can reasonably bear, the "pain tolerance threshold".

The second question, which is obviously more complex, is very relevant to the study of pain, but, owing largely to stimulus control problems, has proved difficult to establish.

Psychophysics has played a useful part in the laboratory investigation of experimental pain, not least in the development of experimental equipment. It is, however, important to remember that no matter how sophisticated the equipment may be on the stimulus side, subjective response is still the vital measure. Traditional psychophysics (and even the recent trends shown by signal-detectability theories, see Tanner and Swets, 1954) deal with a limited problem, namely the construction of a psychological scale which is functionally related to a physical dimension the scale of which is already known. There are, however, important things which are now recognized as affecting perception but which established psychophysical approaches are not intended to measure. These include motives, expectations and a wide range of subjective variables. One of these is language.

Melzack and Torgerson (1971) have shown that language is important in describing the pain experience. They approached the problem of measurement by bringing together and categorizing words commonly used to describe pain. They comment on the scarcity of studies which attempt to classify the boundaries of pain, and also on the tendency to treat pain as a single unique phenomenon which varies only in intensity. The authors examined the pain literature and assembled lists of descriptive words of which 102 were included in their final list. The words were then categorized according to their meaning with regard to sensory qualities, emotional loading, and intensity of the pain experience.

On consideration of the resultant data the following points emerged:

1. There are many words used to describe pain;
2. There is a high level of agreement that the words fall into classes and sub-classes representing dimensions of pain;
3. Substantial numbers of the words have the same relative intensity scale for people with widely divergent backgrounds:

> The fact that there are so many words to describe the experience of pain lends support to the concept that the word "pain" is a label which represents a myriad of different experiences, and refutes the traditional concept that pain is a single modality which carries one or two qualities. ... If logic is to be maintained, then the investigator who contends that A-delta fibres carry pricking pain and C fibres carry burning pain, must also find fibres for cramping, crushing or wrenching pain (Melzack and Torgerson, 1971).

Methods of pain assessment

1. Verbal report

Some of the disadvantages of reporting a sensation such as pain by means of language have been mentioned above, but in spite of this, verbal report has an established place in assessment. In fact, there are those who maintain that for clinical pain no other measure can approach it for reliability. This viewpoint is held by Lasagna (1958):

> The quantification of clinical pain—by which I mean pain occurring spontaneously as a symptom in patients, as opposed to pain produced in the laboratory for experimental purposes—has, as its basic tenet, the postulate that the simplest and most reliable index of pain is the patient's verbal report.

It is not altogether clear why Lasagna makes the above distinction between clinical and experimental pain, for a report, or action congruent with report, is an inherent feature of most laboratory studies.

Perhaps the most detailed study of pain via the medium of subjective report was made by Janis (1958) in a detailed analysis of pain in surgical patients interpreted within a psychoanalytical framework. Although of great interest, widespread adoption of this method is difficult as:

1. It requires psychoanalytic knowledge of the patient for a lengthy pre-operative period;
2. The method involves extensive commitment of trained personnel;
3. A great deal of time is required.

Any verbal report has either to be made to another person or to a recording system. Tape recording may seem an attractive idea at first sight, particularly as possible bias in the experimenter may thus be reduced, but to patients who are not used to technical equipment a tape recorder can be daunting and may restrict the possible range of responses. One advantage of continuous monitoring, however, is that a 24 hour coverage then becomes feasible, a situation difficult to achieve by using observers in a hospital ward.

For recording clinical pain it is desirable to have a particular person (observer) to collect data from patients. This may be a ward staff member, or preferably, a less involved person so that biased interpretation of statements, always possible when the observer is closely associated with patient care, is reduced to a minimum. Patient/observer interaction is obviously a complex interpersonal process, the verbal component of which may represent only a small proportion of the total exchange and in which personality differences may occasion wide variations in response (Argyle, 1969).

The precise way in which patients' reports are kept must be adapted to the research situation and may range from unstructured verbatim records which can be tape recorded and subsequently analysed, to systems of categorizing responses within scales designed for the purpose.

Some of the more obvious problems which can accompany the use of verbal report have been discussed. These are not restricted to the measurement of pain, but are essentially similar to the problems found in any truly subjective report, and it has yet to be demonstrated that consistently more accurate, or more informative results occur from any other method.

2. Rating scales

An unstructured verbal report may produce data which does not easily allow comparisons with other patients. To combat this, and, most important, to reduce possible variations due to different levels of articulateness, it has long been the practice to impose constraints on subjective statements by the use of rating scales. Several types of these exist, perhaps the best known being the Likert Scale an example of which follows.

Strongly Agree	Agree	Neutral	Disagree	Strongly Disagree

Although the above is an example of a five-category scale, this may be extended to seven if deemed appropriate, whilst for pain research the three-category scale used by Keele (1954) has much to commend it.

The use of rating scales to measure pain may be helpful, particularly when comparison between patients is required, but their use invokes certain disadvantages. If the scale contains seven categories, and is purely verbal, it may be difficult for patients to differentiate between these. Additionally there are wide variations in the meaning and importance of words found between people of varied cultural and educational background. Due mainly to these factors Keele (1954) concluded that the use of more than three categories, i.e. "slight, moderate, bad" poses more problems than advantages for the pain researcher.

Evaluation of verbal report scales, even though the categories are constrained, presents problems which are often overlooked by the users of such scales. The recent awareness of how situational and interaction elements may affect subjective reports stresses that, far from being ignored, these variables require as much consideration as the more obvious effects (Rosenthal, 1966).

In spite of their drawbacks, rating scales are useful for some purposes, but, owing to a tendency to impose constraints on responses they tend to be insensitive to material which cannot easily be categorized. Whatever type of scale is used, it is vital to operationally define the categories so that data from different sources may be compared.

3. Bi-polar scales

In an attempt to reduce the forced-choice element which is inherent in the Likert-type scale, investigators have cast around for alternatives which will allow for measurement of information which is not easily categorized. The bi-polar scale is one such method.

This technique was given impetus by Osgood et al. (1953) who reported results of the factor analysis of very large numbers of bi-polar scales in terms of their connotative meaning. This has become known as the Semantic Differential technique, the important assumption being that the components of a concept can be measured by asking subjects to rate that concept on a number of bi-polar adjectives, for example:

Income Tax

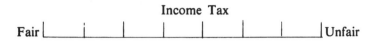

The subject is required to mark the section deemed most appropriate to his subjective judgement.

Although the bi-polar scale above has seven divisions, it is possible to have more, or less than this, or to omit these divisions entirely as described and used by Clarke and Spear (1964) and Bond and Pilowsky (1966). A feature of the bi-polar scale technique has been a tendency to describe the scales as equal interval measure, thus allowing the computation of means, standard deviations, analysis of variance, and other parametric statistics from the data. This is a controversial issue. Although there is a current tendency to ignore the traditional categories of "ordinal" (rank order) and "interval" (equal spacing) data (Baker, 1966; Anderson, 1961), this is a statistical device and does not alter the basic psychological implications of the data. Additionally, under some conditions it may be possible that a Likert scale of orthodox design would produce data more truly "interval" by nature than would a bi-polar scale, but traditionally the Likert scales have utilized non-parametric (distribution—free) methods of analysis.

The present author ran a pilot study using bi-polar scales to measure responses of surgical patients, from which some interesting points emerged. The satisfactory completion of the scale seems largely dependent upon the subject's ability to conceptualize the range of experience which lies between the two poles of the scale.

The vast majority of research on bi-polar scales has used college students as subjects, and has assumed that people of all levels of ability will be able to complete them satisfactorily. In the pilot study mentioned, however, there seemed to be an intellectual "cut-off" point, below which subjects could *not* conceptualize the dimension, thus leaving no recourse but random marking. This difficulty is also mentioned by Jahoda (1969) and may, if found generally, require further scrutiny before this type of scale is widely adopted in pain research.

Response set and question ambiguity effects

An important feature is the use of rating scales in the "Response Set" effect (Edwards, 1957). This investigator describes ways in which subjective responses may vary as a reflection of social, cultural, or educational expectations, and shows that the design of questions is of paramount importance.

The order in which questions are presented is another important consideration. Whitfield (1950) showed that when subjects were given an "imaginary" questionnaire the yes/no responses were not randomly distributed. For example, Whitfield showed that in a list of ten questions, question one is significantly more often answered "yes", while middle questions, irrespective of questionnaire length, are significantly less often answered "yes" than earlier ones, implying that randomization of question order is necessary if this effect is to be controlled.

Where consistency is the aim, the questions should be as unambiguous as possible, aptly put by Joyce (1968):

> What is wanted is the opposite of the "Have you stopped beating your wife?" type of question—traditionally so difficult to answer by 'yes' or 'no'—in which the respondent is neither totally inhibited nor pushed by irrelevancies in one direction or the other but is left entirely free to answer 'yes' or 'no' for valid reasons.

4. Observation scales

Scales may be designed which not only provide an assessment of pain, but which also give an overall picture of the patient's state of wellbeing. As well as being useful in their own right, these will allow relationships to be drawn between pain and other signs and symptoms. Data may be collected from a wide range of physical and psychological behaviour, and are often grouped conveniently in categories.

5. Physiological methods

To the researcher who is interested in the scientific analysis of pain, physiological measures, with their "objective" basis, seem at first sight to present an attractive proposition. However, similar problems of interpretation occur with physiological pain measures as with physiological anxiety measures, for example:

1. Whether or not the recorded response is due to pain (or anxiety) alone.
2. Almost all techniques require a subjective response as the dependent variable, irrespective of the level of sophistication employed in applying the stimulus.

Basically, physiological methods are more useful for the investigation of experimental pain than for the measurement of clinical pain, and it is for this reason that a detailed discussion will not be attempted here.

Relationships between experimental and clinical pain

Most research into pain has tended to follow two main avenues:

a. Experimental pain, created by the experimenter under laboratory conditions.
b. Clinical pain, created by pathological or surgical processes.

It is not at all clear if pain produced under these very different circumstances can be classified and treated in similar ways, and this question has occasioned considerable debate over the past few years. Not all of the arguments have been convincing, and some have contained logical contradictions. Beecher (1959a) has criticized comparisons between clinical and experimental pain, his main reason being that the experimental situation does not contain a "reaction component" (largely anxiety) which is inevitably found with clinical pain. This view is supported by data which Beecher uses to show that:

a. Pain threshold constancy in man has yet to be demonstrated;
b. Many factors are said to affect the pain threshold, but no experiments have controlled even the majority of these;
c. Experimental pain methodology is useless for analgesic efficacy testing, but analgesic efficacy can be tested with a 10% tolerance in cases of clinical pain;
d. Pain relieving drugs appear to act upon the "reaction component", rather than depending entirely on the incoming pain stimuli.

These arguments are strengthened by further evidence (Beecher, 1960) which shows that just as morphine does not reliably relieve experimental pain, it is very effective in relieving clinical pain. Additionally, placebos relieved only 3% of 173 subjects in experimental pain studies, but brought relief to 35% of 831 patients in 10 clinical studies.

Beecher's criticisms focus on the somewhat confused state of pain research, which makes it all the more important that objectives be clearly defined for each individual study, whether experimental or clinical.

Clinical pain research has its critics, for example Houde *et al.* (1965):

> ... on the other hand the clinical yardstick has not in itself been a completely reliable standard, for the medical literature is replete with conflicting reports of the efficacy of many of the analgetic drugs, and there is still a considerable division of opinion on many aspects of analgetic testing in man.

(The author states that "analgetic" is the correct term, *not* analgesic: Analgesia—analgetic, as in anaesthesia—anaesthetic.) When scrutinizing pain research it would seem important to define carefully the objectives the researcher has in mind. To take this further, there may be a great difference in the objectives, methods, and rationale of the pain threshold investigator predominantly concerned with sensory psychophysics, who performs laboratory studies using sophisticated stimulus control equipment, and the worker who wishes to design a clinical tool for use in medical practice. Both are examining a "pain threshold", but the student of psychophysics may be interested in the threshold for its own sake, and not as a correlate of clinical pain. Confusion between these two approaches may contribute to methodological inconsistency. Indeed, adopting a rather extreme position, it is possible to argue that the experimental psychophysics of pain have little, if anything, to do with pathological pain, a point often overlooked by critics who seek meaningful comparisons and perhaps fail to find them.

What factors influence plain?

With such a complex phenomenon it would be surprising to find uniformity of response, either in different people facing a similar situation, or in a particular person facing different situations. Some of these elements have been investigated and a selection is now briefly considered.

1. The nature of the physical stimulus

A specificity theory of pain would argue that the subjective experience of pain is a direct function of the amount and type of tissue injury involved, i.e. p (pain) = t (trauma), and that this relationship would be invariable. That opinions to the contrary have long existed is quite clear from classical and modern literature, whilst more quantitative evidence is submitted by Beecher (1956) who considers two types of wound situations, war injuries and surgery. Beecher showed that military personnel required significantly less analgesic drugs than did the civilian and attributes these findings to the obvious situational differences, i.e. in warfare a wound is sometimes a fairly minor evil compared to what might have been, and may come, therefore, as a relief.

Clinical evidence showing great differences between patients' pain responses to similar operations is common, and is discussed at length by Keats (1956) who uses this evidence to refute a specificity theory of pain. Hence, it is clear that reasons other than the purely physical must be sought to explain the observed variations and of all possible alternative factors, anxiety has attracted by far the most attention.

2. Anxiety and pain

Anxiety has been considered as a variable in both clinical and experimental pain situations, and it is perhaps unfortunate that it suffers from similar problems of identification and definition as does pain itself.

23

In some instances the reference is fairly loose, for example, "the patient seemed anxious", but in others an attempt to measure the degree of anxiety has been made. Perhaps the most important point is that anxiety, like other single-word constructs must always be defined in terms of response criteria so that comparison with other investigators becomes possible.

Any relationship between pain and anxiety suffers greatly from semantic difficulties. Thus Beecher (1959a) contends that the main difference between experimental and clinical pain is that in the latter a reaction component is present, and that this may include anxiety. Although perhaps useful for hypothesis formation, this type of statement is not directly informative as the variable in question has not been demonstrated in isolation from other effects.

In the experimental situation anxiety may be studied as a *dependent variable* (dependent variable—that which is measured by an experimenter) by varying the amount of pain stimulus and at the same time recording subjective anxiety, either continuously or in retrospect. The anxiety recording may be by self-report scales, perhaps accompanied by physiological records. It is important that physiological methods should not be used without some form of verbal report, as factors other than anxiety may cause similar physiological reactions (Martin, 1961).

For experiments where pain is the major interest, it is usual to consider anxiety as an *independent variable* (independent variable—that which is varied by an experimenter so that the effects of this variation can be observed) and then to examine the results of its manipulation on pain reactions. There are several feasible experimental paradigms, for example subjects may be pre-selected on the basis of anxiety inventories so as to isolate the extremes or "tails" of the anxiety distribution in a particular sample; these two groups are then compared in their responses to pain stimuli. Another method is to manipulate pre-instruction, such as, "you realise this will hurt a lot" or "this will not hurt".

Although the isolation of a specific "anxiety factor" seems fraught with difficulties, this is largely because anxiety is such a multidimensional construct. On the basis of research evidence, however, Sternbach (1968) thinks it reasonable to accept that anxiety does act as a relevant variable in experimental pain.

When considering clinical pain the evidence for the effects of anxiety is impressive. There is Beecher's (1956) contention that no dependable relationship exists between extent of injury and magnitude of pain, and in addition to this, there exists a large body of literature concerned with "painless" childbirth (Read, 1943; Chertok, 1959) although, once again, anxiety is not considered in isolation by these authors. After a perusal of available literature, Sternbach (1968) has no doubts:

> All that is necessary for maximising pain responses is that anxiety responses also be great.

On this basis, and following the trend of "Childbirth without fear", the importance of anxiety in other areas, notably surgery, has been considered and will be analysed in detail later.

3. Placebos

The word placebo is derived from the Latin verb "to please" and has been defined by Shapiro (1960) as the

> ... psychological, physiological or psychophysiological effect of any medication or procedure given with therapeutic intent, which is independent of or minimally related to the pharmacologic effects of the medication or to the specific effects of the procedure, and which operates through a psychological mechanism.

Shapiro reviews the history of medication in medical treatment and makes the point that substances such as dung, blood, spiders, ants, earthworms and many similar substances have all, at various times, been used medicinally and after a detailed consideration of these facts he concludes that,

> ... we are led to the inescapable conclusion that the history of medical treatment for the most part, until relatively recently, is the history of the placebo effect, since almost all medications until recently were placebos.

Beecher (1959b) has presented data which indicate that the effectiveness of a placebo operates as a function of level of patient distress. He also comments on the relative failure of placebos in laboratory studies of pain, compared with their success in clinical research, and also the widely demonstrated effectiveness of placebos in conditions as diverse as headache, cough, angina, and seasickness. The 15 studies reviewed contained a total 1,082 patients, of whom 35·2% derived relief from placebos. A similar calculation from experimental pain studies shows the placebo effect to be 3·2%. Drawing on these results, placebos would seem 10 times as effective for clinical pain as for experimental pain, due, says Beecher, to the presence of distress in the former.

As a proportion of distress is certainly anxiety, then it seems reasonable to accept that placebos act through the medium of anxiety reduction, their potency being in direct proportion to anxiety levels at the time.

4. Stress and coping

Although primarily derived from physiological research the term is now used in a wider sense to mean a disruption in personal, social and cultural processes that bear some relationship to health and disease; additionally the concept of stress serves to bring together research from areas such as physiological responses, fear, anxiety and coping behaviour. Research in this area was pioneered by Selye (1956) who examined variations in biological response systems subjected to stress, and who provides the following definition:

> ... the state manifested by a specific syndrome which consists of all the non-specifically induced changes within a biological system.

Selye's work aroused considerable interest in this general area and a number of subsequent investigators have tried to devise lawful relationships between biological stress, as defined by Selye, and socio/psychological stress. At first sight these may seem simply varieties of the same thing, but Janis (1958) argues that physiological stress is quite a different concept from, and not necessarily related to psychological stress (pages 11–13).

Perhaps the most determined series of investigations into psychological stress has been that of Lazarus (1966), whose primary aim was to compare various causes of stress with the ways in which people adapt or "cope". Lazarus identifies six main groups of noxious stimuli which have stress producing effects:

1. Uncertainty about physical survival
2. Maintenance of identity
3. Loss of loved ones
4. Inability to control immediate environment
5. Disruption of community life
6. Avoidance of pain or privation.

Individual responses to stress vary, but Lazarus has found four major reactions to be of prime importance. These are:

1. Disturbance of emotional balance
2. Disruption of motor (neuromuscular) systems
3. Physiological changes
4. Disturbances of cognition (thinking, reasoning, problem solving).

The last point seems of particular importance to the present research with hospital patients.

Lazarus views anxiety as a learnable reaction which has the three properties of being a cue for threat, a drive, and a response, a key feature in this scheme being the "appraisal" process whereby a person becomes aware of threatening features in the environment. Following appraisal of the threat, the next stage is to develop "coping" behaviour, which, says Lazarus, is based upon results of the initial appraisal.

This work seems of great importance, but is quite difficult to relate directly to practical situations. The bulk of the data obtained by Lazarus and his associates has been from subjects who were shown stress-producing films, during which physiological and psychological recordings were made. This inevitably loses some of the complexity of a real-life stress situation. There seems little reason to doubt that admission to hospital for surgery is a stress-producing experience and the sections in which Lazarus describes the processes of appraisal and coping seem of direct relevance to the present work.

Once again the difficulties of measuring such a complex phenomenon as stress are manifest, and as Lacey (1959) has shown, the idea of a comprehensive "stress measure" still seems a distant goal.

5. Individual differences

A detailed analysis of this obviously important area is beyond the scope of this volume. Variations in culture, birth-order, social and educational background, personality and perceptual style have all been scrutinized with regard to possible relationships with the expression of pain. A comprehensive account of this work is found in Sternbach (1968).

CHAPTER 2

The Concept of Anxiety

The concept of anxiety has created intensive public and professional concern in recent years. For example:

> Anxiety is found as a central explanatory concept in almost all contemporary theories of personality, and it is regarded as a principal causative agent for such behavioural consequences as insomnia, immoral and sinful acts, instances of creative self-expression, debilitating psychological and psychosomatic symptoms and idiosyncratic mannerisms of endless variety (Spielberger, 1966; page 4).

The literature relating to anxiety has varied widely in emphasis since Freud formulated his theory of anxiety neurosis in 1894. Since then the topic has received wide attention, particularly in the experimental investigation of anxiety and alternative theories have proliferated. Spielberger (1966) comments on this trend:

> Thus in the period 1950–1966 there have been over 3,500 articles or books related to anxiety (page 6)

There is little reason to think that this general tendency has altered. But there have been changes in the overall theoretical approach to anxiety research—perhaps a reflection of different thinking about the basic nature of the phenomenon, and there has been a rapid extension of techniques purporting to measure anxiety. For example, Cattell and Scheier (1958),

> ... counted more than 120 personality-type tests which have been claimed to measure anxiety (page 353)

Can anxiety be defined?

Anxiety and pain pose similar problems for those who would accurately define them. Both are concepts which, by means of a single word, imply a complex pattern of feelings and sensations and both have suffered from long and laborious definitions. In the case of anxiety the idea running through all definitions is fear of varying intensity. The problems of definition are clearly stated by Levitt (1961):

> We could go on forever in this absurd fashion, adding word after word and phrase after phrase in a vain attempt to define the original single-

word construct. Even if the volume of verbiage becomes infinite, we shall not have added much more clear meaning to the word with which we began (page 19)

The solution, then, is similar to that suggested for pain. Each part of the behavioural response thought to represent anxiety must be operationally defined. If these separate parts combine to form a meaningful construct, they should be positively related (intercorrelated) for a given situation, which has led researchers to develop a "multiple approach" system where data are collected from as many sources as possible from each subject and then examined for relationships.

Theories of anxiety

Before briefly discussing some of the major theoretical approaches to anxiety, it may be useful to consider the purpose of a theory. It is not necessary that a theory be true in an absolute sense, even if this were acceptable, and it is quite feasible to have a number of different theories all of which claim to explain the same event. It is difficult, if indeed possible, to claim that any theory is "true" because new research may produce new information. A "good" theory, therefore, may not be the most "true" but is good because of the number of testable hypotheses it can generate.

Although by no means an exhaustive coverage, some of the major theories of anxiety will be considered here, largely because no one theory seems able to account for all of the known facts.

Freud

To Freud, anxiety was a central concept in his ideas about psychopathology, the major problem being why anxiety and the defences generated against it should persist after circumstances have changed and the individual knows that the original source of anxiety cannot recur. In *The Problem of Anxiety* (1936) Freud clearly states that despite a lifetime devoted to this problem he failed to find a solution, but he distinguished three types of anxiety which differ in causation.

1. Reality anxiety

Is a reaction to a perceived threat from a feared source. This is seen as a useful, built in, protective mechanism, which, if taken further results in "neurotic" and "moral" anxieties.

2. Primary anxiety

The first experiences of anxiety are at birth, says Freud, and are a consequence of the change from intra-uterine to extra-uterine conditions.

This is closely followed by anxiety due to absence of the mother—primary anxiety—which is seen as setting the pattern for all subsequent anxiety reactions, as it represents an external threat to survival.

3. Neurotic anxiety

This is characterized by feelings of apprehension and physiological arousal. The major difference from primary anxiety is that the source of danger is internal rather than external.

Freud (1936) claims that everyone experiences neurotic anxiety to some extent, and it is when this becomes excessive that a condition of anxiety neurosis exists, in fact anxiety is the:

> ... fundamental phenomenon and the central problem of neurosis. (Freud, 1936)

Throughout his life Freud was occupied with attempting to understand the true nature of anxiety, which is apparent following an examination of his theoretical views on the subject. During the 50 years of his professional life Freud continually modified his views on this subject, which he at no time regarded as complete.

Neo-Freudians

Commencing during the 1920s and continuing, with variations, to the present day, a group of psychoanalytically inclined workers developed who accepted some of Freud's basic tenets but who disagreed with Freud in certain areas. For this reason they were termed neo-Freudians. Levitt (1968) comments:

> To summarise neo-Freudianism in one sentence, we might say that it changed the orientation of psychoanalysis from the biological and instinctual to the cultural and environmental.

Although the neo-Freudians accept much of Freud's orthodox theory there are major differences. For example, they regard personality development as a result of social and cultural influences, in which biological drives play a minor role.

Another important variation from Freud lies in the concept of primary anxiety, which the neo-Freudians do not accept; a certain amount of ego (self) development being deemed necessary before this can occur. The frustration of physiological needs, so emphasized by Freud, is not considered important, but priority is given to the frustration of "dependency needs" which then leads to anxiety. An example of this would be parental insistence on the observation of social conventions, with the threat of withdrawal of affection if the child refuses to conform.

Can Freudian theories of anxiety be tested?

Although not without considerable difficulties, it is quite possible to derive testable hypotheses from Freudian theories, a notable example being the attempts of Dollard and Miller (1950). These investigators drew heavily upon the learning theory developed by Hull (1943) who considers that drives, of which there are primary and secondary types, form the basis for learning. Primary drives are similar to Freud's "Id" (basic physiological drives), while secondary drives are acquired by a process of learning, this being mediated by rewards or punishments known as reinforcers. Dollard and Miller (1950) adopt the position that anxiety is a powerful secondary drive, i.e. that it is learned. They start by postulating a *primary* pain avoidance drive, which then leads to pain acting as the reinforcer for the *secondary* drive of anxiety or fear. The strength of this anxiety drive depends upon the number and intensity of reinforcements. As with conditioning, the anxiety reaction may be generalized to objects closely resembling the original fear arousing stimulus, often seen in fear of animals, where an unpleasant event with one type of animal may generalize to a wide range of other animals.

A key area in the Dollard and Miller thesis is that of conflict, a state which occurs when an organism is motivated simultaneously by two strong competing drives. These drives may be of a primary nature, may be learned, or both, and it is the way in which anxiety operates via one or other of these drives that may decide which way the conflict will be resolved.

Anxiety as a drive

Spence (1960, 1964) has been a leading proponent of the idea that anxiety has an energizing function. As in the conflict research of Dollard and Miller, the underlying theory is developed from Hull (1943) who tried to develop a hypothetico-deductive theory which would explain all learning. Starting with a single-response learning situation, in this case eyelid conditioning, Spence has shown that a high anxiety level will facilitate learning, a finding which has received experimental support from other research *providing* that the level of anxiety is not excessive. Spence regards each response tendency (or habit) as possessing a certain strength, or probability of occurrence, which will vary according to the individual's past learning experiences. In this way a "hierarchy of responses" is formed. The fundamental basis of Spence's theory is, therefore, that anxiety will energize or strengthen each of the response tendencies (habits) contained in the hierarchy *in proportion to the initial strength of the habit,* i.e.

$$(R)esponse = (D)rive \times (H)abit \text{ Strength.}$$

31

Spence (1964) reviews research which has tried to establish that anxiety acts as a drive. Not all experiments have been as successful as Spence's, and in order to replicate these results other workers have found that the test situation has to be made extremely threatening and fear-producing before a sufficient level of subjective anxiety, capable of affecting conditioning, is reached. Moreover, although the formula of $R = (D \times H)$ *may* serve as an accurate model of the effects of anxiety on any *one* response tendency, Spence has been unable to develop an equation which will predict the effects of anxiety in *complex* learning situations, i.e. involving more than one response. The major reason here is that there are problems in establishing response hierarchies for complex tasks as the hierarchy will itself vary as a result of past experience and learning. The actual quantification of the part played by anxiety as a drive in complex learning would thus be enormously complex. Another practical difficulty in seeking to apply this type of experimental result is that single-response learning situations do not often occur in everyday life and so in most circumstances an individual can react with a variety of available responses.

In summary, the Hull-Spence theory essentially views anxiety as being primarily brought about by the state of the individual, in which it forms a more or less permanent characteristic, with situational factors playing a secondary part.

Anxiety as a response to situational stress

This approach suggests that situational factors are more important in anxiety causation than the state of individuals, a line of research developed at Yale (Mandler and Sarason, 1952; Sarason *et al.*, 1960; Mandler and Watson, 1966). The essence of this theory of anxiety is summarized by Levitt (1968).

1. Anxiety is a strong learned drive which is situationally evoked. A particular circumstance or class of circumstances may be stressful for a person though he is not made anxious by other situations. Individuals react differently to the same circumstances.
2. The individual has learned or developed characteristic responses to anxiety which he brings to the current situation.
3. The effect of anxiety is also a function of such aspects of the situation as the attitude of the experimenter or teacher, and the meaning of the task as perceived by the individual.
4. There may be a general trait of anxiety, but behavioural science is not yet prepared to investigate it. It is first necessary to thoroughly study important situational anxieties. (page 142)

Although a great variety of stressful situations exist, not all of these are suitable for study under laboratory conditions. To provide a relatively constant situation Mandler and his associates have made a detailed study of the anxiety arousing properties of performance tests, and, supplementary to this, later research which attempts to explore anxiety caused by the *interruption* of behaviour. Mandler and Watson (1966) exemplify this trend:

> The argument to be developed is that the interruption of an organised behavioural sequence will, under certain specifiable conditions, serve as a condition sufficient to evoke anxiety.

Although it is not intended to provide a detailed review of the experimental work on interruption, it is interesting to reflect on the following quotation from Mandler and Watson (1966) as some analogy can be drawn with the predicament of many hospital patients whose everyday behaviour has been interrupted.

> In other words, anxiety should appear when the organism, interrupted in the midst of well-organised behaviour sequences or in the execution of a well-developed plan, has not alternative behaviour available .... *The organism does not know what to do*— ... Helplessness and disorganisation *are* anxiety.

The situational anxiety approach has much in common with the theories of Lazarus (1966) who stresses that an individual's cognitive appraisal (summing-up) of a situation must be closely scrutinized if we are to understand the true nature of stressful agents.

A comprehensive theory of anxiety?

An impressive attempt to relate theory and practice regarding anxiety and arousal has been made by Epstein (1967, 1972) who bases his writings on an extensive series of experiments which have studied psychological and physiological constituents of anxiety in parachutists.

This theory analyses ways in which the individual copes with, and masters anxiety, and postulates on the basis of evidence from self-report inventories, physiological recordings, and specially devised "projective" techniques, that when an individual is exposed to threat two things occur:

1. a broadening, heightening and steepening of a generalisation gradient of anxiety;
2. the development of an inhibitory gradient that becomes increasingly steeper than the anxiety gradient.

These two, says Epstein, account for how, as a result of experience in facing stress, anxiety provides an increasingly efficient warning system which produces earlier warning signals at lower levels of arousal. Following analysis of these experiments, Epstein was led to the conclusion that each individual possesses a defence system in depth, which helps to "buffer" the effects of anxiety and also allows for increasingly effective awareness and coping mechanisms to operate. Hence,

> ... fear is an avoidance motive, arousal is the non-specific excitatory component of all motives and reactions to stimulation, and anxiety is a state of undirected arousal following the perception of danger. (Epstein, 1967)

Summary

Some of the many theories of anxiety have been considered and it is clear that as often occurs with similarly complex phenomena, theory construction is hampered by a lack of clear definition of the fundamental nature of anxiety, and furthermore by the often divergent results obtained by different investigators.

One of the greatest problems lies in providing more satisfactory experimental conditions in which to test hypotheses about anxiety behaviour and perhaps Epstein's work with subjects in a natural environment is a step towards this, particularly as he throws valuable light on some of the differences between physiological arousal and the experience of fear, a major step forward. To conclude this discussion of anxiety theories, a quotation from two of the leading researchers and theorists in the experimental investigation of anxiety may be appropriate:

> To repeat an earlier statement, the development of even limited theories is a difficult undertaking in which progress is likely to be slow. (Spence and Spence, 1966)

Trait anxiety and state anxiety

Recent research has shown an interesting distinction between two types of commonly experienced anxiety: *trait* (or anxiety proneness), where anxiety is considered to be a relatively permanent feature of an individual's personality; and *state* (or transitory), which is a tendency to experience acute anxiety in response to *specific situations*.

The categories are based upon the factor analytic studies of Cattell and Scheier (1958, 1961) who identified two basic factors associated with anxiety. The "trait" factor, which, according to these investigators, is measuring stable individual differences in personality which should remain consistent over time, and a "state" factor, which identified variables concerned with the physiological functioning of the individual. This is consistent with later evidence offered by Schacter and Singer (1962) that all emotional states possess at least two aspects, firstly, physiological arousal, and secondly, situationally determined cognitions.

A trait-state concept of anxiety has been advanced by Spielberger (1966) not so much as a different theory of anxiety, but as a means of clarifying the basic concepts underlying these two conditions. He suggests that there is considerable support for the claim that anxiety *states* are typically characterized by feelings of fear and tension. accompanied by adreno-sympathetic arousal. *Trait* anxiety. on the other hand, implies a type of acquired behavioural disposition which predisposes an individual to perceive non-dangerous situations as threatening and to over-respond with anxiety reactions.

The trait-state distinction is perhaps most important in the choice of a suitable tool with which to measure anxiety. There is obviously little point in a researcher using a "trait" anxiety inventory if he is primarily interested in short-term changes in anxiety "state", a crucial distinction for those who wish to include anxiety as a research variable.

CHAPTER 3

Information and Anxiety in Hospital Patients

It is commonly asserted that admission to hospital causes excessive anxiety in many patients, but direct evidence where anxiety may be clearly separated from other arousal mechanisms is not easy to collect from such a complex situation. There are, however, such numerous accounts of high levels of anxiety in hospitals, that these taken in their entirety form an impressive body of evidence. Neither are these anxieties restricted to patients:

> Hospitals are communities cradled in anxiety. Patients are anxious not only about their own health but about the welfare of their families. Junior nurses are anxious about the difficulties of training, and are often tormented by the fear that they may be inadequate in their treatment of the patients. Sisters are often anxious about the good order of their wards and their relations with the matron and the consultants (Revans, in Weiland and Leigh, 1971, page 4)

Surgical patients face not only the social and environmental pressures of admission, but also the direct physical threat of the operation. But the traditional hospital ward does little to alleviate these anxieties. The patient is usually deprived of his individuality by the removal of clothes and possessions at a time when many are experiencing acute social anxiety in a communal context,

> Altogether two-thirds of the patients described some disadvantages of being in a ward with other patients . . . (Cartwright, 1964, page 61)

In the same study, Cartwright found many specific events which patients found anxiety provoking, including the death of another patient, emergencies, preliminaries to operations, unpleasant sights, and unpredictable behaviour of the elderly and mentally ill.

That these problems are not confined to hospitals in the United Kingdom is shown by what is perhaps the most detailed account of the way in which a prominent American hospital is organized and the stresses, both physical and psycho-social that admission exerts on patients,

> The general hospital possessed many of the characteristics of total institutions. Between admission to, and discharge from the hospital, the

36

patients were subject to the orders of the staff. They were separated from their families. Their street clothes were shed. They were assigned to beds, given numbers, and dressed in bedroom apparel. They had to permit strangers access to the most intimate parts of their bodies. Their diet was controlled, as were the hours of their days and nights, the people they saw and the times they saw them. They were bathed, fed and questioned; they were ordered or forbidden to do specified things. As long as they were in hospital they were not considered self-sufficient adults (Duff and Hollingshead, 1968; page 269)

The text continues vividly to describe patients' fears and, in some cases, patients' desperate attempts to reduce their anxiety.

Anxiety was a characteristic response from the time a person learned he had to be hospitalised, until he was discharged. Even when he returned home he might still be fearful (pages 273–4)

On one of the assessment schedules used for their research was the question, "Did anything happen during the hospitalization which raised anxieties or fears regarding the practice of medicine in this hospital?"

In reply to this, 61 patients (plus spouse and family) reported no incidents, whilst in the remaining 100 cases the patients described specific incidents of an anxiety-creating nature. Each of these reports was then content-analysed with regard to the principal sources of complaint. Summarizing the data from hospitalized patients the authors conclude:

... few of the hospital staff recognised the high anxiety level which patients and family members exhibited. Defective communications with physicians were the most prevalent basis for anxiety-producing events. Ambiguities, evasions, and most of all, simple absence of communication about matters of vital concern to patients were the source of many complaints (pages 286–7)

There are, of course, great differences between Britain and America in the policies and administration of health care, and these differences extend throughout the system, but even allowing for this many areas of complaint voiced by the Eastern Hospital patients would be echoed by their British counterparts.

Information

Perusal of hospital care research clearly shows that communication difficulties, and, more specifically, lack of information form a common area of complaint which links all opinion surveys as with an invisible thread. For example,

The major complaint of patients, as all study groups discovered about this and nearly every other situation in hospital is lack of information.

This comment by Barnes (1961) is based upon the findings of an international study group which investigated psychological problems of general hospital patients. Similar difficulties are reported by Raphael (1969) in a King Edward's Fund study of patient satisfaction: "lack of information" was reported by 95 out of 110 patients.

A major problem in interpreting opinion surveys is that both "information" and "communication" are blanket terms, embracing a whole range of possible activities. For example, most information in hospitals is given verbally, which involves interaction with another person, and so quite often it is far from clear whether the patient is lacking information *per se* or whether this is a plea for more social interaction with a reassuring person.

Writing in the report of the Hospital Internal Communications Project (eds. Wieland and Leigh, 1971) Coghill reports a study of patients' anxieties in relation to clinical ward rounds. Three main points emerged.

1. There were great variations between patients in how much explanation of their illness and treatment they wished to be given.
2. The sense of mounting tension (anxiety) felt by some of the patients who were not seen until the end of the doctors' round.
3. Patients' difficulty in understanding the roles of the different members of the ward team.

This is an opportune moment to ask what for many people is the key question—how much do patients wish to know? As it is impossible to generalize for all patients, no clear answer can be given, a situation not helped by recourse to the literature which reveals considerable disagreement among doctors, nurses and patients as to how much information patients either want to know or need to know.

There seems a considerable difference between the views of hospital staff and the results of patient surveys with regard to how much patients want to know, and, as both groups give tacit approval for the patient to be given the maximum possible information, where, then, does the difficulty lie?

Cartwright (1964) found that 60% of patients reported difficulty in getting information whilst in hospital, the deficient areas including knowledge about general condition, treatment and progress. Many patients were diffident about asking informally, whilst, as recently as 1971, Coghill has found that the atmosphere of the hospital ward round is scarcely conducive to a ready exchange of information.

In a survey entitled *What Patients Expect from their Doctor,* Reader *et al.* (1957) studied the views of 50 outpatients. Of these, 60% wished to know the nature and cause of their illness, 54% wished to know how serious it was, and 44% would have liked much more information about the tests they were given, the results of these tests, and how they were related to the patient's illness.

Spelman, Ley and Jones (1966) studied 80 general medical patients and analysed the results so as to look at specific areas of complaint. The two largest areas of dissatisfaction were,

1. Not being told about diagnosis and prognosis (21·25%)
2. Complained of being told nothing (12·5%)

Following a review of several studies, all of which show similar trends, Ley and Spelman (1967) comment:

> These findings show that most patients want to be told as much as possible about their condition. Their failure to ask questions is probably due more to diffidence than to any lack of desire for information (page 19)

Other studies support this viewpoint. Cartwright (1964) found that 75% of her sample of hospital patients wished to know as much as possible about their illness. Reader et al. (1957) studied a sample of 50 outpatients and found that 68% wished to know about the nature and cause of their illness, 54% wished to know how serious it was, and 44% were curious about the results of laboratory tests which had been carried out and over the resultant implications for their personal welfare. These results are supported by the findings of Spelman et al. (1966) that patients complained of lack of information about diagnosis, prognosis, general progress aftercare and the reasons for laboratory tests.

Consideration of the above evidence may lead the reader to think that there is an unwillingness on the part of doctors and nurses to accept that "putting the patient in the picture" is beneficial; that, perhaps, the "conspiracy of silence" mentioned by Titmus (1958) does, in fact, exist.

Public pronouncements, however, indicate quite the reverse:

> To tell the patient what is to be done for him, and why, is common courtesy. (Lancet, 1963)

The British Medical Association (1961) outlined six reasons for telling acutely ill patients about their illnesses. These were:

1. to assist recovery
2. to obtain patients' co-operation
3. to give patients peace of mind
4. to give patients some idea of the probable length of their illness and absence from work.
5. to suggest means of improving the patients' comfort
6. to prevent infection of other people where infection is possible from the nature of the illness.

The British Medical Journal (1963) commented upon the desirability of patients knowing about their conditions:

> Such an explanation should be limited only by the patient's capacity to grasp the complexities of human disease and by the therapeutic necessity

to withold information which, by alarming the patient, might impede his return to health.

Additionally, there exists a profusion of medical and nursing writings which echo the sentiments expressed above.

When the various findings are compared, a paradoxical situation emerges. All patient surveys report lack of information as the largest single complaint and yet the professions involved have openly deplored such a state of affairs for at least the past 10 years!

Efficient communication between patients and staff is of maximum importance in surgical wards, where patients are under stress from a variety of sources. Responsibility for important decisions, some of which may profoundly affect future life, may have to be delegated by the patient to others. Any surgical patient is placed in a psychologically ambiguous position in that he has to submit to an assault on his person in order to receive treatment, an event which carries definable risks.

Some types of surgery involve the actual or probable loss of a bodily part, or confer a permanent physical and social disability such as colostomy or radical mastectomy. Such operations are inevitably accompanied by anxieties and fears, both as regards mutilation and other possible future consequences for the individual. That some surgeons are very aware of the harmful effects that anxiety can exert upon physical recovery is shown by the following quotations from a surgical text book:

> It is an unfortunate truth that most patients enter hospitals and operating rooms with unnecessary fears and anxieties. A great part of the apprehension stems from lack of knowledge concerning their illness and the operative procedure which is to be performed on them. The persistence of these anxieties often interfered greatly with a healthy post-operative reaction and a smooth convalescence (Rothenberg, 1955)

From the sources mentioned above it seems fairly clear that lack of information, and the subsequent anxiety which this occasions is of paramount importance to those interested in quality of patient care.

These obvious shortcomings are not through lack of official encouragement, for, in addition to the sources named above, the Ministry of Health set up a Joint Sub-Committee to examine the area and their report, *Communication between Doctors, Nurses and Patients,* was published in 1963. The terms of reference were as follows:

1. To consider what general principles and practical procedures may best provide hospital patients (and their relations) with the information they should have on their diagnosis, prognosis and treatment.
2. To make arrangements for any necessary enquiries to that end.
3. To advise on the most appropriate means of drawing any recommendations to the notice of the professions.

Among the Committee's recommendations were the desirability of hospital pamphlets, the concept of a personal doctor, that patients should be treated on an individual basis and that the timing of information should be carefully considered. Considerable importance was attached to the recognition of individual differences between patients, a fact of life which, although given "lip service", is often practicaiiy ignored in hospitals.

> Patients vary greatly in their ability to understand. What seems to the doctor or nurse to be simple, straightforward information may not be understood or absorbed even by the intelligent layman. (Ministry of Health, 1963)

It is easy for the inexperienced doctor or nurse to fall into the trap of thinking that because a patient has "been told", he will necessarily understand and remember what has been said. Nurses spend a considerable proportion of their time in direct patient contact, much more so than doctors, and it is very clear that the giving of information to patients forms a vital part of nursing duties. The teaching and development of skills which facilitate this process are, for this reason, no less important than other more commonly recognized nursing skills, for,

> The doctor cannot live on the ward. Therefore a great deal of responsibility for communication rests with the personal doctor, it is also necessary that one person on the ward staff must accept responsibility for what is said when he is not there. This responsibility can be carried at no lower level than that of the ward sister herself, her deputy acting for her in her absence—she must instruct ward staff in the part they are to play. (Ministry of Health, 1963; paragraph 23)

An important feature of communication effectiveness is that information given by a high-status figure is remembered more effectively (Hovland and Weiss, 1951), so that the above plea for the ward sister to act as informer would mean that this important function would be the responsibility of the most senior member of the ward team. However, the ward sister has many demands on her time. Numerous work study reports show that the proportion of time most sisters spend in direct patient contact is small, a situation found also by Lelean (1974):

> It was not uncommon to see a house physician visit the ward, followed soon after by the registrar of the same firm, followed a little later by the consultant accompanied by the same house physician and registrar. Doubtless they had both wanted to familiarise themselves with the latest conditions of their patients, but it becomes exceedingly frustrating to a ward sister—not to mention the patient—to be questioned three times about the same thing in a short space of time. When this is multiplied by four or more different consultants on a ward, it can be appreciated that the sister would find little time available for other tasks (page 101)

41

The quotation from Revans at the beginning of this chapter highlights the stressful nature of hospital work, and that role identification difficulties form a basis for much of this stress. There are few, if any, hospitals where the roles of house officers, the various grades of nurses, and the patients are clearly defined—in fact some may argue that this is one of the features of professional practice—and it seems that information-giving often suffers from this lack of clear identification of function. The development of formal responsibilities for informing patients is not helped by the rapid patient turnover in modern surgical wards and the six-monthly rota usually found with house-officer appointments. Role ambiguity may thus cause confusion as to *who should tell which patient what, and when.* This problem is considered by Kutner (1958) who writes:

> The unresponsiveness of some nurses to some of the unmet social and psychological needs of patients may be understood, therefore, as not stemming from ignorance of these needs or a lack of desire to care for them, but from a fundamental disagreement of lack of concurrence as to the areas of professional responsibility legitimately to be covered by physician and/or nurses (page 396)

It is difficult to find justification for a certain category of "informer", for, as Alfred North Whitehead has warned, "the fixed person for the fixed duty in a fixed situation is a social menace"—mentioned by Titmus (1958) when considering the "conspiracy of silence" found in some hospital wards. It seems more feasible to educate all members of the ward team to provide such information *as is within their range of competence.*

Whatever the reasons, the provision of appropriate information to patients seems far from adequate. Two main points emerge from the preceding evidence. Firstly, that medical and nursing staff appear to agree, at least publicly, that patients should be given the maximum possible information about their condition. Secondly, that patients continue to put "lack of information" above all other complaints, which seems to imply either that doctors and nurses "say one thing but do another", or that information is given, but in an ineffectual way.

What can go wrong?

It is evident from the examples mentioned above that several factors may interfere with the assimilation and storage of information. Assuming that some efforts are made to tell patients the facts, there are several features of hospital life which may hamper these:

1. The nature of the situation in which information is given to patients. To the doctor or nurse this may seem a perfectly ordinary daily occurrence, but to an individual patient it almost certainly does not seem ordinary. It is probable that most patients find that interaction with a

doctor or senior nurse is anxiety-producing, and this may be so inhibiting that the patient's attentional and perceptual powers will be severely handicapped. There is ample evidence from experimental psychology that high anxiety inhibits learning (Spielberger, 1966), whilst Janis (1958) showed that more than 75% of surgical patients expressed moderate to high levels of pre-operative anxiety.

> From a psychological standpoint, a major surgical operation constitutes a stress situation which resembles many other types of catastrophes and disasters in that the "victim" faces a combination of three major forms of imminent danger—the possibility of suffering acute pain, of undergoing serious body damage, and of dying (Janis, 1958)

In summary, among the many situational variables which mitigate against successful information transfer it is difficult to envisage a sitatuion *less* conducive to retention than the average hospital surgical ward, particularly if the traditional consultants' round forms the main focus of communication.

2. Differences in social and educational background between some doctors and nurses and the patients they are informing, coupled with the difficulties of communicating with high-status figures, who often use a general and technical vocabulary very different from the patient's own, present formidable communication barriers.

In recent years a considerable volume of research has shown very distinct differences in the use and comprehension of language by people who vary in social and educational background. Bernstein (1971) has clearly shown, in his descriptions of "public" and "private" languages, that great variations, largely a reflection of social background, exist in the way language is interpreted and comprehended. No matter how explicit the content and how carefully the informant tries to "put the patient in the picture", unless these linguistic and semantic barriers are overcome the effort may be wasted. This is nicely illustrated by a study undertaken by Hugh-Jones *et al.* (1964) who made a special effort to inform patients and to ascertain that they understood about their condition. In spite of these efforts 39% of patients were dissatisfied with the information given, and although the authors had taken special pains to inform patients what was wrong with them, 20% gave the wrong diagnosis on recall four weeks later.

It may be that the doctor is not always the best person to inform patients about their condition if his presence is particularly anxiety provoking, which may happen if patients are from a very different social and educational background. Cartwright (1964) found that working-class patients were more likely to regard nurses as an appropriate source of information than were middle class patients—perhaps because communication was easier?

A more colloquial account of social barriers is given by Cohen (1964) who writes of her observations whilst a patient in a large hospital,

A gap as wide as the River Thames divides the Lambeth mums from the nursing elite with their hockey-team accents and unpowdered complexions (page 27)

Although these experiences may not be typical, this does seem an area towards which many medical and nursing educationalists give scant attention in their teachings.

3. Perhaps the major weakness with the method of information-giving used in hospitals is that the overwhelming majority of patients are *told*, i.e. a verbal approach.

Ley and Spelman (1967) have reviewed attempts to measure the amount of information that patients remember at various intervals of time following instruction. General findings are that the content and accuracy of recall is dramatically affected by the passage of time, this particularly being the case when the information is given on one occasion only. The authors suggest that more attention should be paid to developing ways by which patients can be given information in writing so that it can be easily assimilated. The repetition which then becomes feasible on re-reading will possibly help memory, in spite of possible adverse situational features such as anxiety.

Perhaps less tangible than either information or memory factors are those psychological processes which form an integral part of an individual's personality, and which may operate, via the mechanisms of denial and projection, to protect the personality from excessive trauma. These features were considered by Janis (1958) in his psychoanalytic investigation of anxiety in surgical patients, an important study which is considered in detail in the next section.

Is anxiety reduction beneficial?

As little direct evidence exists, perhaps this question can be tackled by another question, namely, "is there an optimum level of anxiety at which a person can best organize his abilities to cope with a stressful situation".

This is considered by Janis (1958), with specific regard for surgical patients, who found a moderate to high level of preoperative anxiety in 75% of his sample. The percentage of patients expressing fears became higher as the time of operation approached and reached a peak when actually in the operating room. An interesting finding was that individual differences in anxiety reactions to major surgery, minor surgery and routine dental treatment were slight in the immediate preoperative period.

However, following surgery the picture is very different. The anxiety levels of those patients who underwent minor operations fell sharply, in contrast to the more serious cases where anxiety remained high.

Perhaps the main feature revealed by Janis concerns relationships between the pre-operative levels of anxiety, as measured by a self-report inventory, and subsequent post-operative behaviour. Patients who displayed moderate anxiety displayed fewer evidences of emotional disturbances at the recovery stage, whereas those patients who recorded high *or low* pre-operative levels manifested significantly more symptoms such as acute anxiety states, hostility and depression. The most satisfactory adjustments are made by those patients with moderate anxiety. Janis carried out extensive qualitative analysis of the data and makes the following points which highlight the effects of denial mechanisms:

> When actual suffering occurs, it comes as a somewhat shocking surprise and is frequently interpreted as meaning that someone has failed to treat them properly. The usual pains, discomforts and unpleasant post-operative treatments tend to be regarded as unnecessary accidents caused by the hospital staff. Thus, instead of regarding their suffering as an unavoidable consequence of surgery, they are inclined to place the blame upon danger-control personnel, who are now perceived as being inept, unprotective, or malevolent (Janis, 1958; page 400)

From his extensive psychoanalytical study of these patients Janis concludes that the patient with *very* high pre-operative anxiety usually has a chronic psychoneurotic disposition and has probably suffered from a variety of acute episodes in the past. Those with high levels expressed fears of permanent injuries, or of mistakes on the part of the surgeon. Attempts to reassure both these groups met with little success, even when assayed by high-status people.

Those patients who exhibited moderate pre-operative anxiety levels, says Janis, are basically emotionally stable and are able to form a rational assessment of their predicament. They trust the authority figures around them and believe the information they are given.

In the "very low" anxiety patients, the denial mechanism seemed to operate from the very beginning, and, like the "very high" patients, this group was characterized by post-operative emotional disturbances.

For summary purposes two particular findings are of interest from this research:

1. Patients who are undergoing relatively minor operations appear to be just as anxious pre-operatively as those selected for more severe surgery.
2. Post-operative emotional disturbances were found in both high and low anxiety groups, with the moderate anxiety group making the best overall post-operative adjustment.
3. The detailed insight into patients' fears can be accomplished by means of detailed content analysis of qualitative data, but any real exploration of these complex feelings is quite clearly expensive in time and manpower.

It is apposite at this point to consider the effects of excessive anxiety on the physiological functioning of the body, a complex but nevertheless pertinent question. Williams and Jones (1968) have investigated pre-operative anxiety with particular reference to anaesthesia and they direct attention to the advantages that their method of continuous physiological monitoring has over verbal report assessment, namely that it can be carried on through anaesthesia and during the operation itself.

Adopting the view that stress may produce different patterns of response in different individuals, e.g. a rise in blood pressure in one patient may be paralleled by an increase in muscle tension in another, these investigators recorded pulse rate, digital volume, arterial pulse wave velocity and galvanic skin response, for six patients before and during the operation. Within the limitations of their small sample, Williams and Jones found:

1. Each patient showed a similarity of reaction for the same measure.
2. The pattern of responses for different measures were not necessarily similar.
3. The level of autonomic arousal was modified by pre-medication of Meperidine 50 mgs plus Atropine 0·2 mgs.
4. Noxious stimuli *do* reach the central nervous system under anaesthesia.

Those patients who received no premedication required a higher dosage of induction anaesthetic than did premedicated patients.

These interesting variations in response style at the level of basic physiological functioning are supportive of the situational anxiety theory of Mandler and Sarason mentioned on page 32.

Williams and Jones conclude that pre-operative anxiety significantly affects a patient's physiological state at the time of operation, which,

> Suggests that a high level of anxiety may be more physiologically disruptive than many realise.

In a further study, Williams *et al.* (1969) examined the hypothesis that the quantity of thiopentone required for induction anaesthesia is related to pre-operative anxiety level. Induction was deemed to have occurred by the disappearance of spontaneous galvanic skin responses, and pre-operative anxiety level was assessed by the IPAT test (Cattell and Scheier, 1961).

When dosage of thiopentone was correlated with pre-operative anxiety, for a sample of 10 patients, the figure of 0·69 was significant at the 5% level of probability. The authors therefore suggest that the amount of thiopentone required to induce anaesthesia could be a useful measure of pre-operative anxiety—albeit a retrospective one for some purposes and conclude,

> The study emphasised our previous findings that there is an imperative need for adequate management of patients' preoperative anxiety, not only to reduce the thiopentone sodium required for induction, but, more generally to optimise his overall physiological status.

46

Edwards *et al.* (1956), in a survey of 1,000 deaths following anaesthesia, found that almost 20% of all deaths were occasioned by cardio-vascular collapse following thiopentone overdosage, so it is certainly desirable to reduce dosages of this drug.

Anxiety, communication, and pain

Some of the inadequacies of hospitals as learning environments, particularly for the receipt and storage of information, are cogently assessed by Ley and Spelman (1967) who include the following suggestions for improving these seemingly ubiquitous shortcomings:

1. Patients are usually told more than they can remember.
2. Patients should have a record of what has been said to them.
3. Patients remember best the statements to which they attribute most importance.
4. Patients tend to remember information given early in the interview.
5. Patients who are knowledgeable about medical matters remember more.
6. Least and most anxious patients remember *less* than moderately anxious patients.

It seems, therefore, that research into memory shows that people organize and store their information around a few central concepts or "schemata" which are then organized into a plan or strategy which helps them to cope with a given predicament. This claim has extensive experimental support from the work of Bartlett (1933) and Miller *et al.* (1960).

Additionally, evidence exists to support the contention that when patients have a clear idea of events appertaining to treatment and recovery, the incidence of disruptive symptoms is reduced. For example, Raven and Rietsema (1957) demonstrated that membership of groups which possessed unclear goals, or unclear paths to attain goals, produced very unpleasant emotional states among group members.

Although the terms "information", "anxiety", and "reassurance" are frequently encountered in the literature relating to patient care, wide variations exist both in the apparent meaning of the words, and in their descriptions. It is, therefore, imperative that ambiguity be reduced by careful operational definition, especially if the resultant data are to be compared with results from other sources.

In a notable attempt to examine the effects of reassurance and information on post-operative pain, Egbert *et al.* (1964) utilized an experimental method, an approach rarely found in patient care research of a behavioural kind although common in biochemical comparisons and drug trials. The patients studied were undergoing abdominal surgery of various kinds and were divided into an "informed" group of 51 and a "control" group of 46. The former were visited pre-operatively by the anaesthetist, who provided information about the nature and severity of post-operative pain, and how this may partly be alleviated by relaxation and careful movements. The precise nature of what was said is not reported but,

> The presentation was given in a manner of enthusiasm and confidence; the patients were not informed we were conducting a study. The surgeons, not knowing which patients were receiving special care, continued their practices as usual.

Post-operative narcotics were prescribed by the surgical residents and administered by the ward nurses, "who were also unaware that we were studying these patients"—a statement which makes considerable assumptions about the experimental milieu. In order to examine the effectiveness of the procedures post-operative narcotic-consumption was compared between the two groups. Over a five-day period informed group patients made fewer requests for drugs and also exhibited more rapid improvements in general condition than did control group patients.

This was one of the earliest examples of the use of a natural science design to test the "reassurance" hypothesis and it is reasonable to assume that, at least in part, the results were achieved by anxiety reduction.

However, information-giving did not seem to produce anxiety reduction in the study reported by Keller (1965), although, for reasons which will be discussed, the results should be interpreted with caution.

A total of 36 patients formed equal experimental and control groups. After completing two anxiety inventories, the IPAT (Cattell and Scheier, 1961) and the Anxiety Differential, patients were given information derived from a definite plan, rather than the loosely described "reassurance and encouragement" used by Egbert in the study described above. Selection of items was on the basis of the author's general orientation towards the concept of "safety needs" described by Maslow (1954). To provide comparative scores, the anxiety tests were administered on three occasions before admission, after the operation, and three weeks following discharge from hospital.

When the results of these tests were compared, Keller found no support for the hypothesis that the experimental group would exhibit less anxiety than the controls, *as measured by the anxiety tests used*. This is an important point, because, although Keller finds a variety of possible explanations for these results, what she does not do is to question the appropriateness of the measures used.

As discussed in Chapter 2, it is now generally recognized that there are at least two major types of anxiety; "trait" or anxiety proneness, and "state" which may fluctuate according to circumstances. The IPAT test is for the measurement of "trait" anxiety, easily seen by the frequency of words such as "often" and "always" which appear in the questions, and is, therefore, a totally unsuitable tool for the assessment of short-term changes in anxiety state.

Attempts have been made to modify post-operative pain by varying the type of nursing employed. A study by McBride (1967) is typical of this approach, in this case the nursing approach being varied in three ways,

1. The investigator tried to ascertain what the patient meant by 'pain' and then tried to design nursing practice which would alleviate the pain. Comfort measures were taken, and medication given as usual.

Control 1. This approach viewed the patients' complaints as a request for medication. Only two questions were asked, where is the pain? How long have you had it? All of this group received medication.

Control 2. Received the usual hospital approach.

Relief from pain was measured initially and long-term by verbal statements of improvement, decreases in pulse/respiration rates and changes in non-verbal behaviour.

Results—on the basis of three groups of seven patients—indicated that the first approach brought more relief than the other two. The author concludes that drugs may not always be indicated for pain relief, i.e. that they may be necessary but not sufficient for maximum patient welfare.

Several similar investigations have been reported. Riehl (1966), Barron (1964), Moss and Meyer (1966), are a selection, but, as in the above study by McBride, results are often marred by methodological weakness. The numbers are often small, very often the investigator is single-handed thus exposing the data to observer bias, personality and sex characteristics are often ignored, and the measurement tools used, particularly in the assessment of anxiety, are often inappropriate.

Research which allows insight into the ways by which nurses infer suffering in patients and some of the variables which affect this process has been reported by Davitz and Pendleton (1969). The authors point out that,

—there has been almost no research concerning nurses' inferences of patients' suffering.

The authors examined possible effects of cultural differences, clinical specialities, patient diagnosis, and patient characteristics upon ways in which judgements are made about suffering. Findings suggest that inferences of suffering differ according to the social and cultural background of the nurse, patient diagnosis, and age and socio-economic background of the patient.

Graham and Conley (1971) tried to evaluate anxiety and fear in surgical patients by means of a checklist of physiological and psychological manifestations. They used a trained observer who interviewed patients the evening before surgery took place. If, from the checklist of

26 items, six items were observed to be present on at least three occasions during the visit, and anxiety was inferred from the tone and content of the patient's speech, the patient was then given an "anxiety grade".

The sample consisted of 70 patients, 50 male and 20 female, entering two surgical wards. The authors claim that elevated systolic blood pressure and verbally expressed apprehension can be accepted as significant evidences of pre-operative anxiety and summarize by stating,

> The most useful and frequently occurring indicators of preoperative anxiety or fear were the subjective responses of the patients during both the preoperative period and post-operative visit.

Summary

As nurse/patient communication is essentially a two-way process, the recognition of anxiety in patients is based on selective cues, such as facial expression, eye contact, involuntary movements, all of which have been examined by Argyle (1969) when studying interpersonal communication. The recognition of appropriate cues is a complex process, and one which may be affected by a wide range of social, cultural and educational differences on the part of both nurses and patients; an area worthy of further detailed investigation.

From a consideration of the research reviewed in this and preceding chapters, it is clear that pain is influenced by anxiety, that anxiety is influenced by information about future events, and the lack of information, acting via the medium of increased anxiety, can occasion more pain and suffering in post-operative patients than perhaps need be the case.

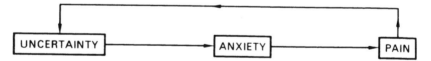

The above diagram represents these relationships and shows how a circular or "loop" effect can develop, with an increase in pain causing further uncertainty and anxiety in turn.

When considering anxiety, a major shortcoming has often been that doctors and nurses have claimed to know precisely what incidents occurring in hospital life occasion anxiety in patients, rather than these incidents being specified by patients themselves. For purposes of the present study, it was therefore decided to ask patients directly, by means of pre-discharge interviews of a representative sample, to identify anxiety-producing incidents which may have occurred during their stay.

SECTION II

The Pilot Study

CHAPTER 4

Interviews with Patients and Development of Information Schedule

The hospital in question is situated in a Metropolitan Regional Board Area and has approximately 180 beds. The catchment area from which most patients are drawn is of a predominantly working-class urban type.

Following initial correspondence, a meeting with senior hospital officers took place during which the aims and objectives of the project were discussed. It was then arranged for the author to observe two surgical wards for a period of four weeks, with the following objectives:

1. To assess the feasibility of these wards being used for a controlled experiment.
2. To assess attitudes of nursing staff to the presence of a research worker on the ward for several hours each day.
3. To examine statistics of patient "turnover" for a representative period so as to establish what size of sample might reasonably be expected.
4. To sample patients' attitudes towards the idea of being interviewed and participating in a research project generally—a very important objective.
5. To spend the third and fourth weeks on interviewing a selected group of patients about their stay in hospital with particular emphasis on anxiety-creating circumstances, if no serious problems emerged in the first weeks.

Findings

The two wards in question appeared quite suitable for the intended research and shared several common features. They were structurally similar, containing 30 beds laid out in the open or "Nightingale" style, and were of approximately similar appearance. Senior medical staff treated patients on both wards, with the exception of the gynaecologist, and house officers divided their time in a similar way. This latter fact was important as the prescribing of post-operative analgesics is almost always the responsibility of junior medical staff.

Before entering the hospital, some anxiety was felt as to the feelings and attitudes of nurses towards the idea of having a research worker on the ward. This proved to be unfounded for the author received considerable help in the collection of patient turnover statistics, explanations of the way drug records were kept, days and times of admission, and innumerable introductions.

The patient turnover figures needed careful investigation, for, if as was hoped, the initial interviews with patients were to be followed by a more extensive evaluation of the effects of pre-operative information, the numbers of patients suitable for a research sample had to be accurately ascertained.

Attitudes of patients from both wards were extremely encouraging. During the first two weeks, lengthy spells on the wards and many informal conversations failed to elicit hostility to the questions asked, so it was decided to go ahead with the more formal interviews.

The aim of these preliminary interviews was to gain insight into anxiety-creating events which had occurred during the patient's stay in hospital. Whenever possible they were conducted on the day before discharge home, covered a representative sample of 22 male and 18 female patients, and took approximately four weeks to complete. Sample characteristics are shown in Tables 1 and 2. The interview technique was loosely structured, with the conversation being "steered" in the desired direction rather than a series of formally organized questions.

A formal introduction was always followed by the statement, "I am particularly interested in things which may have caused worry or anxiety during your stay". A brief outline of the aims of the Study of Nursing Care project followed. It was deemed essential to point out that the in-

TABLE 1

Initial interview patients: operation type

Table 1	Operation type	Numbers
	Pyeloplasty	4
	Hysterectomy	11
	Appendicectomy	6
	Cholecystectomy	3
	Varicose vein stripping	4
	Partial gastrectomy	4
	Prostatectomy	3
	Vagotomy and pyloroplasty	2
	Nephrectomy	2
	Partial thyroidectomy	1

54

TABLE 2

Initial interview patients population
characteristics

Variable	Number	Sex	
		Male	Female
Sex			
Male	18		
Female	22		
Age			
16–29		6	7
30–44		4	5
46–60		5	6
60+		3	4
Socio-economic status	1	–	–
Registrar General	2	2	3
Classification	3	7	7
	4	5	9
	5	4	3

vestigator, and others who would be actively involved, were trained nurses, particularly as some reports have noted a reluctance on the part of patients to be critical of nurses (Cartwright, 1964; Raphael, 1969); the patients, therefore, would not be criticizing to "outsiders", a situation of which some openly disapproved.

The response rate was 100%: not one patient who was approached failed to co-operate while many openly said they enjoyed the experience. Results were analysed by content from tapes of the interview. Those comments relating to fears and anxieties were noted, and then categorized according to the relevant sphere of activities, e.g. anaesthesia, pre-operative nursing, pain and discomfort, an account of which now follows.

1. Anaesthesia

Over 70% of patients found one or more aspects of anaesthesia caused anxiety, a finding which made this the "most mentioned" area. Thirty-six per cent of the sample were uncertain how the anaesthetic would be given; in particular, older patients recalled frightening childhood experiences connected with gas anaesthesia.

> The thing that worried me most before the operation was the idea of the gas. I was worried I would panic when they put the mask over my face.

As would perhaps be expected, patients mentioning the face mask were somewhat older than average, although one man aged 22 recalled a frightening experience of this type at a school dental clinic.

> They had to hold me down in the chair when I had the gas. If I think about it I can smell the gas all this time after.

and,

> If I had realised that it was just an injection in the arm, I would not have been half as worried.

Some of the more articulate patients spoke with great feeling about the disruptive effects of anxiety upon rational thought processes.

> I knew that any rational person would not worry about such a silly thing (recovering consciousness before the surgeon had finished operating) but somehow in the hospital surroundings one tends not to think rationally and becomes concerned with trivialities.
>
> I remember reading in the paper that a patient had died after inhaling vomit on his return to the ward. I thought, "suppose that happened to me" but I suppose I am the worrying kind anyway.

From the above and many similar comments, it is clear that patients are generally uncertain about facts as basic as the way in which the anaesthetic is induced, whether by gas or injection, or even as the next section will explain whether they will "go under" in the ward or operating theatre.

2. Pre-operative preparation

Sixty per cent of the sample mentioned the "ritual" nature of pre-operative preparation almost in the manner of sacrificial rites. These included the donning of gowns, shaving, isolation behind curtains, feelings of loneliness and depersonalization, and, most of all, acute anxiety sometimes bordering on terror.

> I didn't feel too bad until they (the nurses) pulled the curtains round the bed and gave me the gown to put on. I had to put it on back to front, and my fingers felt all weak and shaky. When I found I had it on the wrong way round and had to do it all again I was close to tears. Then I think it was about two hours before the trolley came. It seemed endless. I think it would have been kinder to have seen the other patients rather than to lie behind the curtains stewing.

Not all patients found this procedure stressful. Whether this was for individual reasons, or better support services could not be clearly identified at the time, but the overall importance of this immediate pre-operative phase was emphasized by the accuracy and vividness of recall.

> Whilst waiting to go to the operating theatre I felt very anxious and inadequate. The worst thing was that I didn't really know what was going on so my imagination was working overtime.
>
> I couldn't seem to find out anything definite. I asked a nurse who said, 'don't you worry your head about all that, just lie down and try to get to sleep.' I think it was kindly meant, but it made me feel worse rather than better.

56

Perhaps the most ambiguous pre-operative procedure is the premedication injection, which, unless explained carefully, allows a variety of interpretations. As may be seen from the quote under "Anaesthesia" it was not uncommon to find that some patients confused the premedication injection with the actual anaesthetic, and as time went by, and the expected effects did not occur, it is no wonder that feelings of anxiety became increasingly hard to tolerate. Some patients found this part of the pre-operative procedure less of a strain.

> I had my injection, put on the gown, then the nurse said, "lie there quietly and you will become drowsy and I did. I remember going on the trolley and holding the nurse's hand in the lift. I didn't feel too bad."

In certain cases patients appeared to derive support by "opting out", i.e. abdicating decisions to others, often described by means of an analogous situation with which they were familiar,

> I think it is the same as getting someone, a skilled person that is, to do a job for you.

> You don't keep interfering and asking questions do you? So I just let them get on with the job they were trained for and let them do whatever they liked.

> I don't really understand anything about what was done, but they know better than you do so I just let them get on with it.

Personal preparation, such as genital shaving worried approximately 30% of the sample:

> I know it has to be done, but I felt embarrassed for the nurse as much as myself. I would have thought that we could have done some of it before coming into hospital.

The necessity for shaving was far from clear to some patients:

> I don't really know why I was shaved as the operation was several inches away. I sometimes think this is another bit of hospital ritual.

3. Medication

Nearly 60% of patients interviewed expressed uncertainties over medication, especially pain-relieving drugs and night sedation. The majority of this group said that there were times when they would have liked to request drugs, but due to multiple reasons, of which diffidence rated highly, they were unsure of when, in what manner and to whom the appeal should be made.

The comments of many patients carried the implicit assumption that someone, usually a doctor or nurse, would automatically know when medication was required and provide it. An interesting feature of these comments was the awareness that most patients were "automatically" given one or two doses of pain-relieving drugs during the initial post-operative period, which was then followed by apparent ambiguity as to whether this practice would continue or the initiative left with the patient. In consequence, a lengthy period of time might elapse before the patient was driven to complain, or a nurse to recognize that severe pain existed. Many patients hesitated to ask.

> I thought that if I needed them I would have been given them without having to ask (pain-relievers). If ever I had to come in again I would know better.

> I knew the nurses were busy and I didn't like to bother them too much.

Obtaining medication at night presented vexing problems to many patients:

> I couldn't get to sleep for the first two nights owing to the strange surroundings. I did ask the night nurse, but she said the night sister would have to see me. When the night sister came round I asked her. She said I couldn't have any as I was not written-up for them. I didn't get much sleep, but you don't like to keep asking.

In complex organizations like hospitals a great many procedures become "routinized", a state of affairs which works satisfactorily for most of the time, but which can occasionally operate to the detriment, rather than to the advantage of patients, as in the following case:

> I was in quite a lot of pain with my kidney before the operation. I asked for something but the sister said I must ask the doctor as I had not been prescribed pain-killers until after the operation. I didn't see the doctor all day and in the evening I felt worn out with the pain. When my wife came to visit she went to see the sister in a bit of a temper about it. The sister rang the doctor and he came up in a few minutes.
>
> I was better off at home really because my own doctor had given me some quite strong tablets and I took a couple when the pain was bad. I felt angry at being treated in such an offhand manner when I was in real pain, like they thought I was putting it on.

During these initial interviews it was most noticeable that patients categorized analgesics on the basis of "hierarchy of potency", with injected drugs—irrespective of kind—judged as the most potent, and "aspirin-like" tablets judged as the least potent. The majority of patients exhibited fears about taking pain-relievers for other than the very minimum of time, many stating that it was "better" to do without drugs even if that meant tolerating considerable pain and discomfort. Many comments were made which linked pain-relievers with drugs taken illegally, with the attendant risks of addiction clearly in mind.

The overwhelming assumption was that these drugs are harmful under all circumstances;

I never have been one for tablets and pills. Some people are always taking aspirins and things but not me. I think they are a form of poison to the body, so I did without them most of the time and tried to stick it out.

You hear so much about drugs these days. I had an injection for the pain, but it made me feel queer and lightheaded—not at all nice.

Prompt

Did you have any other injections?

No! I felt I would sooner put up with the pain than be in a drugged state again.

The risk, and speed of acquiring dependency on drugs appears widely misunderstood by patients:

I think the injections helped the pain but I felt so dopey afterwards. You have to be so careful with these strong drugs, you don't want to get hooked on them do you?

I had three injections at intervals of about six hours as the pain was pretty bad. Then I started thinking, 'You've had rather a lot of that stuff my girl, better ease it off a bit.' I stuck it out for a few hours and then asked the sister if I could have tablets instead.

The idea that tablets were less harmful than injections was common.

I was glad to get off the injections and on to the tablets. They didn't work quite so well but at least they are less harmful to you.

On consideration of these statements it is clear that considerable misunderstandings about medication exist on the part of many patients; a situation not helped by the present nature of analgesic prescription and administration in hospitals where, in practical parlance, the doctor occupies a relatively minor role. Analgesic prescription is often routinized (unless medically contra-indicated), rather than individually determined, and as the dosage is usually "p.r.n." (when required), all subsequent decisions are a nursing matter providing that they fall within the scope of the prescription. It is therefore clear that whether a patient receives an analgesic drug every six hours, or whether he receives none at all, is fairly and squarely the responsibility of the ward nursing staff.

4. Post-operative

Thirty-five per cent of patients interviewed said that the severity of post-operative pain had taken them by surprise, this particularly being the case with younger patients, some of whom were resentful about the apparent lack of information about severity, and the fact that individuals vary in their reactions to pain:

If I'd known it would be that bad I could have prepared for it. but in fact nobody mentioned it.

Prompt

How would you have prepared?

Answer

I don't know really, but if I had been prepared in my mind I would have felt less of a shock, I think.

I thought as soon as the immediate postoperative period was over I would have been able to get on with my study, but the pain was really bad. I hadn't really thought about pain before and I resented not being told. Thinking back I feel annoyed about it as though I had been treated like a child.

I think people react so differently to operations and pain that some recognition of this would help. Its not much use saying to me, "Look at Mr. . . . , he had the same operation as you and he is running about all over the place". I know how I feel and this attitude seems to deny that people are different. I find this irritating.

5. Recognition of staff

The confusion created in the minds of many patients by the multifariousness of hospital staff has found comment in most surveys. Very few patients appear to completely understand the medical, nursing and lay hierarchies, nor are there particularly convincing arguments as to why they should do. However, it is important that the immediately responsible staff should be recognized as such, their names known somewhat after the style of the "personal doctor" mentioned on page 41. At present this seems far from being the case;

I had a sign over my bed saying Mr. . . . ; but whether I ever saw him or not I wouldn't know.

I never really knew who my doctor was as several different ones dealt with me during my stay. I don't think I had any particular one. This concerned me a bit as they were never really introduced in a proper fashion and I didn't really know whom to approach, or who to ask to see.

These identification difficulties also encompassed nurses, in spite of their spending a much greater time on the wards than doctors. It was also noted that an orderly was little better off as she was overheard telling a patient that the enrolled nurse would be a staff nurse after a further six months' service. Identification difficulties appeared worse in

60

the elderly, many of whom were concerned at their lack of knowledge as to who staff were and how they should be addressed:

> I knew who the sister was because of the dark dress, but all the others were a mystery. This was a bit confusing as I never knew if I was asking the right things of the right people.

> I sometimes worried about whether I was calling people by their proper title. It would have been a help to have some sort of guide—you like to give people their proper title.

Considerable misunderstanding exists about early ambulation, i.e. getting patients out of bed, often within 24 hours of the operation. About 60% of the entire group did not, on the whole, have much idea of the therapeutic value of this, and unfortunately, in some cases, thought it was for the nurses' convenience rather than a "treatment". Consequently, expressions of resentment were not uncommon;

> It seems a sort of ritual which has to be done no matter how dreadful you feel. I felt pretty awful, and asked the nurse if I could go back to bed. She said that if Mr. .... (surgeon) came along and found me in bed she would be for it!

As these same patients were generally less hostile to the idea of physiotherapy—in spite of this being equally unpleasant—the provision of relevant information may make early ambulation, if not exactly popular, at least more bearable.

Interesting comments were made concerning the actual location of recovery of consciousness, often linked to rather "territorial" attachment to a particular bed position in the ward. Those patients who were placed in a recovery room seemed concerned, as they expected to find themselves back in "their own" bed; similar sentiments were voiced by those whose bed position was changed—a factor which occasioned mention even if the patient had only been in the ward a matter of hours.

> I came round from the anaesthetic and was very upset to find that my bed had been moved. I sort of expected to return to the same place.

Bed positioning in an open ward is often a reflection of degree of illness, it being customary to have the more seriously ill patients in positions affording good observation. Quite often patients realise this and commonly speak of bed position as a form of "illness hierarchy";

> I now realise I must have been pretty rough to have been in number one bed. That is where the nurses can keep a good eye on you.

Thirty per cent of the entire sample had received intravenous fluids or blood transfusions: 70% of these could not recall prior warning about this, an event which when discovered upon regaining consciousness, was often interpreted as a sign of complications—intravenous fluids undoubtedly confer a "serious" status to patients;

When I came round and saw the blood bottle I was shaken. I thought, 'this is much worse than I bargained for'.

Summary

The preceding account of the types and distribution of anxieties allows some insight into the observations and feelings of this group of patients. As the sample was representative, there was little reason to think these findings atypical of patients in general who were treated in this hospital; it was therefore felt that the data could form the foundations of an empirical study.

The major features emerging from these interviews were the obviously disruptive effects of anxiety upon rational thought process, together with the distress this occasioned. These largely qualitative data add emphasis to the stress theory of Mandler and Sarason (1952) noted in Chapter 2.

Medical information, particularly that which may be of a personal nature, is of obvious importance to patients (Cartwright, 1964; Joyce, 1964), and its shortcomings were frequently mentioned by the interviewees. It is clearly difficult to compartmentalize information-giving, but it was felt that sufficient scope existed in the nursing information area for purposes of the present study, without the introduction of further variables.

Development of patient information schedule

The interviews yielded data which were both interesting and informative, but of course the essentially qualitative nature of this material would gain in validity if it could be shown that the provision of "nursing" information would. prevent or reduce anxiety. For this purpose, a research design was required which would allow information to be the main independent variable, the manipulation of which would be monitored by a range of dependent variables.

Content analysis revealed five broad areas of information-lack, ranging from everday routine matters to specialized technical knowledge. Uncertainties existed about:

1. Hospital matters generally
2. Ward practice
3. Pre-operative procedures
4. Post-operative procedures
5. Pain and discomfort aspects.

For purposes of standardization information relating to these five areas was assembled into a "schedule", selected according to the following criteria:

1. Its relevance to the expressed uncertainties of the patients who were interviewed.

62

2. Appropriateness to the operation concerned.
3. The vocabulary and phraseology, which must be understandable to the widest possible range of individuals.
4. The stressing of a "core" of important information.
5. As little information exists as to the "precise" uncertainties which arouse anxiety in patients, a fairly wide range would be incorporated, at least initially.

SECTION III

The Main Study

CHAPTER 5

Formulation of Hypothesis and Research Design

The main experimental hypothesis was formulated as follows: patients who were given information appertaining to their illness and recovery would, when compared to an appropriate control group, report less anxiety and pain during the post-operative recovery period.

Adequate testing of this hypothesis required a suitably controlled situation. In planning the effects of treatment or experience on a group of patients it is usually necessary to observe a control group, the characteristics of which largely resemble those of the experimental group. As comparison may be influenced by a wide range of personal characteristics such as age, sex, and number of previous admissions, a process of "matching" is frequently adopted. This involves the comparison of "pairs" of subjects who share common characteristics including the operation type, e.g. two males, aged 31–40 years, with similar social and educational backgrounds, admitted for partial gastrectomy, one of whom would join the experimental group, the other the control group, i.e. a "matched pairs" design.

There are, however, two varieties of possible matching (Billewicz, 1964). In the former, patients are matched pair for pair as described above. The second method, described by Billewicz as "frequency matching", is where the identity of actual pairs is not preserved, but the composition of the experimental and control groups is so manipulated that the distribution of sampling between the matching categories is the same in each group. Therefore the experiment is performed on two comparable groups rather than on several comparable pairs. As really close matching of the type described is difficult in clinical research (it may be difficult to "match" patients on more than two or three variables) frequency matching is a useful approach.

Before finishing the research design, the following underlying assumptions were isolated:

1. That pain is a combination of physical and psychological factors which, taken in their entirety, form the pain experience.
2. That pain and anxiety are closely related phenomena, i.e. as anxiety increases the awareness of pain increases.

3. That the reduction of uncertainty about future events is a viable way of reducing anxiety.
4. That considerable evidence exists to show that the reduction of excessive anxiety in surgical patients is desirable.
5. That nursing information is that information which a trained and experienced surgical nurse could reasonably be expected to possess and to pass on to patients at opportune times and in an appropriate manner.

The investigation commenced in the two surgical wards from which patients for the initial interviews were drawn, and involved two researchers who alternated in role between "informer" and "observer". To help eliminate bias from the observations, or at least to balance inevitable bias, the following procedures were incorporated into the experimental design.

1. After considerable rehearsal of aims and objectives, the initial "informer" was selected from the two researchers by the spin of a coin. This person was responsible for the selection of suitable patients and their random allocation to either informed or control groups *without communicating this information to the observer,* so that the subsequent post-operative data were collected by someone who was "blind" as to whether the patient belonged to the informed or control category. After every 10 patients, the roles of informer and observer were reversed.
2. After perusal of past records and discussion with medical staff, appendicectomy was chosen as the "least serious" operation for inclusion. The sample was drawn largely from patients whose operations were deemed of "moderate severity", e.g. cholecystectomy; the upper limit was left open at this stage, but in fact tended to be determined by necessity for transfer to intensive care.
3. Male and female patients were included and it was hoped that possible observer bias due to sex differences would be nullified by having a male and female researcher.
4. Patients were seen by the informer as soon as possible after admission, an interview room was provided for this purpose. Their approval and cooperation was sought, after which the admission procedure (described later) took its course.
5. Following their operation, patients were visited thrice daily by the observer who recorded progress for the first five days of the recovery period.

Measurement tools used (dependent variables)

1. The S–R Inventory of Anxiousness—used on admission

As anxiety formed an important feature of this investigation, it was obviously desirable to incorporate some type of measure. The *S–R*

Inventory (Endler *et al.*, 1962) attempts to measure anxiety-proneness of individuals in response to specified situations, e.g. during a visit to the dentist, or after accidentally cutting a finger. It is, therefore, an estimate of the way a person habitually responds, i.e. "trait anxiety", and should not be particularly sensitive to short term fluctuations in anxiety state (Appendix C).

The inventory was originally devised by considering the relative contribution of situations and individual differences in the production of anxiety. Furthermore it allows the effects of specific situations to be separated from the modes of response which serve as reactions, e.g. one person's response to a visit to the dentist may emerge in the cardiovascular mode—"my heart pounds"—whereas another may react by sweating.

The original inventory consisted of 11 situations thought to be familiar to college students. It included both social and non-social situations, which varied from innocuous to threatening. Choice of situations for inclusion was largely dependent upon the use to which the inventory was directed; therefore, in the present case, half of the situations chosen were relevant to the present research which were presented with half from the original inventory (Endler and Hunt, 1969).

The format consisted of 10 situations and nine modes of response, plus two supplementary questions. Each response was rated on a five-point scale, with a high score indicating high anxiety.

The *S–R Inventory* was thought suitable for this particular research as situations appropriate for the purpose could be specifically chosen, leaving modes of response virtually the same as in the original version. Some initial concern was felt about the number of responses required—a total of 110—but these fears were not realized, perhaps owing to the repetitive nature of the layout.

In summary, the main objective in using a pre-operative measure of anxiousness was to test its ability to predict post-operative pain as measured by analgesic consumption and patients' verbal report. If this is the case, it should then be possible to establish this relationship statistically.

2. Patient Subjective State Scale (PSS)

This included a number of questions relating to patients' state of well-being which were documented by the observer three times a day. The response was rated on a five-point scale and entered on the data sheet. Considered in order of presentation the questions were:

i. The pain thermometer (a visual cardboard scale)

Some of the difficulties of measuring pain are considered in Chapter 1. However, the pain thermometer was used by Joyce (1968) and Lasagna (1958) and received favourable mention from both:

The researcher presents a pain thermometer to subjects, asking them to place at appropriate "temperatures" the main points, very severe, severe, moderate and slight. By then calculating the number of degrees between pain levels, it was hoped that one would have some measure of the relative importance assigned to these levels by different people. (Lasagna, 1958)

In order to keep to a five-point scale the following "temperatures" were used;

a. I have no pain at all
b A little pain
c Quite a lot of pain
d. A very bad pain
e. As much pain as I could possibly bear.

The colloquial nature of these phrases reflect the comments of ward patients when replying to the question, "How much pain have you?" Patients were shown the pain thermometer at the pre-operative interview and given an explanation of how it worked.

Question ii.

Is your pain local, that is, just around the site of the operation, or is it widespread?

It is a common clinical observation that wound pain may sometimes be restricted to the immediate area, whereas at other times, or in other patients, it may be widespread. It is accepted that the origins of widespread pain may be diverse, e.g. "wind", nevertheless the question was included on clinical evidence that widespread pain often appears to be reported by more anxious patients.

Question iii.

How do you feel in yourself, by that I mean what sort of mood are you in and how is your morale?

It was hypothesized that less anxious patients would report higher morale; a major finding of Egbert *et al.* (1964). Clinically speaking, high morale should be characterized by alertness, increased level of overall activity and an interest in decision taking, all of which should expedite both biological and psychological recovery.

Question iv.

Have you any feeling of sickness (nausea)?

For many years clinical evidence has suggested the existence of a positive relationship between level of anxiety and post-operative

70

vomiting in surgical patients, a hypothesis tested by Dumas and Leonard (1963) and upheld following a well-controlled experiment. Anxious patients vomited in the recovery room significantly (the word *significantly* denotes statistical significance when used in this report) more than did less anxious ones.

These four questions were asked three times daily; the following three questions were asked only on the morning visit:

Question v.

How did you sleep last night?

Causes of sleeplessness vary widely and include individual variations in sleep patterns, insomnia due to anxiety, noise in the ward, pain and the necessity for night-time treatments. Despite these variations it was decided to compare informed and control patients' ratings of this variable.

Question vi.

How are you managing your food?

A general assessment of appetite.

Question vii.

During the initial interviews with post-operative patients the following question was asked "What single thing contributed most to your comfort and wellbeing whilst recovering from your operation?" Answers varied considerably but the six most· frequently occurring were (in random order), visiting time, talking to other patients, tablets or injections, talking to your doctor, nursing attention, and talking to sister or nurses. These findings were subsequently assembled to form a multiple choice question which was printed on a card and shown to patients on the morning visit. The question "Which of these, if any, have been the greatest source of comfort to you over the past twenty-four hours" was asked and the choice recorded. If none of these factors was relevant, patients' own feelings were noted.

It is important to recognize that recordings on the PSS are observers' ratings of patients' statements, which are, in effect, a translation of the patients' comments and run the risk of bias. In order to minimize the risk, pilot trials, during which both investigators visited a patient simultaneously and recorded reactions independently, were carried out. After a number of practice ratings, final trials on eight patients were recorded by both investigators and the agreement between them assessed statistically by means of Spearman's Rank Correlation. (A measure of association between two variables. See appendix note on Statistics.) The resultant figure of 0·88 indicated a high level of observer reliability.

3. Post-operative analgesic consumption

This has been widely used as an indirect index of pain and seems, at first sight, to offer an objective measure. Although requests for analgesics might reasonably be expected to reflect levels of pain, the issue is complicated by individual differences between patients, especially in their willingness, or otherwise to request drugs. The protocols reported in Chapter 4 indicate some of the uncertainties expressed by patients as to the procedures for requesting drugs and their fears about side effects. Hence, it is perhaps too optimistic to consider analgesic consumption as a truly accurate measure of pain, but, when considered with other measures, it forms useful and easily quantifiable data.

A record of all analgesic drugs given for the first five post-operative days, calculated from the time of operation, was therefore added to the patients' records. To compensate for differences in the type of analgesic used, e.g. omnopon or pethidine, the drug dosages were reduced to a "morphine equivalent score". This was achieved by establishing the dose of a given drug which was, according to the pharmacological literature, equal to 10 mgs of morphine sulphate, and calling this 10 units (Lasagna and Beecher, 1954; Egbert *et al.,* 1964), thus making comparison possible.

4. Post-operative vomiting

Incidence of vomiting was recorded by a small chart attached to the patients' chartboards. This was completed by nursing staff who entered each incidence of vomiting day and night, supplementary information being provided by Question 3 of the PSS.

5. Ward sisters' assessment

Sisters were asked to rate the post-operative progress of each patient on the basis of her own professional judgement on a five-point scale ranging from "unusually well" to "very slowly" (Appendix F). This served the important double functions of, firstly, involving the ward nursing staff in the research, and secondly, seeing if variations in other measures of post-operative progress would be paralleled by a rating based upon professional insight. The scale was completed on the sixth post-operative day.

6. Patients' discharge rating

This was an attempt to obtain patients' feelings about participating in the research, particularly the thrice-daily post-operative visits. Again, a five-point scale ranging from "very helpful" to "a nuisance" was used (Appendix G). The ratings were anonymous and patients were asked to seal the answers in the envelope provided, which would not be opened until the end of the trials. Although it was difficult to obtain unbiased statements under such conditions it was felt that these scales would provide some feed-back about the visits.

The aim, therefore, was to provide a fairly extensive insight into the post-operative recovery of each individual patient by means of the above records.

Procedure for patients' admission

Most patients' first encounter with hospital took place in the out-patients' department, usually following referral by their general practitioner and with the aim of seeking a consultant's opinion. If an operation was then required, the patient was usually informed at the time and then waited a length of time which varied according to factors such as the urgency of the medical condition, the length of waiting lists and whether treatment was being provided privately or under the National Health Service.

Notification of the date and time of admission is sent about 10 to 14 days beforehand. A booklet providing information about the hospital was also sent at this time. After reporting to the ward at the given time, patients were allocated a bed, after which they undressed and gave their day clothes to accompanying relatives or friends, there being no storage facilities available.

Although a distinct procedure for "booking in" patients existed, this was not the responsibility of any particular grade of staff, although it tended to fall to the most senior nurse present. The patient's name, diagnosis, age and religion were entered into the ward book. A label was attached to the right wrist. At this time it was customary for a "consent to operation" form to be signed, by which patients gave formal consent to the administration of an anaesthetic and also acknowledged that it could not be assumed that the operation would be performed by a particular surgeon, a point which occasionally provoked reactions from patients who had assumed just this.

During the period of observation the investigator made an attempt to establish a "pattern" of routine admission procedure, a ploy which brought success only in the more obvious things such as personal details. What sort of information, if any, passed between the nurses responsible for admissions and the patient being admitted, was almost impossible to isolate beyond the fact that some nurses were largely silent, at best answering direct questions, at worst adopting a discouraging demeanour. The majority of nurses attempted to allay fears by "cheering up" rather than by giving information which may have been more effective. Most routine questions were answered readily, but more specific things were often referred either to the doctor or ward sister.

Perhaps the most striking thing to emerge was that no one person was designated for admitting patients. It depended upon who was available at the time, which meant that some patients were admitted by the ward sister, others by an enrolled nurse.

Occasionally, patients were admitted 48–72 hours before they were to undergo surgery, but usually it was one day before. Following the admission procedure, patients may or may not be confined to bed, and at some time during this pre-operative stage a routine medical examination was performed, followed by an anaesthetist's assessment. During this time, specific pre-operative instructions relating to diet, rest, or any restriction where the patient's co-operation is essential were given, but although questions about general post-operative procedures may be answered, little information of this sort was directly offered. It is obviously difficult to generalize where no specific data were recorded, but the contention of Cartwright (1964) that more information appears to be given to patients in the higher socio-economic groups, finds support from the present observations, largely it would seem, because of their greater articulateness and more questioning manner.

Experimental procedure

Following the cross-checks on observer reliability, the procedure was as follows:

Operation lists were obtained several days in advance of admission, so as to identify suitable patients, i.e. those admitted for appendicectomy or more severe operations. If doubts arose about suitability, medical staff opinion was sought.

The initial choice of informer/observer was determined by a coin-toss and subsequently followed in random order. The informer then randomly allocated the first group of patients to informed or control groups.

An example of the research admission procedure now follows:

Pre-operatively

1. Self-introduction to patient with brief description of what would be involved, followed by a request for co-operation.

> Good day Mr./Mrs. . . . . , I am . . . . and I am from the Royal College of Nursing. My colleague . . . and I are interested in the way people respond to coming into hospital and having an operation. To do this, we are asking the co-operation of patients having certain operations. This involves asking you some initial questions, followed by a short interview, and then we keep in touch with you during your stay. Would you care to participate?

2. If the patient agreed to co-operate, main personal details were recorded. Then,

We are particularly interested in the sort of things that worry you. We have a scale here (produce scale) which asks you to grade some common situations.

The S–R inventory was explained. To facilitate this, some examples of five-point scales were devised which patients completed under supervision until they were demonstrably competent.

3. "Informed group" patients then received the schedule of information based upon Appendix D but tailored to each type of operation. Again, if uncertainties existed with regard to individual patients, the doctor was consulted. Every effort was made to make the interview as informal and free from tension as possible and emphasis was laid on major issues in each category rather than giving a wealth of information.

Control group patients were engaged in conversation for an equivalent time. It would be naive to assume that this had no effects, but direct information-giving was avoided.

4. On the morning of the operation, a bedside visit was made to informed patients during which the informer reiterated the central points of information covered during the admission interview. Control patients were visited for an equivalent time and engaged in conversation.

Post-operatively

A morning visit was made by the informer for the first five post-operative days. A record of relevant data was collected by the observer on three separate visits; morning, midday and evening.

The research team were initially very concerned about the effectiveness, or otherwise, of the system of grouping patients and how successfully the observer could be kept "blind" to this grouping when patients were being visited thrice daily. It was soon realized that the greatest threat would come from the patients themselves who could easily "leak" some details of the pre-operative interviews and thus "give the game away". In view of these anxieties, patients' cooperation was sought. It was explained that different groups were being followed and it was important that the observer remained unaware of what transpired at the interview. Therefore, patients were asked to refrain from volunteering information relating to admission, a policy which was successfully followed in the majority of cases.

CHAPTER 6

The First Hospital—Results and Analysis

A total number of 92 patients were approached and invited to participate in the project. From this number complete data were obtained from 68 patients. Reasons for discarding the 26 others included:

1. Two patients preferred not to participate; one because she had not written anything for 20 years and was concerned at the idea of so doing, the second refusal gave no reason.
2. After being interviewed on the day of admission, a history of recent psychiatric illness was subsequently discovered in five patients. Data were collected as arranged and discarded.
3. Post-operative emotional instability developed in four patients which rendered data collection uncertain.
4. Seven patients developed post-operative complications which delayed, or rendered atypical, their recovery.
5. Eight patients went straight from the operating theatre to the intensive care unit. They were visited and the data discarded.

Table 3 gives the range of operations. Tables 4 and 5 show the sample characteristics of those patients for whom data were complete.

The outcome of this first experiment was obviously of great importance, firstly, to assess the feasibility of this type of research in hospital wards and secondly, to assess possible effects of information on pain and anxiety.

Data collection

There were no apparent problems relating to the collection of operation lists and selection of sample patients proceeded as planned. The varied days and times of admissions necessitated both investigators working irregular hours, an unimportant factor for the first research assistant, but one which created problems for subsequent ones.

The research assistant in this type of project was much more than a relatively uninformed data collector. Owing to the "crossover" nature of

TABLE 3

The First Hospital:
Operation types for sample patients

Number of patients	Operation
8	Pyeloplasty
18	Hysterectomy
4	Gastrectomy
4	Vagotomy and pyloroplasty
4	Nephrectomy
2	Resection of colon
2	Cholecystectomy
10	Appendicectomy
4	Haemorrhoidectomy
6	Herniorrhaphy
2	Partial thyroidectomy
4	Others
68	

TABLE 4

Sample characteristics of those for
whom data were complete

Variable	Number	Sex	
Sex		Male	Female
Male	26		
Female	42		
Age			
16–29		8	14
30–44		5	14
45–59		5	12
60+		8	2
Socio-economic status			
Registrar	1	1	–
General's	2	4	4
Classification	3	10	13
	4	3	18
	5	8	7
Marital status			
Married		17	29
Single		8	11
Widow/er		1	–
Divorced		–	2

TABLE 5

Sample characteristics

(i) Total sample

Variable	Mean	Standard deviation	N
Age	40·02	15·46	68
Social class	3·60	0·98	68
Previous admissions	1·35	1·29	68
Birth order	3·57	2·30	68
Length of stay in days	11·45	6·52	68
Total analgesic units	69·41	44·34	68
Admission anxiety score	195·87	55·30	40

(ii) Experimental group

Variable	Mean	Standard deviation	N
Age	41·73	16·20	34
Social class	3·56	0·925	34
Previous admissions	1·33	1·28	34
Birth order	3·52	2·28	34
Length of stay in days	11·55	7·33	34
Total analgesic units	59·85	35·38	34
Admission anxiety score	200·04	53·74	26

(iii) Control group

Variable	Mean	Standard deviation	N
Age	38·85	14·56	34
Social class	3·61	1·08	34
Previous admissions	1·31	1·29	34
Birth order	3·40	2·26	34
Length of stay in days	11·35	5·69	34
Total analgesic units	78·97	50·50	34
Admission anxiety score	188·14	59·35	14

the study design, i.e. alternating between informer and observer, the assistant played an integral part in the organization and day to day running of the project, a role calling for considerable commitment, therefore it was difficult for this role to be carried out by other than a full-time assistant.

A rather unexpected problem occurred with patients who were admitted on Saturdays or Sundays. Owing to the policy of virtually unlimited visiting, it was often difficult to interview patients without them having to leave relatives or friends waiting at the bedside. It was thought preferable to wait for visitors to depart before interviewing as it was thought the alternative may cause patients to hurry their responses, not to mention inconveniencing visitors.

The procedure for pre-operative interviewing worked satisfactorily, a side-room offering suitable accommodation for this stage. No untoward difficulties arose over the giving of information, as this was preceded by careful preparation in line with the operation type and other relevant factors. The *S−R Anxiety Inventory* is one of the longer self-report scales and some concern was felt initially that patients may find its completion tedious. In fact, the average time for completion was 20 minutes, which, although long by some other test standards, seemed quite acceptable to these patients. To some extent this problem of length was helped by the similarity of scoring on each page, the only change being the situation described at the top.

The demonstration five point scale was extremely useful. It ensured that no patient could start the anxiety inventory without firstly demonstrating competence.

Objectives in these first trials of the *S−R Inventory* were:

1. To ascertain whether variations in post-operative state, especially pain as assessed by analgesic consumption, could be predicted by the anxiety score on admission.
2. To gauge patients' reactions to the inventory.
3. By administering the inventory a second time, usually the day before discharge, it was hoped to gain insight into its test−retest reliability, i.e. would patients' second completion relate closely to their first? A total of 34 patients completed two inventories.

Findings

1. To detect possible predictive validity, admission anxiety scores were compared with post-operative analgesic scores from the 40 patients who successfully completed this inventory. For this purpose, the statistical calculation of product-moment correlation (see Appendix note on correlation) was performed, a technique which allows the relationship between two variables to be expressed. The resultant figure of 0.264 signified a moderate positive relationship, which was subsequently shown to be significant at the 5% level (see Appendix note on test of significance). Thus, the implications are that the admission anxiety score acted as a moderately good predictor of post-operative analgesic consumption for this group of patients.

2. Similar correlations were calculated between admission anxiety and all other variables, but of these, only the "length of stay" result was significant (1% level). This very interesting finding does not support the

79

contention of Janis (1958) discussed in Chapter 3, who suggested that similar levels of pre-operative anxiety were experienced by all patients irrespective of severity of the impending operation. The present findings do not strengthen this viewpoint, for in this research the major factor in length of stay was operation type (patients who developed post-operative complications were excluded from this calculation) and, quite clearly, the higher levels of anxiety were recorded by patients undergoing operations of greater severity.

3. Correlations were calculated relating analgesic consumption to each of the 10 situations forming the anxiety inventory. From these comparisons the relative contribution of each situation can be examined and an "hierarchy of relevance" established. Table 6 shows correlations between analgesics and each situation, calculated for informed and control patients. It may be seen that situations 7, 8 and 5 are significant contributors for informed patients, while situations 2, 3 and 6 appear to exert little influence.

An unfortunate error in data collection meant that only 14 control patients completed the inventory. Significant comparisons were rendered less probable because of low numbers, only situation seven reaching the 5% level. However, the overall pattern appears similar with situations 7 and 5 showing the highest and situations 2, 3 and 6 the least relationships with analgesic consumption.

An attempt was made to provide two separate categories of "Threat" situations in the S—R inventory designed for this project. Situations 4,

TABLE 6

Correlations for S–R situations 1–10 and post-operative analgesics, informed and control group

| Situations | Analgesics | |
	Informed	Controls
1. (Crowded room)	0·23	−0·13
2. (Blackout)	0·01	0·08
3. (Visiting the ill)	0·03	0·07
4. (Opened letter)	0·26	−0·09
5. (Dentist)	0·35*	0·37
6. (Standing on ledge)	0·11	0·05
7. (Operation necessary)	0·47†	0·46*
8. (Medical examination)	0·39†	0·12
9. (Cut finger)	0·22	0·23
10. (Crowded train)	0·31	0·22
	N = 26	N = 14

* Significant at 5% level.
† Significant at 1% level.

80

TABLE 7

Type of threat situations compared with analgesics informed group

Variable		Mean	St. deviation	N
Analgesics		59·86	35·39	34
admission } Physical	Physical	105·65	30·64	26
Inventory }	P/S	94·38	25·42	26
Discharge }	Physical	93·19	32·63	21
Inventory }	P/S	83·57	33·14	21

Pearson Product-Moment Correlations

Variable	Analgesics	Adm. P.	P/S	Dis. P
Analgesics				
Admission P	0·364*			
Admission P/S	0·290 n.s.	0·836		
Discharge P	0·336*	0·938	0·792	
Discharge P/S	0·332*	0·879	0·852	0·912

* Significance level of $p < 0.05$ (1 tailed)
  P = Physical threat
P/S = Psycho-social threat

Control group

Variable		Mean	St. deviation	N
Analgesics		78·97	50·51	34
Admission }	Physical	99·14	32·82	14
Inventory }	P/S	89·00	29·07	14
Discharge }	Physical	83·62	23·77	13
Inventory }	P/S	80·00	28·29	13

Type of threat situations compared with analgesics

Pearson Product-Moment Correlations

Variable	Analgesics	Adm. P.	P/S	Dis. P
Analgesics				
Admission P	0·251 n.s.			
Admission P/S	0·099 n.s.	0·839		
Discharge P	0·436 n.s.	0·864	0·719	
Discharge P/S	0·209 n.s.	0·700	0·924	0·817

P = Physical threat
P/S = Psycho-social threat
n.s. = not significant at $p < 0.05$.

5, 6, 7 and 9 provided physical threat whilst situations 1, 2, 3, 8 and 9 represented psycho-social threat. In order to assess possible relationships between these two categories and analgesic consumption the correlations shown in Table 7 were calculated for both informed and control groups. Means and standard deviations are also shown.

For both groups the mean scores for physical threat situations were higher than the corresponding scores for psycho-social threat situations while for the informed group a significant positive correlation between physical threat and analgesics emerged. The psycho-social threat correlation for the same group failed to reach significance. A similar pattern was found for the control group, although neither correlation reached significance.

Although not exposing great differences in response to physical and psycho-social threat situations, these results indicate that higher anxiety was recorded for those situations concerned with direct physical threat.

4. Thirty-four patients completed an *S–R Inventory* on admission and then again before discharge from the wards. This second test was to gain insight into the test–retest reliability of the inventory, using correlations between the admission and discharge scores to examine this. The total included 21 informed group and 13 control group patients and the correlations were 0·88 and 0·83 respectively. These results imply that the inventory is robust in the test–retest sense. It must also be remembered that the patients concerned underwent surgery involving varying degrees of trauma during the intervening period, a fact which supports the contention that the *S–R Inventory* measures anxiety-proneness rather than "state" or transient anxiety.

The above findings indicated that this particular method of measuring anxiety had advantages such as ease of completion and relevance to hospital situations. Additionally the results showed that the inventory possessed reasonable predictive validity for post-operative pain as assessed by analgesic consumption. Further testing of this measure was thus indicated.

Post-operative data—Patients' Subjective State Scale

The pain thermometer

Patients reported few problems in understanding and using this device and data collection was straightforward. It was hypothesized that informed patients would record lower ratings than control patients, and scores for each of the five post-operative days were compared between 34 informed and 34 control patients. Although these scores were rated on a five-point scale, it was felt that they were not a truly "equal interval" measurement (a scale where the distances between any two numbers on the scale are of known size). For this reason the Mann-Whitney test (Siegel, 1956) (see Appendix note) was used to detect

82

possible significant differences between informed and control patients. In spite of the informed groups' consistently lower scores, the only significant differences were for Day 5, which was the final day of data collection, when informed patients were significantly recording less pain. In other words, informed patients seemed to be reaching a relatively pain-free state more rapidly than the patients in the control group, a finding which provides support for the anxiety-reduction hypothesis.

Pain: local or general

This question proved rather difficult for the observers to rate satisfactorily, as patients' answers tended to be rather non-specific. It is also possible that sources of pain other than from the wound made accurate delineation a matter of guesswork for some patients. However, data were recorded for all 68 cases, but subsequent statistical analysis failed to reveal significant differences between the two groups.

Morale

Observers reported that this question presented few difficulties to patients who seemed able to differentiate their answers clearly and without ambiguity. Following data analysis the hypothesis that informed patients would report higher morale than controls was supported on Day 4 (2% level), Day 5 (5% level), with Day 2 narrowly missing significance (6%).

This was an encouraging result as other workers have reported an increased sense of wellbeing in patients who are well informed. When the data from Questions 4 (Nausea) Question 5 (Sleep) and Question 6 (Appetite) were compared, analysis failed to show significant differences.

Comfort and reassurance

This was the multiple-choice question where patients were asked to rate, randomly, the presented six sources derived from initial interviews or, alternatively, to add their own comments. Table 8 gives the percentages of items given a rank of one, i.e. those considered most important.

Ward Sisters' assessments

Sisters completed this scale on the sixth post-operative day. Results are shown in Table 9.

Although the ratings tended to classify the informed group as making better progress than controls, the scores did not differ significantly. Thus patients' own ratings of their level of morale (Question 3) were not reflected in the Ward Sisters' ratings of progress.

TABLE 8

Patient State Scale, Question 7
5th day following operation:
Patients' first choice as percentages

Sources	%
Other patients	19·4
Visiting time	14·6
Talking to sister or nurses	10·4
Tablets or injections	11·8
Talking to your Doctor	10·3
Nursing attention	33·4
Total	100·0

TABLE 9

Ward Sister's assessment of patient progress

Statement	Informed	Controls	Total
Unusually well	5	2	7
Better than usual	8	7	15
About average	13	15	28
Not as well as usual	4	5	9
Very slowly/not well at all	4	5	9
Totals	34	34	68

Post-operative analgesics

The procedure for analgesic administration was similar for the male and female wards, and, as house officers were responsible for patients in both wards it was possible for analgesics to be standardized (unless medically contra-indicated). By far the most commonly prescribed analgesic was Omnopon (Papaveretum), usually in 20 milligram doses given by injection. The main supporting analgesic was Fortral (Pentazocine) given either by injection or tablets. The manufacturers state that 40 milligrams of Pentazocine are equivalent in analgesic effects to 10 milligrams of morphine sulphate.

Following the doctor's prescription, the major responsibilities as to when patients "needed" analgesics fell upon the nurses. The actual time that elapsed between patients' request and the administration of the drug varied considerably, due largely to administrative problems, e.g. unless a registered nurse was on duty the drug had to be taken from the cupboard and checked by a registered nurse from another ward, or by a nursing officer. This process was often further complicated by factors such as staff shortages, meal times and the general availability of trained staff. Patients reported these problems as being especially pressing at night.

For purposes of analysis the time of operation was noted for each patient and Day 1 was the 24 hours after this, right through to Day 5, thus analysis was for "patient days" rather than for orthodox time. The procedure followed by nurses when recording analgesics was standard throughout; the date, time and dosage of each drug being entered on a medicine chart kept at the foot of the bed. This made data collection very straightforward.

The method envisaged of matching informed and control patients by operation type and as closely as possible on other variables was so that a "matched-pairs" type of analysis could be used. However, in some pairings the ages were rather disparate, and as the sample contained a preponderance of females the "frequency-matching" approach, considered earlier, was used.

The hypothesis under test was that due to decreased post-operative anxiety, informed patients would request significantly fewer analgesics than control patients. The mean dosage for informed patients was 59·86 units, whilst for controls the mean dosage was 78·97. When the 34 pairs of scores were compared statistically using a "t" test (see Appendix A note on statistics used) the result was significant at the 2·5% level. Figure 1 shows these differences in graphical form.

The influence of age

It was hypothesized that an inverse relationship would emerge between these two variables based upon the following assumptions:

1. Older patients tend to complain less.
2. Pain tolerance increases with age as a function of learning.
3. The age disparity between nurses and elderly patients may hinder communication of distress.

This hypothesis received statistical support for the entire sample at the 5% level of significance, for the control group at the 2·5% level, while the informed group failed to reach significance. This latter finding is of particular interest as it is possible that informing patients of all ages how to request pain relieving drugs partly nullified the effects of age which are seen clearly in control patients' data.

It is clear from these results that younger patients tended to receive more analgesics, especially in the control or non-informed group. This finding was supported by considerable observational evidence as it was the experience of all concerned that younger patients complained strongly if they were not warned to expect severe pain. The pain came as an unpleasant shock. A moment's reflection will, however, reveal that it is quite possible for a young adult in present-day society never to have suffered the experience of severe pain, in fact a type of learning deficit. In

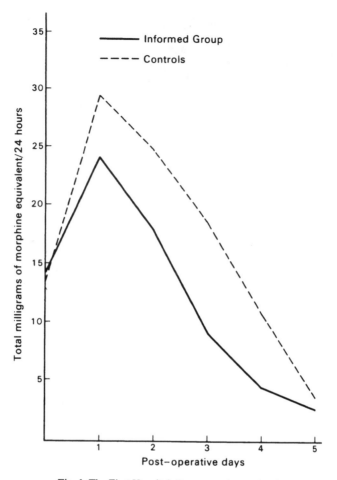

Fig. 1. The First Hospital: Post-operative analgesics.

view of the major aims of the experiment it is interesting to note that Table 10 shows correlations for both the age and social class variables as being lower for informed than for control patients. Therefore it seems a reasonable suggestion that informing patients of all ages and classes will reduce the differentials usually found in analgesic requests.

The influence of social class

The relevant literature often suggests that social class plays a part in analgesic requests, it being considered that the greater articulateness and social competence of the higher social groups allows a more rapid

TABLE 10

Correlates of age and social class

Informed group

Variable	Mean	Std. deviation	N
Social class	3·59	0·93	34
Age	41·74	16·19	34
Analgesics	59·85	35·39	34
Anxiety	200·04	53·74	26

Pearson correlations

	Social class	Age	Analgesics
Social class			
Age	−0·22		
Analgesics	0·35*	−0·27	
Anxiety	0·09	0·11	0·34

Control group

Variable	Mean	Std. deviation	N
Social class	3·62	1·07	34
Age	38·85	14·60	34
Analgesics	78·97	50·51	34
Anxiety	199·14	59·35	14

Pearson correlations

	Social class	Age	Analgesics
Social class			
Age	−0·35		
Analgesics	0·43†	−0·37	
Anxiety	0·71	−0·22	0·188

* Significant at 5% level.
† Significant at 1% level.

formation of communication links with medical and nursing staff. Such patients are likely more often to adopt a "consumer" view of medical care and are frequently better informed about citizens' rights. In view of these factors it was not surprising to find a positive statistical correlation between social class and analgesics for both informed (2·5%) and control (1%) patients. The reduction mentioned above, in the effects of age found for informed patients, seems reflected in the social class findings, in that the influence of class was much more pronounced for control patients than for informed. This is entirely reasonable as the effects would operate as though under ordinary conditions.

Post-operative vomiting

The collection of these data presented unforeseen problems, particularly for night duty, during which time nurses were unable to record with accuracy. As a result this part of the investigation was abandoned. A further complication was that nausea and vomiting are associated with certain analgesic and other drugs, thus confounding the situation further.

Discussion

Any discussion of the actual findings must be preceded by a consideration of two crucial factors: firstly, the reactions and views of those patients who participated in the research, and secondly, the reactions of ward staff. As a direct indication of what patients felt about being visited by the research team the results of Patients' Discharge Ratings are shown in Table 11.

TABLE 11

Patients' statements regarding
research visits

Statement	%
1. Very helpful	19·3
2. Slightly helpful	35·3
3. No effect	35·3
4. Unhelpful	8·8
5. A nuisance	1·3

These statements show a preponderance of favourable responses, which, although the conditions under which these ratings were collected may allow room for bias, nevertheless provide a direct statement. In addition to discharge comments, the very high response rate was a favourable index. All patients were told that participation was voluntary and that they could ask to withdraw from the project at any time. In fact, only three patients out of almost 100 preferred not to collaborate, and of those who consented, only two asked to withdraw during the course of data collection. Several favourable letters were received after patients had gone home.

88

Co-operation of doctors and nurses from both wards was excellent. Considerable interest in the project was shown by a wide range of staff and it was especially encouraging that junior nurses were among the most avid questioners. To a certain extent the study design hampered a free exchange of information between researchers and staff, because involving nurses too closely would have increased the bias risk.

A less satisfactory aspect of data collection was an imbalance between numbers of patients admitted, resulting in a preponderance of females. This was due primarily to lack of demand. At the time there seemed few indications that these numbers would balance, therefore data were collected in spite of the relative lack of males.

A disadvantage arising from male and female patients being nursed in separate wards was that sex differences tended to be confounded by differences in ward staffs. For some areas of research this may not be important, but where analgesics are concerned the differences are crucial. It is true that the prescription of analgesics was as standardized as circumstances allowed, but prescription forms only a small part in the chain of processes which decide whether or not a patient receives the drug. As the investigation progressed it became quite clear that the major responsibility for these decisions fell on the nurses and that discernible differences in approach existed between the male and female wards.

The male ward tended to use a "routine" method of analgesic administration, based largely on assumptions that certain operations required certain dosages of analgesics. Some male patients did not obtain relief from pain following the "routine" drug dosage and consequently requested more. This departure from normal practice led some nurses to express slight resentment when referring to those patients who persistently requested analgesics over and above the "recognized quantity" for their particular operation. Conversely, female patients were encouraged to request analgesics rather than "suffer in silence", therefore the total dosage received was determined more by individual demand than by ward routine.

Of course, an important variable to consider is that both male and females patients are nursed mainly by female nurses, and that this may, in itself, lead to variations in the decision-taking that precedes the giving of drugs, a factor noted by Bond and Pilowsky (1966) in a discussion of analgesic administration by nursing staff:

> Comparison of the average pain scores of those patients (who had not communicated pain) with those of patients who requested or received drugs indicates a more satisfactory therapeutic relationship between women patients and nursing staff than between male patients and nursing staff.

The authors develop this further by suggesting that female nurses identify more easily with their own sex than with male patients, and consequently are able to recognize need more quickly and easily in women; they continue,

> The greater need for males to communicate distress may be linked with the popular conception that women tolerate pain better than men, and that complaints made by women were more readily accepted as an indication of genuine discomfort.

The point which plainly emerges from the above discussion is that the doctor's prescription which legitimizes the giving of analgesics, is, when compared with the nursing contribution, a relatively minor influence as to whether or not a patient ever receives the drug.

In spite of the equal distribution of "contact time" between informed and control patients significant differences emerged in analgesic consumption and level of morale. Additionally informed patients reported significantly less pain than controls on Day 5. These findings indicate that just "talking to the patients" is less effective in reducing anxiety (as measured by the indices used) and pain than "informed talking". That social interaction may play an important part in relieving fear and anxiety would not be denied but, from the present evidence, social interaction plus information is still better.

The *S–R Inventory of Anxiety* gave encouragement to the view that this type of test could be especially useful in identifying sources of anxiety in patients. There were few problems associated with completing the scale and the high test–retest reliability showed that patients were consistent in response. Furthermore, the significant (5%) positive correlation between admission anxiety and analgesics showed that the inventory could claim a certain predictive validity for this purpose. The contention receives further support when the mean admission anxiety scores for the informed and control patients are compared with analgesics received.

This comparison must obviously be considered when evaluating the correlations involving prediction, for if the mean anxiety score of control patients was substantially higher than that of informed patients interpretation problems would arise. Table 12 shows that the reverse occurred, i.e. that admission anxiety was higher for informed than for controls.

TABLE 12

Means of admission anxiety and analgesics compared
for informed and control groups

Group	Mean admission anxiety score	Mean post-operative analgesic drugs
Informed	200·03	59·86
Control	188·14	78·97

90

It was apparent that some of the situations used for the $S-R$ *Inventory* were more relevant than others, a point which would need discussion if further use were contemplated.

Patients' answers to the wide range of questions used for the PSS were each recorded on a five-point rating scale. With the exception of the pain thermometer and morale sections, the scale generally failed to reveal major differences between the groups. This leaves the possibility that differences in patients' condition were restricted to these two areas, or that the scale was insensitive to subtle differences in condition. The fundamental nature of rating scales may account for some of these problems, for, although useful for many purposes where standardization and reliability are involved, by their very nature they tend to be insensitive to material that cannot easily be categorized. However, it was difficult to visualize a reasonable alternative in view of the clinical constraints on data collecting which operate under hospital ward circumstances.

Again, although the pain thermometer only detected significant differences on Day 5, it is problematic whether replacement of this device by another form of pain "measure" would be entirely advantageous. The ease and simplicity of this method makes it ideally suitable for post-operative use, where any lengthy or complicated process is obviously undesirable.

The significant differences in morale between informed and control groups were an encouraging finding. When morale is high, patients tend to be more alert and active and require fewer analgesics. This increased mobility is especially important in the prevention of complications such as deep-venous thrombosis and chest complications; additionally, the improved circulatory rate provides more satisfactory healing of wounds. The desirability of high morale for a patient's own state of well-being scarcely requires mention (Revans, 1964).

It is interesting to consider the answers to Question 7 relating to sources of comfort. These tended to be answered fairly consistently from day to day, with the "Tablets or Injections" response more prominent in the first three days than in the last two, although these differences were not significant. Table 8 (page 84) shows all patients' first choice as percentages on Day 5. No significant differences emerged between informed and control groups.

The relative importance to "Nursing attention", "Visiting", and "Other patients" is roughly comparable with other survey findings, although the high rating given to "Other patients" deserves mention. Talking to Sister or Nurses was included to compare its position with "Nursing attention" and it is seen that to these patients talking, whether by doctors or nurses is not a magical panacea. Without question, a large part of nursing attention involves what Argyle (1973) has called non-verbal communication. This author presents the findings of many experiments involving human communication and finds non-verbal communication far more effective than language in the understanding of attitudes, feelings and emotions. As so much of nursing attention is concerned with these particular aspects of behaviour it is hardly surprising that the "mere word" falls far short of what is required by patients in distress.

It is encouraging to find that the Ward Sisters' ratings of patients' progress followed the research findings. Although differences were not statistically significant, they rated the informed patients as making better progress than the controls on the basis of professional judgement. One sister felt that there was a tendency to rate the progress of all patients as slightly better than would be the case if a completely objective answer were given, largely because unfavourable ratings may be taken as a reflection on standards of care.

The significant relationship (5%) between length of stay and admission anxiety, coupled with the higher average scores for the "physical threat" situations on the *S–R Inventory* indicates that patients in this sample showed higher anxiety for the more serious operations. This is quite different to the findings of Janis (1958) who considered that severity of operation made little contribution to pre-operative anxiety, but a major contribution to post-operative anxiety.

Although not a main feature of this investigation, an attempt was made to note excessive emotional or physical reactions of patients who either scored very low on admission anxiety or who strongly denied anxiety during the pre-operative interview, i.e. exhibiting the psychological mechanism of denial. Janis (1958) found that these patients tended to show severe emotional upset during the post-operative phase, sometimes to such an extent that recovery was retarded. Similar cases did occur during the present investigation, but infrequently. However, it is an interesting aspect of anxiety in patients and one in which further study is merited.

The information schedule as used in this first experiment was rather an unrefined instrument. For individual patients the items included almost certainly formed a hierarchy of relevance, in which some items were more important than others in reducing anxiety, but as this obviously varied according to individual needs and requirements, the data allowed little insight into these differences. One of the more interesting issues concerned the type of information provided and the possibility of its being obtained from alternative sources. Therefore, it is quite possible that routine information about everyday procedures on the ward could come from a variety of sources, but that this may be less so for information considered as "technical or professional". Further trials could usefully determine if the anxiety-reducing effect would still be found if the "schedule" were restricted in this way. Furthermore, the reduced length would allow patients to concentrate upon central issues without being swamped by minutiae.

The "open" or "Nightingale" wards in which the investigation was carried out provided a "social" environment in which many patients derived comfort and reassurance from contact with their neighbours. At the same time, many patients who participated in this research echoed the findings of surveys (e.g. Cartwright, 1964) in that most open wards are noisy, sometimes unpleasant, and make few concessions to privacy; e.g. in response to the question "How did you sleep last night?" a patient replied archly that this was decided by the noise level of the ward rather than by any differences in his condition. Additionally, the open ward system possessed serious drawbacks when trying to examine relative differences in analgesic consumption between male and female patients; any such variation could be also accounted for by differences in policy between male and female ward staffs, i.e. the effect would be "confounded". (A statistical term denoting an uncontrolled variable which could also account for the findings.) One way out of this predicament would be to find a ward in which male and female patients are nursed by the same staff. In newer hospitals containing small wards or cubicles this seemed a feasible proposition and so attention was turned to this type of ward for the next phase of the project.

CHAPTER 7

The Second Hospital—
Design Modifications

The encouraging results of the first study indicated that extension and modification of this information–giving technique might produce further items of interest. Moreover, with any research it is sound practice to attempt replication of findings; for although sound design and the use of appropriate statistics reduces the risk of error, the possibility remains that local factors may influence findings in such a way that erroneous conclusions may be drawn. With this in mind, attention was turned towards a second experiment which would include certain modifications, the completion of which would perhaps throw further light on the relations between information, pain and anxiety.

A constant problem of data analysis from the first hospital was that differences in response between male and female patients were confounded by the fact that they were cared for by different nursing staff. These differences are important where analgesic administration is concerned (Chapter 3). Analysis of this problem is difficult since most hospitals have separate wards for men and women.

In view of this, this investigator felt it worth while to obtain the co-operation of a hospital where male and female patients were nursed by the same staff. Not without tribulation this aim was finally achieved, and, following correspondence and consultation with appropriate personnel, access was gained to a "mixed" ward in a newly-constructed hospital which had been operational for three years.

After a one-week orientation visit the hospital seemed quite suitable for the proposed "next stage" and attention was turned towards finding an observer who would serve for the whole data collection period. The project was fortunate to obtain the services of an experienced SRN who had previously served as a research assistant to another member of the Study of Nursing Care project.

Patient accommodation and admission procedure

The type of ward on which the research was to be centred differed substantially from the "open" or "Nightingale" wards of the first

94

hospital. Patient accommodation consisted of four small rooms, each containing five beds; one smaller room containing four beds, and six single rooms. The total of 30 beds was thus identical to the first hospital wards, but of course this represented only half of the total numbers of patients available for inclusion in a sample in the first hospital.

Patients' admission procedure commenced with an introductory letter from a general practitioner, after which an out-patient appointment was made to see a surgeon. Following a variable period of delay patients were then informed of the date and time of admission. After presenting themselves at the appropriate time patients were "booked in" by the admissions officer and subsequently escorted to the ward by a voluntary worker.

Unlike the first hospital a specific "admissions nurse" was designated to receive all patients who were admitted during a particular shift and whose duties entailed providing patients with a welcome followed by an orientation tour of the ward and its facilities. This was greatly appreciated by patients, many remarking upon how it helped combat the strangeness which inevitably surrounds admission. Information provided by the "admissions nurse" was almost always of a general nature, specific enquiries being referred to the doctor or ward sister.

The ward geography consisted of a corridor, with a centrally situated "nurses" station with the small wards and single rooms on either side. During the investigator's orientation visits patients' comments about the small wards fell into two distinct groups. Those patients for whom this was the first hospital experience expressed very favourable attitudes, privacy and quietude being frequently mentioned. These factors also found favour with patients who had, on a previous occasion, been nursed in "open" or "Nightingale" wards, but with the rider that being in the smaller wards occasioned feelings of isolation at times. "I like to see the nurses busying about" was a typical comment. It was most noticeable that only patients who had previous experience of open wards made these comments, the others perhaps feeling that they would intuitively dislike the open ward milieu.

Nursing uniforms differed from the first hospital, being white for all trained staff and various colours for other grades. Once more it was interesting to note patients' comments, the most common being that it was difficult to recognize the relative status of staff at a distance. Name badges were worn but elderly or infirm patients seemed not to find these very helpful. There was a common fear of "Not giving people their correct title".

Where patients are nursed in side wards and are outside the range of direct observation it is obviously desirable to have some form of communication system between patients and nurses. This particular hospital had installed a proprietory call system, each patient having access to a control panel by means of an adjustable arm. The rather limited information collected suggested that the system worked satisfactorily, with the exception of some elderly patients who found the manifold rather awe-inspiring and consequently used it as little as possible.

A main feature of this hospital was its close relationship with community nursing services which enabled suitable patients to be discharged in a much shorter time than usual, further care being provided by community nurses.

Design modifications

The design of the second experiment was basically similar to the first, but included modifications based upon the experience and findings already gained.

The second hospital catchment area consisted of a predominantly rural area of the home counties, in marked contrast to the first hospital which was a densely populated industrial urban area. Differences in patients' social and educational background would therefore be expected and it was hoped that Groups 1 and 2 of the Registrar-General's classification would be more in evidence, thus providing a more balanced sample.

It was decided to restrict the range of the information schedule to "professional/technical". The reasons for this have already been discussed (Chapter 6) and include the possibility that a shorter information-giving session will result in improved retention of information on the patient's part. If, following analysis of results, evidence still existed that anxiety and pain had been reduced, further progress would have been made towards the establishment of a "hierarchy of importance" of information. In practice, this meant that the pre-operative information-giving interview with informed group patients consisted of Part 4 (Pre-operative Nursing Information) and Part 5 (Pain and Discomfort Aspects) of the original schedule.

The first experiment had collected data for the Patients' State Scale three times daily. As the midday recordings seemed to offer little information that was not covered by the first and third visits it was decided to omit this during the second experiment. There was also some element of doubt as to whether the five-point scale technique should be retained or whether an alternative form of scaling could be utilized. After considerable discussion there seemed little prospect of any suitable alternatives providing a more discriminatory measure and so the rating was retained. It was felt also that the services of one observer for the whole of the second experiment would aid consistency during the second trials.

As the *S—R Inventory of Anxiety* had provided useful data, it seemed feasible to extend its use to all patients who could complete it. When correlated against drug scores, situations One and Two had yielded non-significant results and so were replaced by "You are to stay in a hospital ward which may mean sharing facilities with others", and, "There has been an accident; you are first on the scene and have to take charge". Owing to the high test–retest reliability obtained during the first trials it was considered unnecessary to repeat this manoeuvre at the second hospital.

The first hospital data contained no record of either the amount of pain patients suffered before admission, or of the amount of pain patients expected to suffer during the immediate post-operative period. It had been noticeable that certain patients who suffered from conditions causing extreme pain, e.g. renal calculi, commented that their post-operative pain was mild by comparison with that suffered before the operation. Patients' expectations of pain varied widely, from severe apprehension in some instances to almost complete lack of awareness in others (young patients especially). To obtain information about pre-operative pain, and patients' expectations of post-operative pain, five-point rating scales were used, based upon the same categories used for the pain thermometer.

There is some evidence of a positive relationship between pain tolerance and the personality dimension of extraversion (Lynn and Eysenck, 1961) the extraversion variable being measured by the *Eysenck Personality Inventory* (EPI). The EPI sets out to assess the major dimensions involved in Eysenck's theory of personality, namely extraversion and neuroticism, the evidence for which concepts has been extensively reviewed by Eysenck (1960). The time required to complete the EPI is about six minutes therefore it was felt that this inventory could usefully be included in this second part of the investigation without being excessively onerous for patients.

In view of the successful operation of the "crossover" technique in the first experiment, i.e. informer and observer switching roles periodically, there seemed little point in varying this, so that following these modifications in procedure the regime for an informed-group patient was as follows:

1. Self-introduction, followed by request for cooperation.
2. *S–R Inventory* produced and explained. After practice with the model rating scale used in the first trials patients then completed the inventory.
3. Pain thermometer explained and its use demonstrated. Ratings of pre-admission pain and expectancy of post-operative pain were then recorded.
4. Information relevant to the type of operation given. For these trials, only Section 4 and Section 5 of the original schedule were used.
5. On the morning of operating day and also on the five subsequent days the patient was visited by the informer.
6. Patient was visited morning and later afternoon by the observer, who collected data for the PSS.
7. On the day prior to discharge from hospital each patient was asked to complete:

a. The EPI.
b. The PSS. Question 7 (Comfort) for the entire post-operative period.
c. Patients' discharge rating.
8. The ward sister was asked to complete her assessment of progress on Day 6.

Control patients differed only in that general talk replaced the information-giving in (4).

CHAPTER 8

Data Collection and Analysis

The total sample again contained a preponderance of women patients, due partly to the inclusion of a sub-group of hysterectomy patients. The electricity supply crisis of 1972 also restricted hospital admissions. An attempt was made to increase the numbers of male patients by selective sampling, but a lengthy time span would have been required for this to have been effective.

Data were again transferred to punch cards so that some parts of the analysis could be computerized. The choice of statistical tests used to test the various hypotheses followed the conventional pattern, i.e. when the data were seen to be of an interval nature, parametric tests were used, if of nominal or ordinal nature non-parametric tests were employed (see Appendix notes on Statistics).

Upon examination the data seem more closely matched than those obtained from the first hospital, especially on the age variable. Table 13 shows characteristics of the total sample, while Tables 14, 15 and 16 show close agreement between the means of the informed group and of the control group for age, length of stay, extraversion, neuroticism, pre-operative pain and birth order. A mean difference of 6·85 occurred between the groups in admission anxiety, the scores being almost equally dispersed. The average length of stay for patients was approximately equal for the first and second hospitals, being 11·45 days and 12·28 days respectively.

Social class

Comparisons of social class and birth order reveal differences between the hospitals, perhaps a reflection of catchment area characteristics. These are shown in Table 17.

In one sense birth order may provide a more useful comparison as the social class categories do not adequately reflect population characteristics. This is mainly because most populations of patients receiving care under the National Health Service are "skewed" towards the lower income groups, while classes one and two of the Registrar-General's list are under-represented. The birth-order comparisons indicate that the average family size of second hospital patients is less than the corresponding figure for the first hospital; the lower standard

TABLE 13

Sample characteristics: general distribution
Second Hospital

Variable	Number	Sex	
		Male	Female
Sex			
Male	22		
Female	44		
Age			
16–29		1	4
30–44		7	22
45–59		7	15
60+		8	5
Socio-economic status			
Registrar 1		–	–
General's 2		4	5
Classification 3		9	22
4		4	11
5		4	5
Marital status			
Single		3	4
Married		17	34
Widow/er		2	1
Separated		–	3
Divorced		–	2

TABLE 14

Characteristics of total sample

Variable	Mean	Std. deviation	N
Sex	1·68	0·47	66
Social class	3·33	0·92	66
Age	46·47	13·20	66
Length of stay	12·28	4·62	66
Admission anxiety	204·21	57·40	66
Extraversion	12·68	3·90	66
Neuroticism	12·52	4·10	66
Pre-operative pain	3·11	1·27	66
Birth order	1·99	1·24	66
Pain expectancy	3·06	1·06	66
Analgesic drugs	31·52	28·14	66

TABLE 15

Informed group characteristics

Variable	Mean	Std. deviation	N
Sex	1·66	0·47	33
Social class	3·33	1·08	33
Age	46·75	13·51	33
Length of stay	12·18	3·98	33
Admission anxiety	197·36	59·88	33
Extraversion	12·66	4·01	33
Neuroticism	12·33	4·48	33
Pre-operative pain	3·18	1·35	33
Birth order	2·00	1·27	33
Pain expectancy	2·87	1·14	33
Analgesic drugs	26·12	21·70	33

TABLE 16

Control group characteristics

Variable	Mean	Std. deviation	N
Sex	1·69	0·46	33
Social class	3·33	0·74	33
Age	46·18	13·04	33
Length of stay	12·36	5·26	33
Admission anxiety	211·06	54·86	33
Extraversion	12·69	3·84	33
Neuroticism	12·70	3·74	33
Pre-operative pain	3·03	1·18	33
Birth order	1·97	1·23	33
Pain expectancy	3·24	0·96	33
Analgesic drugs	36·91	32·82	33

TABLE 17

Comparisons of social class and birth order

	First hospital N=68		Second hospital N=66	
	Mean	s.d.	Mean	s.d.
Social class	3·59	0·97	3·33	0·92
Birth order	3·57	2·35	1·99	1·24

101

deviation suggests that family size is smaller. The slight differences in social class may thus be an underestimation.

Age

The average age of second hospital patients was 46·47 years as opposed to 37·62 years. This difference was thought to be within the normal limits of sample variation for such a project.

Table 18 shows a matrix of intercorrelations for the total second hospital sample, while Tables 19 and 20 show similar comparisons for informed and control groups respectively. The figure of 0·41 for age against length of stay would be expected on the assumption that older patients tend to stay in hospital for longer periods. Again the negative correlation of −0·24 between age and extraversion scores on the EPI reinforces other findings that extraversion tends to decrease with increasing age of subjects. However there are marked differences between informed and control groups when age is related to admission anxiety, the correlations being −0·31 for informed and 0·24 for control patients. The correlation for the total sample of −0·06 does not allow very much insight into this relationship.

Although the anticipated inverse relationship between age and analgesic consumption was not found, the control group again produced a higher correlation than the informed group (0·23 as against 0·19) and is consistent with the findings from the first hospital that giving information about how and when to request analgesics reduces age differences found in control patients, i.e. that older patients request fewer drugs.

S−R Anxiety Inventory

A total of 67 patients completed this satisfactorily. Few adverse comments were made. The main form of analysis was correlation of anxiety scores (item 5) against other variables, which are shown in Tables 14 to 16. Correlations of particular interest include:

a. The positive relationship between the *S−R Inventory* scores and the neuroticism dimension of the EPI (0·49, significant at the 0·1% level). This result gives additional support to the contention that the *S−R Inventory* is measuring "trait" anxiety or "anxiety-proneness" because the EPI attempts to measure stable personality characteristics.

b. The hypothesis that patients whose pre-operative pain had been high would rate their anticipated post-operative pain low was upheld. The negative correlation (−0·37, significant at the 0·1% level) clearly implies that high pre-operative pain scores resulted in low anticipated pain scores.

c. The correlation of 0·29, significant at the 5% level, gives some

TABLE 18

Intercorrelations for total sample N = 66

	1	2	3	4	5	6	7	8	9	10	11
1. Sex											
2. Social class	0.03										
3. Age	-0.28	0.07									
4. Length of stay	-0.31*	-0.01	0.41†								
5. Admission anxiety	0.27*	0.17	-0.06	0.05							
6. Extraversion	0.02	-0.02	-0.24*	-0.17	0.01						
7. Neuroticism	0.09	0.14	-0.02	0.02	0.49‡	-0.13					
8. Pre-operative pain	-0.15	-0.16	0.09	0.21	-0.37†	-0.04	-0.03				
9. Birth order	-0.27*	0.21	0.08	0.04	0.07	0.01	-0.08	-0.06			
10. Pain expectancy	-0.23	0.05	-0.13	0.05	0.29*	-0.17	0.31*	-0.34†	-0.01		
11. Analgesic drugs	0.07	0.13	0.21	0.33†	0.01	0.06	0.05	0.07	0.01	-0.13	

* Significant at 5% level.
† Significant at 1% level.
‡ Significant at 1% level.

TABLE 19

Intercorrelations for informed group
N = 33

	1	2	3	4	5	6	7	8	9	10	11
1. Sex											
2. Social class	−0·08										
3. Age	−0·29	0·08									
4. Length of stay	−0·28	−0·04	0·33								
5. Admission anxiety	0·38*	0·02	−0·31	−0·38*							
6. Extraversion	0·18	0·18	−0·05	0·02	0·24						
7. Neuroticism	0·07	−0·10	−0·17	−0·19	0·46†	−0·13					
8. Pre-operative pain	−0·09	−0·17	0·19	0·23	−0·46†	−0·02	0·02				
9. Birth order	−0·56†	0·27	0·38*	0·20	−0·25	−0·09	−0·32	0·05			
10. Pain expectancy	0·15	−0·06	−0·18	0·04	0·45†	−0·15	0·48†	−0·36*	−0·34*		
11. Analgesic drugs	−0·22	0·05	0·19	0·41*	−0·19	0·02	−0·23	0·07	0·31	−0·14	

* Significant at 5% level.
† Significant at 1% level.

104

TABLE 20

Intercorrelations for control group
N = 33

	1	2	3	4	5	6	7	8	9	10	11
1. Sex											
2. Social class	0·12										
3. Age	−0·27	0·06									
4. Length of stay	−0·35*	0·02	0·49†								
5. Admission anxiety	0·14	0·41†	0·24	0·41†							
6. Extraversion	−0·15	−0·31	−0·44†	−0·34*	−0·25						
7. Neuroticism	0·12	0·57†	0·17	0·22	0·53†	−0·24					
8. Pre-operative pain	−0·21	−0·15	−0·01	0·20	−0·24	0·21	−0·31				
9. Birth order	0·04	0·11	−0·24	−0·08	0·13	0·12	0·21	−0·19			
10. Pain expectancy	−0·03	0·03	0·07	0·06	0·04	−0·21	0·04	−0·27	0·21		
11. Analgesic drugs	−0·26	0·23	0·23	0·29	0·12	0·08	0·31	0·10	0·19	−0·19	

* Significant at 5% level.
† Significant at 1% level.

105

indication that high anxiety scores indicated a more apprehensive attitude towards the possibility of post-operative pain.

d. So as to compare the present results with those of other users of the *S−R Inventory* the statistical technique of analysis of variance was used. The results of this are reported elsewhere (Hayward, 1973).

e. When admission anxiety was compared with post-operative analgesic consumption for first hospital patients the resultant correlation of 0·26 (significant at the 5% level) indicated that the *S−R Inventory* may prove a useful predictor of post-operative state. The second hospital results failed to support this finding.

Patients' State Scale (PSS)

The method used to collect data was similar to that used in the first hospital, the main difference being that patients were visited twice, instead of thrice daily for the pain thermometer test and once daily for the remainder of the questions.

All observations were recorded on five-point rating scales so as to provide a convenient format for comparisons between informed and control groups. The main statistical test employed for these data was the Mann-Whitney test (see Appendix notes on Statistics) which is suitable where data are in rank order and a significance test for two independent groups is required, as in the present case. The separate results of these comparisons are discussed below:

a. The pain thermometer

The method of presentation appeared quite acceptable to patients and was identical to that used in the first hospital (see page 69). However, differences between informed and control patients only reached a significant level on Day 5 for the first hospital, whereas this applied to both Days 4 and 5 for second hospital groups. This result gives strong support to the idea that informed patients become relatively pain-free more rapidly than usual.

b. Pain: local or general

Few differences emerged between first hospital groups and little advance was found in the second hospital. Although all differences were positive, perhaps indicating a tendency for informed patients to view their pain as being more localized, none of these differences reached significance. Some patients found this question rather difficult to answer precisely; a view shared by the observers who found corresponding difficulty in rating patients' replies.

106

c. Morale

Results from the first hospital showed that informed patients reported their morale as being significantly higher than controls for Day 4 and Day 5. Although the second hospital informed patients averaged higher ratings than controls, the differences failed to reach significance.

d. Nausea

For two of the post-operative observation days, informed patients reported significantly less nausea than controls (Day 2 significant at 2% level, and Day 4, significant at 2% level). But there are interpretation difficulties here as nausea is a frequent side effect of analgesic drugs. Control patients received, on average, more analgesics, therefore this means that the "nausea" results must be interpreted with caution.

e. Sleep

One of the more interesting findings from the second hospital was that informed patients reported that they slept consistently better than controls. These differences were statistically significant on Day 2, Day 3 and Day 4.

The difficulties experienced by many patients when trying to sleep in an open ward have been mentioned, and it was suggested that even if differences *did* exist, the higher level of noise generally found in open wards may well obscure them. The small wards and single rooms of the second hospital were reported by most patients as being quiet at night.

f. Appetite

For those patients where appetite was uncomplicated by dietary factors the informed patients reported a significantly quicker return to normality than controls on Day 4 and Day 5.

g. Comfort

The results for this multiple-choice question are shown in Table 21 where the Day 5 results from both hospitals are compared. Results are arranged in order of choice, i.e. commencing with nursing attention which was ranked first by patients from both hospitals.

The higher priority given to "talking" categories by second hospital patients tends to support the contention that some of these patients felt relatively isolated.

TABLE 21

Comfort: Patients' first choices as percentages

Source (presented randomly)	First hospital	Rank	Second hospital	Rank	Difference
Nursing attention	33·4	1	37·7	1	4·3
Other patients	19·4	2	13·3	4	6·1
Visiting time	14·6	3	18·3	2	3·7
Tablets or injections	11·8	4	3·0	6	8·8
Talking to sister or nurse	10·4	5·5	15·4	3	5·0
Talking to your doctor	10·4	5·5	12·3	5	1·9
	100·0		100·0		

Analgesic drugs

It was hoped that the second hospital trials would provide a more balanced sample, but regrettably this was not the case. For the reasons described at the beginning of this section there was a preponderance of women patients.

To test the hypothesis that informed patients would receive significantly less analgesics than controls the results were compared in three ways; firstly, informed against controls (total sample), secondly, a sub-group of 18 closely-matched cholecystectomy patients, and finally another sub-group, this time of 18 hysterectomy patients.

Two types of analysis were used:

1. Comparison of analgesic units by means of "t" tests (see Appendix notes on Statistics).
2. Examining relationships between analgesic consumption and other selected variables by means of correlation.

The analgesic drug scores were reduced to "base units" by the same method as was used for first hospital results and the three comparisons noted above were made. For the total sample (N=66) the "t" test for related pairs was 2·02 (significant at 5% level) showing that, as was the case with first hospital results, informed patients received significantly fewer drugs than controls (Figure 2).

The cholecystectomy sub-group (N=18) "t" test was 3·18 (significant at 1% level) a very significant result in favour of informed patients.

The hysterectomy sub-group produced a "t" of 1·30 which failed to reach significance. Table 22 summarizes these results.

There were differences in the types of analgesics used routinely. In the first hospital Papaveretum (Omnopon) was routinely prescribed, followed by Pentazocine (Fortral) at a later stage. Pethidine Hydrochloride was the first choice in the second hospital, followed by

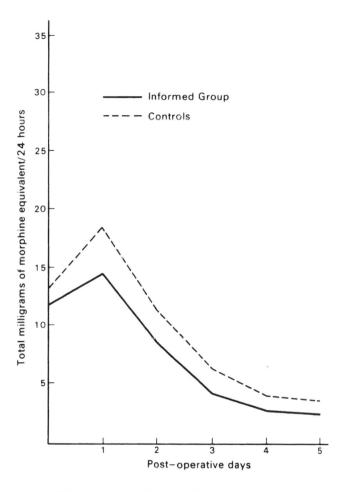

Fig. 2. The Second Hospital: Post-operative analgesics.

TABLE 22

Second hospital comparisons of analgesic units
between informed and control patients

Sample	"t"	p
Total sample N = 66	2·02	5%
Hysterectomy N = 18	1·30	non-sig.
Cholecystectomy N = 18	3·18	1%

109

Codeine Compound B.P. Only if there were medical contraindications did these patterns vary, thus making useful comparisons possible.

The much lower mean analgesic consumption for the second hospital is worthy of comment, 31·52 against 69·41 for the first hospital. Perhaps the major variable concerned is type of ward, the open or Nightingale as opposed to small wards and single rooms. This point will be discussed later.

The Eysenck Personality Inventory (EPI)

All 66 subjects for whom data were complete scored within the normal range as defined in the test manual (Eysenck and Eysenck, 1964). The questions were easily understood and completed by patients of widely differing age and backgrounds.

According to Eysenck's theory of personality extroverts should show greater pain tolerance than introverts. For the present investigation this means that a negative correlation between extraversion and analgesic consumption should emerge if this claim is to receive support. For the total sample the correlation was 0·06, for the informed group 0·02, and for controls 0·08. Therefore the postulated relationship received no support from these results.

The neuroticism factor of the EPI produced some interesting results. Although not significantly related to post-operative analgesic consumption, several other correlations were significant, in particular 0·49 (significant at 1% level) with the *S–R Inventory* and 0·31 (significant at 5% level) with pain expectancy. Although the predictive validity of that particular version of the *S–R Inventory* is questioned by the second hospital results, this highly significant relationship with the neuroticism factor of the EPI supports the view that it measures anxiety proneness.

Ward sisters' assessment

These assessments utilized the same five-point rating as the first hospital sisters. Table 23 shows the results compared by hospital and patients sub-groups.

It may be seen that the first hospital ratings tended to be more widely dispersed than the more clustered second hospital scores. To examine differences between ward sisters' ratings Table 24 shows the ratings summed and the mean rating for informed and control groups from both hospitals.

The scores favour the hypothesis that informed patients' progress would be facilitated, although the differences are not significant statistically. Variations in the distribution of "operation types" created interpretation difficulties for these comparisons.

110

TABLE 23

Ward Sisters' assessment of patients' progress

Statement	First hospital N=68			Second hospital N=66		
	Informed	Control	Total	Informed	Control	Total
Unusually well	5	2	7	2	0	2
Better than usual	8	7	15	9	5	14
About average	13	15	28	18	23	41
Not as well as usual	4	5	9	4	4	8
Very slowly/not well at all	4	5	9	0	1	1

TABLE 24

Ward Sisters' Assessments: Comparison of summed ranks and mean ranks between Hospitals

	Informed groups		Controls groups	
	Sum	Mean	Sum	Mean
First hospital N=68	96	2·8	107	3·2
Second hospital N=66	89	2·7	100	3·0

Patients' discharge statements

The rating scale (Appendix F) was identical for patients from both hospitals and represented an attempt to record actual feelings about the research visits to the bedside. Table 25 shows the scores from both hospitals compared on a percentage basis. Considerable differences emerge between hospitals, the very positive result from the second hospital being particularly striking. Reasons for this are far from being obvious but may be concerned with the relative isolation from social contact experienced by second hospital patients, perhaps making the researchers' visits a relief from boredom.

The disproportionate numbers of male and female patients meant that detailed analysis of sex differences was not feasible.

The most obvious differences between the two hospitals were ward size and layout; the 30 bed open wards of the first hospital forming a marked contrast to the four- and five-bed wards and single rooms of the

TABLE 25

Patients' discharge statements as percentages of totals

Statement	First hospital	Second hospital
1. Very helpful	19·3	39·3
2. Slightly helpful	35·3	52·1
3. No effect	35·3	8·6
4. Unhelpful	8·8	0
5. A nuisance	1·3	0

second. Although no specific questions were included about patients' preferred ward size (to avoid excessive length of interviews), in retrospect this question could have been usefully included as some patients in single rooms openly confessed to feelings of isolation.

It was also notable that nursing staff in the second hospital frequently commented upon the difficulties of consistently observing patients who were hidden from the centrally-placed nurses' station. There are also considerable problems in devising a "schedule" of visits to ensure that patients are seen by a nurse at frequent intervals, a predicament that was an obvious source of worry to the ward sisters. It seems clear that open wards allow more indirect observation to occur, i.e. clinical inference, and that nurses can detect a change in the state of a particular patient without consciously observing him. This very interesting area of professional practice has been examined closely by Hammond *et al.* (1964) who found that the process is one of extreme complexity and considerable research, energy and resources would be required to investigate this further.

These observational factors seem particularly important in the administration of analgesics. In an open ward a patient may emit "cues" which can be recognized and acted upon by a nurse who may be engaged in an entirely different task, a situation unlikely to occur with small wards or single rooms. Second hospital patients were quite at liberty to call a nurse via the communication system, but before doing this a chain of decisions must be made, each one of which acts as a barrier to be overcome before the patient actually rings. Patients often referred to these problems of decision-taking by saying that they felt "uncomfortable" at the idea of ringing for a nurse, frequently adding justifications such as "I know the nurses are busy". The above viewpoint receives considerable support from the finding that second hospital patients received about half of the total analgesics given to first hospital patients, a situation difficult to explain by the relatively minor variations in types of operation.

112

CHAPTER 9

Discussion and Implications for Practice

Overall relevance of the second hospital results are summarized below, some lending support to findings from the first hospital trials, others requiring further evaluation before firm conclusions can be drawn.

1. The results firmly established the feasibility of ward-based experimental nursing research. No major difficulties emerged from the presence of investigators on the wards concerned, and the Patients' Discharge Statements clearly indicate that patients were among the most willing participants in the entire investigation; this being particularly so in the second hospital.

To some extent the research design precluded active involvement on the part of ward nursing staff. Although in some ways regrettable this was unavoidable in the interests of preventing bias. There are many areas of nursing research where this situation may not occur and the resultant closer involvement could benefit both ward staff and investigators.

2. The major experimental hypothesis that giving relevant pre-operative information would reduce post-operative pain and anxiety was upheld for total samples from each hospital, and for one of the two sub-groups from the second hospital. This finding supports the contention that "informed" talking is more effective in this context than "just talking".

3. The modified *S–R Inventory of Anxiety* performed well as a measure of trait anxiety, this claim being supported by its relationship to other variables particularly the Eysenck Personality Inventory (EPI) in the second hospital. The high correlation obtained for the test–retest situation was encouraging in terms of test reliability. In the first hospital the S–R acted as a significant predictor of levels of post-operative pain (as assessed by analgesic consumption) but this finding was not supported by the second hospital results. It is possible that sampling problems occurred in the second hospital and therefore further trials are advisable before firm conclusions may be drawn.

4. The research design was robust in the field situation, the use of the "blind" observer and the cross-over design proving less difficult than was

originally envisaged. The major weakness was the disparate numbers of men and women patients. Any future projects would need to "build in" a method of compensatory sampling to overcome this.

5. The Patients' Subjective Scale resulted in a comprehensive account of patients' state in terms of the variables chosen. Further developments in scaling methods may enable this technique to be refined, thus evolving a more sensitive discriminatory measure which would involve the establishment of "profiles" for each patient. Perhaps the major problem is covering the whole 24 hours of the patient's day, therefore, in this context day time observations are not truly representative. In the context of qualitative care, the proposed "patient profile" would need to be matched against a "nursing profile" so that differences between these may be examined. There seems little point in studying patients in a ward situation and neglecting the major control variable of nursing staff.

6. The Ward Sisters' Assessment tended to rate informed group patients more favourably than controls although these differences did not reach statistical significance. To some extent this may have been due to the simple rating scale used, which could not encompass fine differences; once again the development of a more comprehensive scale would seem a possibility.

7. The analysis of Patients' Discharge Ratings indicate that the majority of patients are quite willing to participate in investigations of this type, This tendency being particularly marked in the second hospital.

Relationship with theories of stress and anxiety

A major problem in testing hypotheses relevant to pain, stress and anxiety lies in finding appropriate experimental situations. Laboratory studies contain elements of artificiality, important in pain and anxiety studies where subjects realize there is little danger of actual bodily harm. Field situations often possess multiple control variables, any of which may affect results, and over which the investigator often has little influence.

Very relevant to the present research is the concept of "appraisal" by which the individual assesses incoming stimuli along a continuum from innocuous to threatening (Lazarus, 1966). It is when innocuous stimuli become outweighed by threatening stimuli that the "appraisal" process leads to one or more of four patterns of response defined by Lazarus as: disturbance of affect; disruption of motor systems; physiological changes and changes in the adequacy of cognitive functioning. Following his "appraisal" of the situation, the individual has next to decide upon an optimum "coping" policy. This "coping" becomes increasingly difficult as situational ambiguity increases and may, in extreme cases, lead to completely inappropriate behaviour.

Information lack as a causative agent in stress formation is fundamental to this theory. In highly ambiguous situations there is insufficient information available for efficient appraisal and faulty conclusions at this stage predispose the patient to inappropriate coping behaviour. This inappropriate coping was strikingly demonstrated when protocols of initial interviews with patients were examined. An additional feature is that, in retrospect, inappropriate coping becomes obvious to the individual concerned when his overall stress is reduced. The initial protocols demonstrate this specifically in the example of a patient who feared recovering consciousness during the operation (page 56):

> somehow, in the hospital surroundings, one tends not to think rationally and to become concerned with trivialities.

Within the framework of the Lazarus approach to anxiety and stress the role of information is readily apparent. It allows an accurate appraisal of the stimuli which bombard a patient at the time of admission, and hence the adoption of appropriate coping behaviour. Both of these processes reduce the overall stress level, thereby enabling the appraisal of new situations to be more efficient.

Research directly concerned with information transfer under stressful situations is reviewed by Spielberger (1966). Typically the studies involve the learning of tasks under varying conditions, some of which are stressful. The majority of these studies support the contention that high levels of anxiety inhibit storage and retention of information.

Ley and Spelman (1967) consider studies dealing with memory aspects of informing hospital patients and it is clear from this review that only a small proportion of the information is retained after 24 hours. In fact a great deal is being asked of the patient in these circumstances. He is asked to learn a mass of unfamiliar material after one verbal repetition (one trial learning) and this under conditions of high stress. It is not, therefore, surprising that rapid forgetting occurs. As alternatives to verbal information are rudimentary, and hospital booklets tend to deal only with general information, one approach is to examine methods of improving and systematizing presentation. Perhaps the concept of "schemata" advocated by Bartlett (1933) is useful here. This postulates that an individual stores a small quantity of key facts, around which elaborations and rationalizations occur, but he retains much of the central theme. It was noticeable that patients in the second hospital tended to retain more of the information given at the pre-operative interview, due perhaps to the shortening of the total amount of material presented. Even so, considerable loss occurred which needed reinforcement at the daily visit. In view of these difficulties the old teaching adage may provide a practical guide.

1. Tell 'em what you're going to tell 'em.
2. Tell 'em.
3. Tell 'em what you've told 'em.

Results, particularly from the first hospital, tend to support the view that anxiety and pain are closely related variables. The significant correlation between admission anxiety and analgesics found in the first hospital was not repeated in the second, but seems worthy of further research. With a more detailed analysis it should be possible to examine the effects of modes of response and situations which characterize pain-prone individuals in hospital.

Evaluation of research tools

1. Information—the independent variable

The first hospital trials used a wide range of information (described in Chapter 3) and thus gave little insight into the relative importance of individual items. Cartwright (1964) found that hospital patients obtain general information from a variety of sources, any of which may vary according to the patient's social and educational background. The initial interviews for the present investigation suggested similar trends.

After the success of the overall schedule in the first hospital it was realized that the results gave no clue to relative efficacy of the items involved. As the evidence implies that patients obtain general information from many sources it was decided to include only professional/technical items for the second hospital trials, i.e. Sections 4 and 5 of the original schedule. These deal specifically with pre-operative nursing information and pain and discomfort aspects of the operation. This shortening of the original schedule also had the advantage of reducing the total amount patients were required to remember. It was therefore easier to concentrate upon central points with the idea of establishing a viable "schema".

The overall sample results for the second hospital supported the information-giving hypothesis; the cholecystectomy sub-groups showed highly significant differences between informed and control patients, while group differences between the hysterectomy sub-groups did not reach significance.

These results give credence to the idea that technical/professional information is perhaps more difficult for patients to obtain from casual sources than might be the case for more general items and there seems no reason why a ward nurse should not obtain similar results, providing that she has a competent knowledge of surgical nursing procedures. The question has arisen in discussion as to whether the information-providing person need be a nurse, or a non-nursing person trained for the role. A major problem with this latter suggestion is that patients often ask detailed questions, some of which may be tangential to the immediate topic. The fully-trained nurse could cope with these whereas other personnel may be unable to give a satisfactory explanation. In view of research into communication effectiveness (Hovland and Weiss, 1951) it seems essential that the information comes from an authoritative source, i.e. the source must be credible to the patient.

As a further development, information could be more finely separated and its relative effects determined by a further series of experiments, preferably with refined samples of one operation type.

It is important to note that in spite of possible advances into the precise relevance of various items of information, little actual progress will be made until problems associated with the total pattern of ward care are tackled. This implies modifying the anxiety-producing regime of typical hospital wards. The majority of doctors and nurses encountered during this investigation agreed in principle that patients should receive as much information as possible, but felt that without extensive reorganization the idea was unrealistic.

Additional methods of supplying information exist, and it may well be possible to improve upon the verbal method, either in a supplementary or replacement manner. There is a need for detailed comparison and assessment of booklets, the spoken word and video-tape recordings, all of which may play a future role in informing the patient.

The modified S—R Inventory of Anxiety

The original impetus for developing this approach to anxiety measurement came from Endler *et al.* (1962). For the present research, modifications involved substituting situations which were deemed more relevant to the process of admission to hospital. This modified inventory was originally envisaged as a research tool in two ways. Firstly as a general measure of trait anxiety, and secondly, as a possible predictive device in terms of post-operative patients' pain as assessed indirectly by relating anxiety to analgesics.

The first hospital results were encouraging. In spite of this being a first trial of the inventory, the following results emerged:

1. The inventory could be completed by patients drawn from widely differing backgrounds.
2. The range of scores obtained indicated a fairly wide discriminatory function.
3. The test—retest reliability after an interval of at least 7 days was very high for inventories of this type.
4. The positive relationship between anxiety and analgesics ($P < 0.05$) allowed the predictive hypothesis to be accepted. This was further strengthened by the higher mean anxiety scores of the informed group.

It was felt that the first hospital results indicated further testing of the inventory, therefore, following modifications of two situations the inventory was used in the second hospital. The test—retest reliability was not assessed this time but a further dimension was added by relating the

S–R results to the Eysenck Personality Inventory (EPI) given to the same patients prior to discharge. The emergent correlation of 0·49 (significant at 0·1% level) with the neuroticism factor of the EPI supports the claim that the S–R inventory is a useful measure of trait anxiety.

The second hospital results were less consistent in some of the relationships, rendering interpretation difficult. An example is seen in the correlation between anxiety and length of stay which for the total sample is 0·05, for the informed group −0·38, and for the controls 0·41. Both group correlations are highly significant, but in opposite directions.

For future investigations the S–R Inventory possesses useful features. The significant correlation with analgesics could profitably be followed up, using a more refined sample. The relationship with the neuroticism factor of the EPI raises the question that if an overall trait anxiety measure is all that is required, then one of the shorter and less time-consuming inventories may perform as well. However, if the true nature of anxiety in hospital patients is to be understood, the situations and modes of response variables can supply valuable additional data.

The Patients' Subjective State Scale

This was primarily an attempt to gather data covering a wide range of behaviour and to study responses made by patients to the hospital environment. This information is essential to any investigation involving pain and anxiety as both phenomena encompass a wide range of individual differences. It has yet to be demonstrated that a completely reliable alternative to subjective report exists for either anxiety (Martin, 1961) or pain (Melzack and Torgenson, 1971). The latter authors discuss verbal differences in subjective pain reports, but claim that if these are suitably grouped a high level of consistency becomes possible.

The problems involved in scaling patients' statements are far from a total solution. If the scaling is recorded on too broad a basis, the procedure becomes unwieldy; if too few choices of categories are offered, constraints are imposed. The five-point scaling used throughout the present investigation allowed meaningful comparisons of between-group differences, this process being aided by improved observer consistency in the second hospital.

Interesting future developments must, at some stage, include nursing staff ratings of similar variables to enable comparisons with patients' data, both of these could then be related to more "objective" variables such as medications.

There are, of course, humane considerations which preclude too much data collection from stressed patients. The development of videotape monitoring techniques as a supplement to verbal report would possibly be a compromise here. This would enable a wider range of the patients' day to be covered, possibly by activity sampling followed by analysis of predetermined content.

Analgesic consumption as a dependent variable

This has the initial attraction of being "objective", i.e. it can be recorded along an internal scale of measurement thus allowing the most powerful statistical methods to be employed. In practice, this objectivity is seen to be profoundly affected by control variables in the hospital ward environment. Individual differences exist between patients in response to analgesics, although these can be minimized by careful sampling coupled with large sample numbers.

Perhaps the major variable in analgesic consumption is nursing staff policy. Differences between wards were very apparent in the present investigation, and were mentioned as a major difficulty by Bond and Pilowsky (1966). A wide range of nursing staff attitudes exists, and discussion brings out similar "fears and misconceptions" about the use of narcotics and analgesics as were expressed by some patients at the initial interviews (Chapter 4). Attitudes among nurses vary, being affected by a wide range of cultural and religious beliefs. Some wards appear to have a fixed "routine" for analgesic administration, thus tending to deny individual differences between patients, whereas other wards give analgesics almost on demand within the limits set by the doctors' prescription.

Future research involving analgesic consumption as a measure must take account of these control variables if valid comparisons are to be achieved. It is difficult to see how improvements will be made in method unless there is also close scrutiny of the nurses' decision-making processes.

Implications for nursing practice

Chapter 3 reviewed some reports appertaining to information and hospital patients. The concept of the "personal doctor" who was seen as a key informative figure by the Ministry of Health Report (1963) is now 11 years old, but little progress seems to have been made towards this ideal. The interview sections of the present investigation would support Cartwright (1964) and Raphael (1969) both of whom found lack of information to be the largest single complaint of hospital patients. Many patients still do not know who their doctor is.

The same Ministry of Health report states quite clearly that if the doctor is unable to supply patients with information, the responsibility for this then lies with nursing staff.

> This responsibility can be carried at no lower level than that of ward sister—She must instruct staff in the part they are to play. Ministry of Health (1963) para. 23.

119

The present project shows the viability of this statement by demonstrating that nursing information can result in improved patient welfare. It is also possible that this resultant increase in patient welfare reduced the post-operative nursing load. The 30 minutes or so spent at the pre-operative stage may thus be seen as an "investment" which has a profitable sequel.

It is clear that the important influence of anxiety in patient welfare is insufficiently stressed by some of those providing a patient care service and informal enquiry during the present project showed that many nurses viewed information-giving as an extremely minor aspect of their nursing duties.

Under the present system there is no doubt that considerable reorganization would be required to allow a ward sister 30 to 40 minutes with each newly admitted patient. For this degree of organizational change to become reality, the rethinking of the ward sister's role needs support from the highest levels of nursing management. Organization and method studies indicate that the average ward sister spends a very low percentage of each duty shift in actual patient contact. This is predominantly because of other duties, some of which are far removed from patient contact, so that practical, as well as attitudinal changes are required for reform to occur. During informal discussions with hospital nursing staff, the advantages of providing an efficient patient-information service are freely acknowledged by most nurses; it is in the implementation of such a scheme that problems are seen.

Changed attitudes are also required in order to recognize that the doctor and nurse do not *always* know best. A surgical operation is a joint venture with the patient's welfare as the ultimate objective. Surely it is right that, wherever possible, the patient should participate in this venture and that he should be given enough information to anticipate events intelligently.

Nurse educators bear a heavy responsibility for the formation of nursing attitudes. For example, are student nurses made aware of the undesirable physiological and psychological concomitants of excessive anxiety, all of which have a direct bearing on the quality of care provided?

Progress in ward and equipment design may require the reorganization of traditional practices. Ward design involving multiple small wards may need extensive redeployment of duties if patients are to be satisfactorily observed. There is also less "chance contact" between nurses and patients, therefore the initial "information session" becomes even more important.

The experience and status of the person who acts as "information-giver" is a point of some importance. There is evidence (Hovland and Weiss, 1951) that the effectiveness of a communication is enhanced if it is seen to come from an authoritative source. Some wards appoint an "admission nurse" whose duty it is to supply information to newly

120

admitted patients. Although useful, the nurse may be inexperienced, often giving information of a general nature which may be obtainable from other sources. Research literature indicates that the information is transferred more efficiently if the source credibility is high.

In discussion many nurses display ambivalent attitudes towards the idea of a specially employed "information-giver" who would greet new admissions. Some resentment is created at this possible encroachment into the traditional nurse/patient relationship, but, at the same time, most nurses view an efficient information service as quite impractical under present circumstances. One drawback of the special "information-giver" would be possible lack of "continuity of care", the need for which was very apparent following initial interviews and which applies to both relationship formation and the physical environment.

Research has an important future role in the development of a high quality nursing service and the ultimate aim of nursing research must be to examine the effects of various nursing procedures in terms of patient welfare. It is thus the *process* of nursing which requires detailed scrutiny, and this involves studying the ward as a social unit, no one part of which can be satisfactorily examined without considering the others. Quality of care is obviously a multifactorial process and, as so often occurs in complex situations, the interactions between factors may exert more significant influences than the major factors themselves.

It is therefore hoped that the present investigation will make a small contribution towards the ideal situation where a programme of high quality nursing care is individually planned for each patient.

Statistics

Before giving a short account of the statistics used in the study it may be useful to define some of the terms used in the text.

Statistics

This term is now commonly used in two ways. Firstly, as a plural noun, when it means a collection of numerical facts, e.g. "vital statistics" of population, births, deaths, etc., secondly, as a singular noun it denotes certain methods utilized in the collection and analysis of such facts. Whichever meaning is used the subject deals with facts expressed in a numerical form.

Hays (1960) has included the following objectives of statistics:

1. To give facts in a definite form, i.e. numerical facts give more precise information than facts expressed in general terms. The statement that many people were killed as a result of industrial accidents in August 1952 does not give the same amount of information as the statement that 81 were killed in August 1952 as a result of industrial accidents.

2. To simplify and clarify large masses of facts.

3. To furnish methods of comparison. The significance of a series of figures is often better appreciated when these figures are compared with others of a similar kind.

4. To indicate trends and tendencies and so help in determining present policy and action and in the forecasting of future conditions.

Population

The term "population" refers to groups of people, but it is used in statistics to refer to any defined group of people, animals, objects, measurements, and the like. Distinction is sometimes made between finite and infinite populations, e.g. a pack of cards or the number of first-year nurses in a certain hospital are finite, i.e. they can be counted. The possible number of rolls of a die are infinite. Many populations are finite but very large, e.g. all trained nurses in the world, or indefinitely large, e.g. the possible number of observations in an experiment. In these cases it may be impractical to involve all members of a population, and if a population is indefinitely large it is, of course, impossible to produce complete population statistics and the investigator must draw a sample.

Sample

Any sub-group or sub-aggregate of scores drawn by an appropriate method from a population. Statistical procedures used in *describing* the properties of samples, or of populations, when applicable, are referred to by some authors as descriptive statistics, i.e. they describe the characteristics of a sample or population. Procedures used in the drawing of *inferences* about the properties of populations *from samples* are known as inferential statistics, i.e. we infer certain characteristics of a population from information derived from a sample.

Variable

This term refers to a property whereby the members of a group or set differ from one another, e.g. age, sex, race, occupation, are all variables which may influence the findings of an investigation.

Where using an experimental method it is usual to describe *independent variables,* as those conditions which can be varied by an experimenter and *dependent variables* as measures of the effects of the independent variables on a situation, i.e. they are functionally related, the latter being dependent on the former.

Data

Systematically collected information. Usually, but by no means always, it is numerical. To a large extent the type of data collected determines what statistical tests may be used. Siegel (1956) describes three main classifications of data:

1. Nominal scale

Measurement at its weakest is found where numbers or other symbols are used to classify an object, person, or characteristic, i.e. nominal naming. An example of this would be psychiatric diagnosis. The terms "neurotic" or "schizophrenic" represent a nominal classification.

2. Ordinal or ranking scale

Here the objects within a scale are not just different, but they stand in some relation to one another. For example, a wine taster can order or rank a series of wines on a scale from the best to the worst tasting in his view.

3. Interval scale

When a scale has all the characteristics of an ordinal scale, and when in addition the *distances* between any two numbers on the scale are of known size, this constitutes an interval scale. For example, temperature is measured on an interval scale, the difference between 6 and 7 degrees being the same as the distance between 8 and 9, or 28 and 29 degrees. Although most researchers who use numerical methods aspire to create interval scales, success in this aim is rare for the type of data discussed in the present report.

Hypothesis

Hypotheses may be of two types. The first stage of using a statistical test involves stating a *null hypothesis*, i.e. a hypothesis of no differences which is usually formulated for the express purpose of being rejected. When the null hypothesis can be rejected at an appropriate level of significance (see below) the alternative or experimental hypothesis may be accepted, i.e. that differences do exist between the sets of scores.

Significance levels for rejection of a null hypothesis

When the null hypothesis (Ho) and the experimental hypothesis (Hi) have been stated, the next step is to specify a level of significance at which the Ho can be rejected. Common values used in research are $0 \cdot 05$ (5%) and $0 \cdot 01$ (1%). This means that if an experiment is performed and the statistical test results are significant at less than ($<$) the 5% level, then this result would only occur by chance 5 times in 100 experiments of this kind. Correspondingly, if the result is significant to 1%, it would not occur by chance more than once in a hundred such experiments.

Statistical tests

Descriptive statistics describe two main features of a sample of scores. Firstly the central score (mean or arithmetic average) which gives an idea of the *average score* (even though no one score may be identical to this); secondly, an estimation of the spread or *dispersion of scores,* for which purpose the standard deviation is often used.

However, some statistical tests are based upon the assumption that the groups of scores to be compared are *normally distributed* (see references to statistics texts below) and, providing certain other assumptions are met, parametric (within defined boundaries) tests may be used. These are the most powerful statistical tools, an example of which is the "t" test used to compare analgesic consumption in the present report.

One of the assumptions to be satisfied before parametric tests can be used is that data should be measured on an interval scale. Hence, on occasions where data are either nominal or ordinal by nature these tests are inappropriate and a range of alternative tests (not based on "normal distribution" assumptions) has been developed. Not surprsingly these are known as "distribution free" or "nonparametric" tests. Therefore to a great extent the data decide the choice of test which is available for use.

Tests used in this report

1. The "t" test

This test was devised originally in 1908 by W. S. Gosset who wrote under the pen name of "Student". It is widely used to test for the significance of differences between the means of two sets of scores and assumes normality of the distributions of the variables in the populations from which the samples are drawn. It can be used to analyse two sets of related or independent scores. For comparisons of analgesic consumption between informed and control patients the independent "t" test was used, for although the design is based upon frequency matching (Chapter 5) some patients were not closely matched on all variables.

2. Correlation

This is concerned with describing the degree of relation between variables and the data consist of pairs of measurements, e.g. admission anxiety paired with post-operative analgesic consumption for each patient in the present study. The most widely used measure of correlation is the Pearson Product-Moment Correlation Coefficient, and its use requires that the variables are quantitative, i.e. of the interval scale type. Application of the formula (see references) results in a figure lying somewhere between minus one (-1), through zero to one:

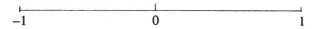

$$-1 \qquad\qquad 0 \qquad\qquad 1$$

A correlation of one represents a perfect positive relationship, whereas minus one shows a perfect negative relationship. In practice such extremes are rare.

Other types of correlation may be used where data are of nominal or ordinal nature, perhaps the best known being Spearman's Rank-Order Correlation. Interpretation remains the same as in the diagram above.

For establishing the significance level of between group differences, the correlation coefficient can be converted to "t" and the resultant figure checked by means of tables. This method was used in the present study.

Limitations of correlational methods

1. When an amount of correlation is used as a basis of argument it should be calculated from a sufficient number of persons to make its general application possible.

2. A high correlation must not be taken as evidence for a causal relation between variables. On the other hand, a high degree of correlation might be used to support a case for *one* cause.

3. Before assuming cause and effect, it is desirable to see if both sets of figures may not be the result of some third factor. This is especially important when considering ward-based research findings.

3. The Mann-Whitney Test

When ordinal scale measurement has been achieved, this test may be used to determine whether two independent groups differ significantly, i.e. are not drawn from the same population. It is a non-parametric test and is a useful alternative to the "t" test when the data are not in interval scale.

In the present study the Mann-Whitney test was used to compare the PSS scores of informed and control patients. For a useful review and explanation of this test see Siegel (1956).

Useful references in statistics include:

CROCKER, A. C. (1969). *Statistics for the Teacher.* Harmondsworth, Middlesex. Penguin Books.

MORONEY, M. J. (1962). Facts from Figures. Harmondsworth, Middlesex: Penguin Books.

SIEGEL, S. (1956). Nonparametric Statistics. New York: McGraw-Hill.

Data Collection Schedule

Name: _____ Sex: _____ S. class: _____

Case No.: _____ E/C

Age: _____ Birth order: _____

Marital status: _____

Previous admissions: _____

Date of admission: _____ Discharge: _____

Operation _____ on _____ duration _____

Anxiety scores

Admission													
	A	B	C	D	1	2	3	4	5	6	7	8	9	10
Discharge													

Pain and subjective state

	1	2	3	4	5	6	7	8	9	10
Day 1										
Day 2										
Day 3										
Day 4										
Day 5										

Analgesia	Time							Drug and dosage					
Day 1													
Day 2													
Day 3													
Day 4													
Day 5													

Total in units

Day 1	
Day 2	
Day 3	
Day 4	
Day 5	

Other drugs:

Other comments:

Sister's assessment score:

Vomiting Day 1						
Vomiting Day 2						
Vomiting Day 3						
Vomiting Day 4						
Vomiting Day 5						

S–R Inventory of Anxiety

Ways in which people react to different situations

These questions are a way of looking at the ways in which people react to different situations. The idea is that on the following pages you will see examples of common situations. You may have experienced these, or if you have not, you can perhaps easily imagine them.

Below each situation there are two questions which ask if you have ever actually seen or been in such a situation, and whether or not you can easily imagine yourself in it. If you now look at the first page you will see the questions. Do ask if they are not quite clear.

The two questions we have mentioned are numbered 1 and 2. These are followed by further questions which indicate some common reactions which people experience when they are placed in worrying situations. An example of this would be, "My heart starts pounding". Underneath this you will see:

very much   5   4   3   2   1   not at all.

If you experience this reaction to a considerable extent when you meet a situation of this type you would put a ring round the number 5. On the other hand if you never experience such a reaction, you would put a ring round the number 1.

The numbers 2, 3 and 4 which lie between these two are used to indicate different levels of reaction, and this will be explained fully by the person asking you to fill in the form.

You will find that only the situations at the top of the page change. The reactions which are listed below remain the same on each page, so that when you have done one page the rest will be easy.

Important

There are no right or wrong answers to these questions. We are only concerned with your reactions to the situations.

Thank you for your co-operation

"You have to walk into a crowded room full of strangers and make an announcement."

1. This has happened to me.   This has never happened to me.

                  5   4   3   2   1

2. I can easily imagine, as I sit here, what it would be like.   I find it very hard to imagine.

                  5   4   3   2   1

3.   My heart starts pounding.

very much   5   4   3   2   1   not at all.

4.   My mouth feels dry.

very much   5   4   3   2   1   not at all.

5.   I break into a cold sweat.

very much   5   4   3   2   1   not at all.

6.   I feel rather excited.

very much   5   4   3   2   1   not at all

7.   I feel I need to talk to someone.

very much   5   4   3   2   1   not at all.

8.   I feel "butterflies" and sick.

very much   5   4   3   2   1   not at all.

9.   I feel I need to visit the toilet a lot.

very much   5   4   3   2   1   not at all.

10.   I feel irritated and annoyed.

very much   5   4   3   2   1   not at all.

11.   I feel shaky and weak at the knees.

very much   5   4   3   2   1   not at all.

130

Situation 2   "You have just seen someone having a fit or a blackout in the street."

1. This has happened to me.   This has never happened
                                      to me.

        5   4   3   2   1

2. I can easily imagine, as   I find it very hard to
   I sit here, what it would   imagine.
   be like.

        5   4   3   2   1

3.   My heart starts pounding.

   very much   5   4   3   2   1   not at all.

4.   My mouth feels dry.

   very much   5   4   3   2   1   not at all.

5.   I break into a cold sweat.

   very much   5   4   3   2   1   not at all.

6.   I feel rather excited.

   very much   5   4   3   2   1   not at all

7.   I feel I need to talk to someone.

   very much   5   4   3   2   1   not at all.

8.   I feel "butterflies" and sick.

   very much   5   4   3   2   1   not at all.

9.   I feel I need to visit the
              toilet a lot.

   very much   5   4   3   2   1   not at all.

10.   I feel irritated and annoyed.

   very much   5   4   3   2   1   not at all.

11.   I feel shaky and weak at the knees.

   very much   5   4   3   2   1   not at all.

Situation 3   "You are just about to visit someone who is very ill."

1. This has happened to me.   This has never happened to me.

        5   4   3   2   1

2. I can easily imagine, as   I find it very hard to
   I sit here, what it would   imagine.
   be like.

        5   4   3   2   1

3.   My heart starts pounding.

    very much   5   4   3   2   1   not at all.

4.   My mouth feels dry.

    very much   5   4   3   2   1   not at all.

5.   I break into a cold sweat.

    very much   5   4   3   2   1   not at all.

6.   I feel rather excited.

    very much   5   4   3   2   1   not at all

7.   I feel I need to talk to someone.

    very much   5   4   3   2   1   not at all.

8.   I feel "butterflies" and sick.

    very much   5   4   3   2   1   not at all.

9.   I feel I need to visit the
   toilet a lot.

    very much   5   4   3   2   1   not at all.

10.   I feel irritated and annoyed.

    very much   5   4   3   2   1   not at all.

11.   I feel shaky and weak at the knees.

    very much   5   4   3   2   1   not at all.

Situation 4   "You have just opened the letter telling you to come to hospital."

1. This has happened to me.   This has never happened to me.

         5   4   3   2   1

2. I can easily imagine, as   I find it very hard to
   I sit here, what it would   imagine.
   be like.

         5   4   3   2   1

3.   My heart starts pounding.

  very much   5   4   3   2   1   not at all.

4.   My mouth feels dry.

  very much   5   4   3   2   1   not at all.

5.   I break into a cold sweat.

  very much   5   4   3   2   1   not at all.

6.   I feel rather excited.

  very much   5   4   3   2   1   not at all

7.   I feel I need to talk to someone.

  very much   5   4   3   2   1   not at all.

8.   I feel "butterflies" and sick.

  very much   5   4   3   2   1   not at all.

9.   I feel I need to visit the
              toilet a lot.

  very much   5   4   3   2   1   not at all.

10.   I feel irritated and annoyed.

  very much   5   4   3   2   1   not at all.

11.   I feel shaky and weak at the knees.

  very much   5   4   3   2   1   not at all.

Situation 5   "You are waiting for a dental appointment which you know will be painful and uncomfortable."

1. This has happened to me.   This has never happened to me.

     5   4   3   2   1

2. I can easily imagine, as I sit here, what it would be like.   I find it very hard to imagine.

     5   4   3   2   1

3. My heart starts pounding.

very much   5   4   3   2   1   not at all.

4. My mouth feels dry.

very much   5   4   3   2   1   not at all.

5. I break into a cold sweat.

very much   5   4   3   2   1   not at all.

6. I feel rather excited.

very much   5   4   3   2   1   not at all

7. I feel I need to talk to someone.

very much   5   4   3   2   1   not at all.

8. I feel "butterflies" and sick.

very much   5   4   3   2   1   not at all.

9. I feel I need to visit the toilet a lot.

very much   5   4   3   2   1   not at all.

10. I feel irritated and annoyed.

very much   5   4   3   2   1   not at all.

11. I feel shaky and weak at the knees.

very much   5   4   3   2   1   not at all.

Situation 6   "You are walking on a high narrow ledge for example on a mountain or a high building."

1. This has happened to me.   This has never happened to me.

           5   4   3   2   1

2. I can easily imagine, as I sit here, what it would be like.   I find it very hard to imagine.

           5   4   3   2   1

3.   My heart starts pounding.

   very much   5   4   3   2   1   not at all.

4.   My mouth feels dry.

   very much   5   4   3   2   1   not at all.

5.   I break into a cold sweat.

   very much   5   4   3   2   1   not at all.

6.   I feel rather excited.

   very much   5   4   3   2   1   not at all

7.   I feel I need to talk to someone.

   very much   5   4   3   2   1   not at all.

8.   I feel "butterflies" and sick.

   very much   5   4   3   2   1   not at all.

9.   I feel I need to visit the toilet a lot.

   very much   5   4   3   2   1   not at all.

10.   I feel irritated and annoyed.

   very much   5   4   3   2   1   not at all.

11.   I feel shaky and weak at the knees.

   very much   5   4   3   2   1   not at all.

"The Doctor has just told you that an operation will be necessary."

1. This has happened to me.   This has never happened to me.

        5   4   3   2   1

2. I can easily imagine, as I sit here, what it would be like.   I find it very hard to imagine.

        5   4   3   2   1

3.   My heart starts pounding.

   very much   5   4   3   2   1   not at all.

4.   My mouth feels dry.

   very much   5   4   3   2   1   not at all.

5.   I break into a cold sweat.

   very much   5   4   3   2   1   not at all.

6.   I feel rather excited.

   very much   5   4   3   2   1   not at all

7.   I feel I need to talk to someone.

   very much   5   4   3   2   1   not at all.

8.   I feel "butterflies" and sick.

   very much   5   4   3   2   1   not at all.

9.   I feel I need to visit the toilet a lot.

   very much   5   4   3   2   1   not at all.

10.   I feel irritated and annoyed.

   very much   5   4   3   2   1   not at all.

11.   I feel shaky and weak at the knees.

   very much   5   4   3   2   1   not at all.

1. This has happened to me.   This has never happened
                                  to me.

            5   4   3   2   1

2. I can easily imagine, as   I find it very hard to
   I sit here, what it would   imagine.
   be like.

            5   4   3   2   1

3.   My heart starts pounding.

   very much   5   4   3   2   1   not at all.

4.   My mouth feels dry.

   very much   5   4   3   2   1   not at all.

5.   I break into a cold sweat.

   very much   5   4   3   2   1   not at all.

6.   I feel rather excited.

   very much   5   4   3   2   1   not at all

7.   I feel I need to talk to someone.

   very much   5   4   3   2   1   not at all.

8.   I feel "butterflies" and sick.

   very much   5   4   3   2   1   not at all.

9.   I feel I need to visit the
            toilet a lot.

   very much   5   4   3   2   1   not at all.

10.   I feel irritated and annoyed.

   very much   5   4   3   2   1   not at all.

11.   I feel shaky and weak at the knees.

   very much   5   4   3   2   1   not at all.

Situation 9 "You have cut your finger, and it bleeds quite badly for a few minutes."

1. This has happened to me. This has never happened to me.

         5   4   3   2   1

2. I can easily imagine, as I sit here, what it would be like. I find it very hard to imagine.

         5   4   3   2   1

3.   My heart starts pounding.

    very much   5   4   3   2   1   not at all.

4.   My mouth feels dry.

    very much   5   4   3   2   1   not at all.

5.   I break into a cold sweat.

    very much   5   4   3   2   1   not at all.

6.   I feel rather excited.

    very much   5   4   3   2   1   not at all

7.   I feel I need to talk to someone.

    very much   5   4   3   2   1   not at all.

8.   I feel "butterflies" and sick.

    very much   5   4   3   2   1   not at all.

9.   I feel I need to visit the toilet a lot.

    very much   5   4   3   2   1   not at all.

10.   I feel irritated and annoyed.

    very much   5   4   3   2   1   not at all.

11.   I feel shaky and weak at the knees.

    very much   5   4   3   2   1   not at all.

Situation 10   "You are in a crowded tube. or a lift which unexpectedly stops, perhaps due to a breakdown."

1. This has happened to me.   This has never happened to me.

  5   4   3   2   1

2. I can easily imagine, as I sit here, what it would be like.   I find it very hard to imagine.

  5   4   3   2   1

3.   My heart starts pounding.

  very much   5   4   3   2   1   not at all.

4.   My mouth feels dry.

  very much   5   4   3   2   1   not at all.

5.   I break into a cold sweat.

  very much   5   4   3   2   1   not at all.

6.   I feel rather excited.

  very much   5   4   3   2   1   not at all

7.   I feel I need to talk to someone.

  very much   5   4   3   2   1   not at all.

8.   I feel "butterflies" and sick.

  very much   5   4   3   2   1   not at all.

9.   I feel I need to visit the toilet a lot.

  very much   5   4   3   2   1   not at all.

10.   I feel irritated and annoyed.

  very much   5   4   3   2   1   not at all.

11.   I feel shaky and weak at the knees.

  very much   5   4   3   2   1   not at all.

Method of Patient Instruction

The aim of this procedure is to transmit the maximum amount of relevant information under conditions conducive to retention and storage. Previous research indicates that in highly structured situations, rentention of verbal information by patients tends to be inefficient. In an attempt to counteract this:

(a)   The information was given in conditions which were as informal as could be arranged in a ward situation. (Usually a small side ward.)

(b)   The items of information were delivered in an unstructured manner wherever possible.

(c)   There was a clear statement of the patient's role in the research plan.

(d)   Items were derived from patients' statements during pilot interviews.

1.   *On admission* the first stage is a personal introduction. This is followed by a general statement of the aims. "We are interested in the way people respond to coming into hospital and having an operation. To do this we are asking the cooperation of patients having certain operations. This involves asking the patient some initial questions, followed by a short interview, and then we keep in touch with them during their stay. Would you care to participate?"

   If the patient is aggreeable continue with (2).

2.   *Administration of situational anxiety scale*

3.   *Information interview*
   (i) *Ward.* Name and number of beds. (This is . . . . Ward and has 30 beds. The patients are of varied ages, and are in for many types of operation.) Example of method of delivery.
   This is followed by the following items, again with emphasis upon a conversational rather than an instructional manner.
   (ii) Name of surgeon. Why he is known as "Mr" and not "Dr".
   (iii) Ward sister's name. I/c of ward nursing.
   (iv) Role of other Doctors (briefly).
   (v) Staff nurse/SEN mentioned. Other grades also but not in detail.
   (vi) Ward facilities (referred to booklet whenever relevant).
   (vii) Extra, i.e. telephone, library books.

4. *Pre-operative nursing information*
(i) Impressed on patient that specific medical information will be given by the doctors. We are merely giving general information about pre- and post-operative care.
(ii) Reinforcement of patient's decision to undergo surgery. Stressing of long term benefits.
(iii) Relevant selection from following items of nursing care. This will obviously vary according to the type of operation.
(a) Who to ask for information, i.e. ward sister, who will then arrange other appointments if appropriate.
(b) Idea of pre-operative care. Why following may be necessary. (Selected for relevance of operation type.)
Medical examination.
Consent form.
Dietary restrictions (if any).
Laboratory specimens.
Pre-operative shaving.
Premedication; and other preanaesthetic procedures.
May have blood transfusion or I.V. fluids.
May recover in recovery room, or intensive care unit.

5. *Post-operative pain and discomfort aspects*
(i) Pain is a normal reaction to an operation, but its severity can often be affected by the patient's attitudes.
(ii) Pain is amplified by muscle spasm or tenseness in the muscles surrounding the operation site—the tighter these are, the more it hurts.
(iii) Therefore, relaxation of the immediate area and of the whole body may help the pain. Practice beforehand.
(iv) Avoid strain on the injured part by rehearsing changes of position, etc.
(v) Information on physiotherapist and early ambulation.
(vi) Patient is told about any item of post-operative care specific to his/her operation; e.g. infusions, tubes, diet.

You have been very helpful. I shall be visiting you again to see how you are getting on and to remind you of the points I have mentioned.

By the way, there is one particular thing I would like you to remember and it is this. After your operation my colleague M ... will visit you and ask some questions (give example). We realize that you may not be feeling very bright for the first few days, but it would be very helpful if you would answer the questions as accurately as you are able.

Explain that we have different groups involved and ask patients to be discreet.

APPENDIX E

Assessment of Patient's Subjective State

Introduction appropriate to situation, i.e. "Good morning. Mr. . . . . . . , followed by explanation of visit.

1. Pain thermometer

Here is a little scale something like a thermometer (show) in fact we call it a pain thermometer. You will see that it has degrees of pain marked on it. Could you show me how much pain you have at the moment? You can choose in between the statements if you wish (demonstrate). Take your time, and think about it before deciding.

2. Pain, local or general

Is yor pain local, that is just around the site of the operation? If not how widespread is it? (Score 1 for local, 5 for all over body.)

3. Morale

How do you feel in yourself? By that I mean what sort of mood are you in? (Suggest categories, i.e. cheerful to "fed up". Score cheerful and content 1, "completely fed up" score 5.

4. Nausea

Have you any feeling of sickness? Score 1 for not at all, 5 if has vomited.

The following questions are asked at the morning visit only

5. Sleep

How did you sleep last night? Score 1 for very well, 5 for no sleep.

6. Appetite

Have you managed your food all right? Score 1 for normal, 5 for totally unable to take food. Indicate if medical reasons prevent eating, i.e. post-gastrectomy.

7. Patient's comfort

We are interested in events which directly help the comfort of patients. I will show you examples of what other patients have said (show list). These are not in order of preference. Is there one which applies in your case? If not perhaps you could tell me what sort of thing *you* find comforting.

8. Any specific points patient mentions, not included in above categories.

Multiple choices for question 7

1. Talking to other patients.
2. Tablets or injections (medication).
3. Visiting time.
4. Nursing attention (bed made and position changed).
5. Talking with Doctor.
6. Talking to sister or nurses.

APPENDIX F

Sister's Assessment Sheet

Could you please put a ring round whichever number below seems to you, in your experience, to fit the post-operative progress of the following patient:

Mr./Mrs./Miss.. has progressed

Unusually well	1
Better than usual	2
About average	3
Not as well as usual	4
Very slowly/not well at all	5

Patient's Discharge Statement

It is important that we should know the effects of the research workers' visits during your stay. Would you mark a cross in the appropriate section with your *honest* opinion and seal your answer in the envelope. Do *not* write your name as your answer is *strictly confidential*.

| Very helpful | Slightly helpful | No effect | Unhelpful | A nuisance |

Bibliography

ABEL-SMITH, B., (1960). *A History of the Nursing Profession*. Heinemann, London.

ANDERSON, N. H. (1961). Scales and statistics: parametric and nonparametric. *Psychological Bulletin, 58*, 305–316.

ARGYLE, M. (1973). *Social Interaction*. Methuen, London.

BAKER, M. (1966). Validating test assumptions. *Educational and Psychological Measurement, 26*, 291–309.

BARNES, E. (1961). *People in Hospital*. Macmillan, London.

BARRON, M. A. (1964). The effects varied nursing approaches have on patients' complaints of pain: A clinical experiment. Unpublished Master's Thesis, Yale University School of Nursing.

BARTLETT, F. C. (1933). *Remembering: A study in Experimental and Social Psychology*. Cambridge University Press, Cambridge.

BEECHER, H. K. (1956). Relationship of significance of wound to the pain experienced. *Journal of the American Medical Association, 161*, 1609–1613.

BEECHER, H. K. (1959a). Generalisation from pain of various types and diverse origins. *Science, 130*, 267–268.

BEECHER, H. K. (1959b). Measurement of subjective responses: Quantitative effects of drugs. Oxford University Press, Oxford.

BEECHER, H. K. (1960). Increased stress and effectiveness of placebos and "active" drugs. *Science, 123*, 91–92.

BERNSTEIN, B. (1971) (ed.). *Social Class, Language and Communication*. The Russel Sage Foundation, New York.

BILLEWICZ, W. Z. (1964). Matched samples in medical investigation. *British Journal of Social and Preventive Medicine, 18*, 167–173.

BOND, M. R. and PILOWSKY, I. (1966). Subjective assessment of pain and its relationship to the administration of analgesics in patients with advanced cancer. *Psychosomatic Research, 10*, 203–208.

British Medical Association (1961). *Health Education*. British Medical Association, London.

British Medical Journal (1963). *Hospital Manners, 2*, 265–266.

BROWN, J. A. C. (1954). *The Social Psychology of Industry*. Penguin Books, Harmondsworth, Middlesex.

BRUEGEL, M. A. (1971). Relationship of preoperative anxiety to perception of postoperative pain. *Nursing Research, 20*, 1, 26–31.

CARR-SAUNDERS, A. M. and WILSON, P. A. (1933). *The Professions*. Oxford University Press, London.

CARSTAIRS, V. (1970). *Channels of of Communication*. Scottish Health Service Studies, Scottish Home and Health Department.

CARTWRIGHT, A. (1964). *Human Relations and Hospital Care*. Routledge and Kegan Paul, London.

CATTELL, R. B. and SCHEIER, I. H. (1958). The nature of anxiety. *Psychological Reports, 4,* 351–358.

CATTELL, R. B. and SCHEIER, I. H. (1961). *The Meaning and Measurement of Neuroticism and Anxiety.* Ronald Press, New York.

CHERTOK, L. (1959). *Psychosomatic Methods in Painless Childbirth.* Pergamon Press, New York.

CLARKE, P. R. F. and SPEAR, F. G. (1964). Reliability and sensitivity in the self assessment of well-being. *Bulletin of the British Psychological Society, 17,* 55. 18a.

COGAN, M. L. (1955). The problems of defining a profession. *The annals of the American Academy of Political and Social Science.* Vol. 297.

COGHILL, N. F. (1971). In WIELAND, G. and LEIGH, HILARY (eds.). *Changing Hospitals,* pp. 183–210. Tavistock, London.

COHEN, G. (1964). *Whats wrong with Hospitals?* Penguin Books, London.

CROCKER, A. C. (1969). *Statistics for the Teacher.* Penguin Books.

DAVITZ, L. J. and PENDLETON, S. H. (1969). Nurses' inferences of suffering. *Nursing Research, 18,* 2, 100–107.

DOLLARD, J. and MILLER, N. E. (1950). *Personality and Psychotherapy.* McGraw-Hill, New York.

DONABEDIAN, A. (1968). Promoting quality by evaluating medical care. *Medical Care, 6,* 3, 181–202.

DUFF, R. S. and HOLLINGSHEAD, A. B. (1968). *Sickness and Society.* Harper and Rowe, New York.

DUMAS, RHETAUGH, G. and LEONARD, R. C. (1963). Effect of nursing on the incidence of postoperative vomiting; a clinical experiment. *Nursing Research, 12,* 12–15.

EDWARDS, A. L. L. (1957). *The Social Desirability Factor in Personality Assessment and Research.* Dryden Press, New York.

EDWARDS, A. L. (1966). *Experimental Design in Psychological Research.* Holt, Rhinehart and Winston, New York.

EDWARDS, G., MORTON, H. J. V., PASK and WYLIE, D. (1956). Deaths associated with anaesthesia: A report of 1000 cases. *Anaesthesia, 11,* 194.

EGBERT, L. D., BATTIT, G. E., WELCH, C. E. and BARTLETT, M. K. (1964). Reduction of postoperative pain by encouragement and instruction of patients. A study of doctor-patient rapport. *New England Journal of Medicine, 270,* 825–827.

ENDLER, N. S., HUNT, J. McV. and ROSENSTEIN, A. J. (1962). An S–R inventory of anxiousness. *Psychological Monographs, 76,* 16 (Whole No. 536), 1–33.

ENDLER, N. S. and HUNT, J. McV. (1969). Generalisability of contributions from sources of variance in the S–R inventories of anxiousness. *Journal of Personality, 37,* 1–24.

ERNSTENE, A. C. (1957). Explaining to the patient. A therapeutic tool and a professional obligation. *Journal of the American Medical Association, 165,* 110.

EPSTEIN, S. (1967). Towards a unified theory of anxiety. In B. A. MAHER (ed.). *Progress in Experimental Personality Research,* Number 4, 1–89.

EPSTEIN, S. (1972). The nature of anxiety with emphasis on its relationship to expectancy. In C. D. SPIELBERGER (ed.). *Anxiety; Current Trends in Theory and Research.* Academic Press, New York.

147

EYSENCK, H. J. (1960). *The Structure of Human Personality*. Methuen, London.

EYSENCK, H. J. and EYSENCK, S. B. G. (1964). Manual of Eysenck Personality Inventory. London, University of London Press.

FREUD, S. (1936). *The Problem of Anxiety*. Norton, New York.

GRAHAM, L. E. and CONLEY, E. M. (1971). Evaluation of anxiety and fear in adult surgical patients. *Nursing Research, 20*, 2, 113–120.

HAMMOND, K. R. and KELLY, K. J. (1964). Approaches to the study of clinical inference in nursing. *Nursing Research, 13*, 4, 314–322.

HAYS, S. (1960). *An Outline of Statistics*. Longmans, London.

HAYWARD, J. C. (1973). Relationships between pre-operative information and post-operative pain and anxiety responses in surgical patients. Unpublished thesis, University of London.

HOUDE, R. W., WALLENSTEIN, S. L. and BEAVER, W. T. (1965). Clinical measurement of pain. In G. DE STEVENS (ed.). *Analgetics*. Academic Press, New York. Pp. 75–121.

HOVLAND, C. I. and WEISS, W. (1951) The influence of source credibility on communication effectiveness. *Public Opinion Quarterly, 15*, 635–650.

HUBERT, M. (1967). British nursing and the universities. *Nursing Times, 63*, 1335, 1375, 1415, 1453, 1485, 1519, 1533.

HUGH-JONES, P., TANSER, A. R. and WHITBY, C. (1964). Patients' view of admission to a London Teaching Hospital. *British Medical Journal, 2*, 660–664.

HULL, C. L. (1943). *Principles of Behaviour*. Appleton-Century-Crofts, New York.

JAHODA, G. (1969). Review of P. B. Warr and C. Knapper (1968). The perception of people and events. *British Journal of Psychology, 60*, 2, 267–268.

JANIS, I. L. (1958). *Psychological Stress*. Wiley, New York.

JOYCE, C. R. B. (1964). What does the doctor let the patient tell him? *Journal of Psychosomatic Research, 8*, 343–352.

JOYCE, C. R. B. (ed.) (1968). *Psychopharmocology: Dimensions and Perspectives*. Tavistock Publications, Lippincott, London.

KEATS, A. S. (1956). Postoperative pain; research and treatment. *Journal of chronic diseases, 4*, 72–83.

KEEHN, J. D. (1964). Consciousness and behaviourism. *British Journal of Psychology, 55*, 89–91.

KEELE, K. D. (1954). The pressure algometer. *Lancet, 1*, 636–639.

KELLER, CHARLOTTE M. (1965). Relationship of anxiety and an information-giving experience. Unpublished Ph.D. thesis, New York State University.

KNOPF, E. W. (1961). Florence Nightingale as a statistician. Quarterly publication of the *American Statistical Association*, NS 13, 138.

KUTNER, B. (1958). Surgeons and their patients. In E. G. JACO (ed.), *Patients, Physicians and Illness*, pp. 384–396. The Free Press, Glencoe, Illinois.

LACEY, J. I. (1959). Psychophysiological approaches to the evaluation of psychotherapeutic process and outcome. In E. A. RUBENSTEIN and M. B. PARLOFF (eds.), *Research in Psychotherapy*, pp. 160–208. American Psychological Association, Washington, D.C.

LANCET (1963). Human relations in hospital. *Lancet, 2*, 77.

LASAGNA, L. (1958). The clinical measurement of pain. *Annals of the New York Academy of Science, 13,* 28–37.

LASAGNA, L. and BEECHER, H. K. (1954). Analgesic effectiveness of codeine and meperadine (Demeral). *Journal of Pharmacology and Experimental Therapeutics, 112,* 306–311.

LAZARUS, R. S. (1966). *Psychological Stress and the Coping Process.* McGraw-Hill, New York.

LELEAN, S. R. (1974). Ready for report nurse? Royal College of Nursing, London.

LEVITT, E. E. (1961). *Clinical Research Design and Analysis in the Behavioural Sciences.* C. C. Thomas. Springfield, Illinois.

LEVITT, E. E. (1968). *The Psychology of Anxiety.* Bobbs-Merrill, Indianapolis.

LEWIS, T. (1942). *Pain.* Macmillan, London.

LEY, P. and SPELMAN, M. (1967). *Communicating with the Patient.* Staples Press, London.

LYNN, R. and EYSENCK, H. J. (1961). Tolerance for pain, extraversion and neuroticism. *Perceptual and motor skills, 12,* 161–162.

MCBRIDE, MARY A. (1967). *Pain and Effective Nursing Practice.* A.N.A. Clinical Sessions. Appleton-Century-Crofts, New York.

MCFARLANE, JEAN K. (1970). *The Proper Study of the Nurse.* Royal College of Nursing, London.

MACGUIRE, J. M. (1966). *From Student to Nurse*: Part II, Training and qualification, Oxford Area Nurse Training Committee (B. 13).

MANDLER, G. and SARASON, S. B. (1952). A study of anxiety and learning. *Journal of Abnormal and Social Psychology, 47,* 561–565.

MANDLER, G. and WATSON, D. L. (1966). Anxiety and the interruption of behaviour. In C. D. SPIELBERGER (ed.), *Anxiety and Behaviour.* Academic Press, New York.

MARTIN, B. (1961). The assessment of anxiety by physiological and behavioural methods. *Psychological Bulletin, 58,* 234–255.

MASLOW, A. H. (1954). *Motivation and Personality.* Harper, New York.

MELZACK, R. and SCHECTER, B. (1965). Itch and vibration. *Science, 147,* 1047–1048.

MELZACK, R. and TORGENSON, W. S. (1971). On the language of pain. *Anaesthesiology, 34,* 1, 50–59.

MELZACK, R. and WALL, P. D. (1965). Pain mechanisms: A new theory. *Science, 150,* 971–979.

MERSKEY, H. (1964). An investigation of pain in psychological illness. D.M. Thesis, Oxford.

MILLER, G. A., GALANTER, E. and PRIBRAM, K. H. (1960). *Plans and the Structure of Behaviour.* Holt, Rhinehart and Winston, New York.

Ministry of Health (1963). *Communications between Doctors, Nurses and Patients.* Central Health Services Council, H.M.S.O., London.

MORONEY, M. J. (1962). *Facts from Figures.* Penguin Books, Harmondsworth, Middlesex.

MOSS. FAY T. and MEYER, B. (1966). Effects of nursing interaction pain relief in patients. *Nursing Research, 15,* 303–306.

NOORDENBOS, W. (1959). *Pain: Problems Pertaining to the Transmission of Nerve Impulses which give rise to pain.* Elsevier, Amsterdam.

OSGOOD, C. E. *et al.* (1953). *Method and Theory in Experimental Psychology.* Oxford University Press.

PETRIE, A. (1967). *Individuality in Pain and Suffering.* Chicago University Press, Chicago.

RAPHAEL, WINIFRED (1969). Patients and their Hospitals. King Edward's Hospital Fund for London.

RAVEN, B. H. and RIETSEMA, J. (1957). The effects of varied clarity of Group Goal and Group Path upon the individual and his relation to his group. *Human Relations, 10,* 29–45.

READ, G. D. (1943). *Childbirth without Fear.* 3rd Edition, Heinemann, London.

READER, G. G., PRATT, LOIS and MUDD, M. C. (1957). What patients expect from their Doctor. *Modern Hospital,* July 1957.

REVANS, R. W. (1966). *Standards for Morale.* Oxford University Press, London.

RIEHL, JOAN P. (1965). Effect of naturally occurring pain on heart rate and G.S.R. *A.N.A. Clinical Sessions,* No. 3.

ROSENTHAL, R. (1966). *Experimenter Effects in Behavioural Research.* Appleton-Century-Crofts, New York.

ROTHENBURG, R. E. (ed.) (1955). *Understanding Surgery.* Pocketbooks Ltd., New York.

SARASON, S. B., DAVIDSON, K. S., LIGHTHALL, F. F., WAITE, R. R. and RUEBUSH, B. K. (1960). *Anxiety in Elementary School Children.* Wiley, New York.

SCHACTER, S. and SINGER, J. (1962). Cognitive, social and physiological determinants of emotional state. *Psychological Review, 69,* 379–399.

SELYE, H. (1956). *The Stress of Life.* McGraw-Hill, New York.

SHAPIRO, A. K. (1960). A contribution to a history of the placebo effect. *Behavioural Science, 5,* 109–135.

SIEGEL, S. (1956). Nonparametric statistics for the *Behavioural Sciences.* McGraw-Hill, New York.

SIMPSON, H. MARJORIE (1971). Nursing Mirror Lecture given at Edinburgh University. *Nursing Mirror,* 12th March, 1971.

SPELMAN, M S., LEY, P. and JONES, C. (1966). How do we improve Doctor-Patient communication in our Hospitals? *World Hospitals, 2,* 126–134.

SPENCE, K. W. (1960). *Behaviour Theory and Learning.* Prentice-Hall, Englewood Cliffs, New Jersey.

SPENCE, K. W. (1964). Anxiety (drive) level and performance in eyelid conditioning. *Psychological Bulletin, 61,* 129–139.

SPENCE, J. T. and SPENCE, K. W. (1966). The motivational component of manifest anxiety. In SPIELBERGER, C. D. (ed.) (1966). *Anxiety and Behaviour.* Academic Press, New York.

SPIELBERGER, C. D. (1966). *Anxiety and Behaviour.* Academic Press, New York and London.

STERNBACH, R. A. (1968). *Pain: A Psychophysiological Analysis. Academic Press, New York and London.*

TANNER, W. P. (Jr.) and SWETS, J. A. (1954. *A decision-making theory of signal detection. Psychological Review, 61,* 401–409.

TITMUS, R. M. (1958). *Essays on the Welfare State.* Allen and Unwin, London.

WEDDELL, A. G. M. (1962). "Activity Pattern Hypothesis" for sensation of pain. In R. G. GRENELL (ed.). Progress in Neurobiology, Volume 5, *Neural Physiopathology,* pp. 134–177. Hoeber, New York.

WEINERMAN, E. R. (1964). Medical Care in Transition. Public Health Services Publication No. 1128, 83–88, Washington, D.C.

WHITFIELD, J. W. (1950). The imaginary questionnaire. *Quarterly Journal of Experimental Psychology, 2,* 76–87.

WIELAND, G. E. and LEIGH, HILARY (1971). *Changing Hospitals.* Tavistock, London.

WILLIAMS, J. G. L. and JONES, J. R. (1968). Psychophysiological responses to anaesthesia and operation. *Journal of the American Medical Association, 203,* 415.

WILLIAMS, J. G. L., JONES, J. R. and WILLIAMS, BARBARA (1969). A physiological measure of preoperative anxiety. *Psychosomatic Medicine, 31,* 522–527.

Prescription for Recovery

The effect of pre-operative preparation of
surgical patients on post-operative stress,
recovery and infection

JENNIFER R.P. BOORE
PhD., B.Sc., SRN, SCM

Contents

4

List of Figures and Tables in the Text

Acknowledgements

I would like to thank the many people who made possible this work carried out at the University of Manchester as a Department of Health and Social Security Research Fellow. My supervisors, Professor Jean McFarlane and Dr. B. F. Matthews, and Dr. Charlotte Kratz gave me advice, help and encouragement. Within the Faculty of Medicine Dr. Valerie Hillier and Dr. S. Lucas provided the necessary help with the computers, statistical advice and explanation was provided by Mr. Alan Gibbs, while Dr. Gowenlock facilitated my work in the biochemistry laboratory at the Manchester Royal Infirmary. Finally, the acceptance and friendliness of the nursing and medical staff of the hospital wards used was greatly appreciated.

Jennifer Boore

Preface

Research into nursing has grown steadily over the past 20 years and is now rapidly becoming an accepted part of our efforts to understand health care. Early work tended to concentrate on organisational aspects of nursing, for example, the 1960's were dominated by problems of recruitment, selection and wastage in the workforce. Naturally enough, research directed towards these issues was given high priority. It is important to say also that during this time, those interested in a more detailed analysis of what nursing is all about received much support and encouragement from colleagues in the social and biological sciences, many of whom supervised the early work of nurse-researchers and took a great interest in their development.

It is a healthy sign that it is no longer enough for a nurse to claim to be doing research into nursing, without at the same time specifying more closely the actual area of concern. Furthermore, an encouraging development of recent years is the recognition that research into practice is crucial if we are to assess the effectiveness of nursing care and develop an adequate basis of professional knowledge.

Recent trends which have affected the care of surgical patients include the effects of ever-advancing technology; early-discharge systems which allow for a more rapid through-put of patients, and reduced working hours for staff, all of which tend to reduce the chances of patients forming supportive relationships with those who care for them. It is vital therefore that such time as we *can* spend with patients is used effectively. Consequently, interpersonal skills of a very high order are essential if a suitable "psychological climate" is to be established and maintained.

Jennifer Boore's research is set in surgical wards and concerns stress and pain, both of which involve psychological processes. Unfortunately, these terms are single-word constructs which are often used in such a general fashion as to be of little help to those seeking to understand the phenomena more closely. If practical guidance is sought, more detailed analysis must be undertaken, which is precisely what the research presented here has tried to do. After a thorough review of the relevant literature, an experiment was designed and carried out to try and evaluate the effect of preoperative preparation on the level of stress experienced by patients after an operation. The organisation and day-to-day management of such research is not easy and can be influenced by a great number of variables, none of which may be under the researcher's control. It is to Dr. Boore's credit that, in spite of inevitable and necessarily unforseen setbacks, the research was completed successfully, presented for a Ph.D. degree of the University of Manchester and now forms part of the Rcn Research Series.

Research carried out within a scientific framework is sometimes difficult to relate directly to nursing. But such relations are essential if the findings are to reach nurses responsible for patient care so that practice may be influenced. The present work has two strands by which the disciplines of physiology and psychology are linked to nursing. First, the findings that adequate preoperative care by nurses *can* affect stress in patients. Second, the attempts to fit the research into the Betty Neuman Model and a discussion of the relevance of this model to nursing.

This study represents an important addition to the growing research literature on nursing practice. No doubt others will further explore and develop this fascinating area. In the meantime, the Rcn Research Series is to be congratulated on this latest addition to its now substantial list.

JACK HAYWARD
Professor of Nursing Studies
Chelsea College
University of London

Introduction

This work was carried out at the University of Manchester for a higher degree and is described in full in Boore (1976).

The idea for this study developed from a consideration of Selye's theory of stress (Selye, 1956) and its relationship to nursing, and it was decided to examine one aspect of surgical nursing in the light of this concept.

Most nurses will agree that surgical patients should be given information about their circumstances, and that they should be taught exercises to perform after the operation. However, personal observations indicated that any instruction given was often unplanned and inadequate. Therefore, an experiment was designed to try to evaluate the effect of pre-operative preparation on the level of stress experienced by patients after an operation. It was considered possible that by giving adequate planned instruction pre-operatively, psychological stress, and, therefore, physiological stress, after operation might be reduced.

CHAPTER 1

Literature Review—
Theoretical Framework

1.1 A Model of Nursing

Although this study examines only one aspect of nursing, it is founded on a wider theoretical framework. Nursing has been described in many different ways and one is particularly pertinent here.

Dumas (1966) suggested that "the significance of the nurse's contributions toward this goal (of helping man attain or maintain optimum health) lies in her abilities to facilitate the prevention, mitigation or alleviation of stress; or, if this is not possible, to help individuals sustain themselves through a stress episode and promote rapid restoration of optimum functioning and well-being".

Later a similar concept was expressed in the Betty Neuman Health-Care Systems Model: a total person approach to patient problems (Neuman, 1974) an adaptation of which is shown in Figure 1. In this model emphasis is placed upon each person as a unique individual but with some characteristics in common with others. Each individual interacts with the environment and endeavours to maintain a degree of stability. Stressors have the potential to disrupt this balance. The lines of defence and of resistance which counteract these stressors are influenced by various factors within the individual, "the basic physiologic structure and condition, sociocultural background, development state, cognitive skills, age and sex". The importance of considering all these variables and the relationships between them in determining someone's resistance to stressors is emphasised. The core of the person consists of "the basic survival factors which are common to all members of the species" while the lines of resistance are conditions within the person which help to resist stressors. The way in which stressors are normally dealt with by someone in their usual state is the "normal line of defence". On the other hand, the "flexible line of defence" is a more dynamic structure which helps to "buffer" the effect of stressors.

Neuman described interventions as primary, secondary or tertiary preventions. Primary prevention is implemented before a reaction has occurred and aims to reduce the encounter with the stressor or to strengthen the flexible line of defence in order to minimise the reaction. After a reaction to the stressor has begun secondary prevention is concerned with treatment of the symptoms in the patient and aiding

13

Figure 1. A model of nursing care adapted from the Betty Neuman model (Neuman 1974).

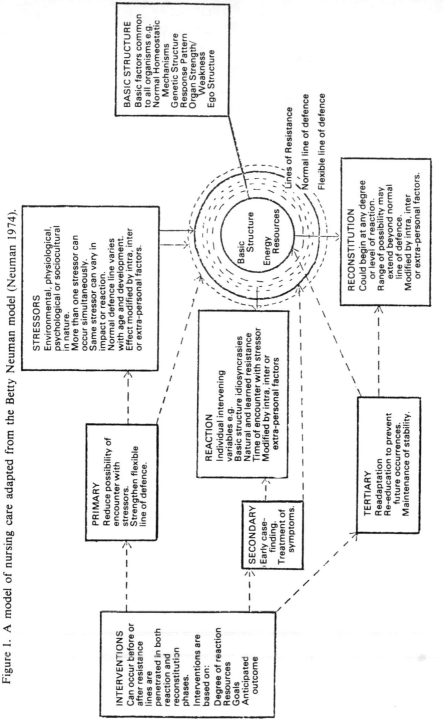

BASIC STRUCTURE
Basic factors common to all organisms e.g.
Normal Homeostatic
Mechanisms
Genetic Structure
Response Pattern
Organ Strength/
Weakness
Ego Structure

Lines of Resistance

Normal line of defence

Flexible line of defence

STRESSORS
Environmental, physiological, psychological or sociocultural in nature.
More than one stressor can occur simultaneously.
Same stressor can vary in impact or reaction.
Normal defence line varies with age and development.
Effect modified by intra, inter or extra-personal factors.

Basic
Structure

Energy
Resources

RECONSTITUTION
Could begin at any degree or level of reaction.
Range of possibility may extend beyond normal line of defence.
Modified by intra, inter or extra-personal factors.

PRIMARY
Reduce possibility of encounter with stressors.
Strengthen flexible line of defence.

REACTION
Individual intervening variables e.g.
Basic structure idiosyncrasies
Natural and learned resistance
Time of encounter with stressor
Modified by intra, inter or extra-personal factors

SECONDARY
Early case-finding.
Treatment of symptoms.

TERTIARY
Readaptation
Re-education to prevent future occurrences.
Maintenance of stability.

INTERVENTIONS
Can occur before or after resistance lines are penetrated in both reaction and reconstitution phases.
Interventions are based on:
Degree of reaction
Resources
Goals
Anticipated outcome

reconstitution. Tertiary prevention is described as "interventions following the active treatment or secondary prevention stage where some degree of reconstitution or stability has occurred". The aims are to maintain a reasonable degree of adaptation and to prevent recurrence of reaction to the stressor. The distinction between tertiary and primary intervention is sometimes blurred.

This research project was examining one aspect of primary intervention—strengthening the flexible line of defence and thus minimising the stress experienced by the patient.

1.2 Stress

In Neuman's Model of Nursing the concept of stress used is that described by Hans Selye (1956). He defines stress as "the state manifested by a specific syndrome which consists of all the non-specifically induced changes within a biologic system". Such changes are provoked by stressors which can be external or internal to the body, for example, environmental conditions, diseases, traumata, emotional states, etc., all of which produce non-specific changes, in addition to changes specific to the stressor. The General Adaptation Syndrome (G.A.S.), with its three constituent parts, is the manifestation of stress within the body. The Alarm Reaction is the first stage and is characterized by increased activity of the adrenal cortex, shrinking of lymphoid tissue and development of peptic ulcers. In the Stage of Adaptation these changes are reversed and only in the third stage, the Stage of Exhaustion, do they return in an intensified form before death ensues. Stress can thus be measured by the intensity of the G.A.S. manifestations provoked. The coining of the term "General Adaptation Syndrome" emphasises the importance of these changes in adapting to altered conditions. Lack of an increased secretion of corticosteroid hormones in stress results in an inability to adapt to stressors, and can result in death. However, although stress is an essential part of living, it causes profound alteration in metabolism and can lead to diseases of maladaptation.

Adrenocorticotrophic Hormone

The primary biochemical change in stress is increased secretion of adrenocorticotrophic hormone (ACTH) from the anterior pituitary gland, which then stimulates production of adrenal cortical hormones, particularly glucocorticoids (Ganong, 1977).

The action of stressors is mediated either through substances carried in the blood, or through nervous pathways, acting on the hypothalamus of the brain. The hypothalamus secretes corticotrophin releasing factor which is then carried in the blood through the hypothalamo-hypophysial portal system to the anterior pituitary gland, where the secretion of ACTH is stimulated. There appear to be two co-ordinating mechanisms involved in the control of ACTH secretion. Negative feed-back, whereby the corticosteroids in the blood regulate the secretion of ACTH, allows adjustments tending to keep steroid levels relatively constant. In addition, it is suggested that a second mechanism is concerned with rapid responses to environmental changes, and the response to stress is due to activity of this mechanism (Ganong, 1977).

Adrenocorticosteroids

There are three groups of steroid hormones formed in the adrenal cortex, glucocorticoids, mineralocorticoids and sex hormones (Bondy and Ronenberg, 1974; Hall *et al*, 1974; Ganong, 1977). For the purposes of this study the most important are the glucocorticoids, the secretion of which is directly regulated by ACTH. ACTH facilitates, but does not regulate, the secretion of mineralocorticoids.

The metabolic actions of glucocorticoids are many, but are primarily catabolic. Protein breakdown and nitrogen excretion are increased and some of this protein is used as a source of glucose contributing to the increased release of glucose from the liver. Although the blood glucose level rises, its utilization by the tissues diminishes. Thus, it has been suggested that corticosteroids produce a relative lack of insulin, and this leads to impaired glucose metabolism. Further evidence of increased protein catabolism is shown by the reduction in the immune response, involution of the thymus and by thinning (from collagen breakdown) of the skin.

Lipid metabolism is also altered, and increased production of ketone bodies occurs as fatty acids are metabolized while glucose utilization is inhibited.

Glucocorticoids also result in decreased resistance to infection and there are several factors involved. The inflammatory reaction is suppressed and new granulation tissue formation is inhibited. In addition, leukocyte motility decreases and phagocytosis may be impaired. Together these will increase the likelihood of widespread dissemination of infection in the body. The production of antibodies from plasma cells diminishes and there is some evidence that transport of antigens to the immune centres is altered by cortisone. The involution of lymphoid tissue and lowered white cell count which occur may also undermine resistance to infection.

Glucocorticoids have been shown to have a number of other effects as well. A study by Cosgriff (1951) of thromboembolic episodes in subjects undergoing treatment with large doses of glucocorticoids suggests that these hormones also alter blood coagulation. In addition, it is accepted that glucocorticoids will sometimes result in the formation of gastro-intestinal ulcers, but the mode of action remains unclear. Moreover, glucocorticoids can have a profound effect on the nervous system either an excess or deficiency of these hormones leading to emotional changes.

Glucocorticoids also have some effect on mineral and water metabolism. Aldosterone is the main mineralocorticoid produced and it is essential for the fine regulation of sodium and potassium excretion. However, glucocorticoids enhance potassium excretion and they also appear to cause release of potassium from cells. On the other hand, excess cortisol over a prolonged period can lead to decreased serum potassium. These hormones also increase sodium reabsorbtion and the increased body sodium, with water, leads to an increase in extracellular fluid volume.

Corticosteroid hormones are metabolized to a variety of compounds, mainly by the microsomal drug-metabolizing enzymes in the liver. Here they are largely conjugated with glucuronic acid and approximately 90% of the hormone and metabolites are excreted in the urine.

Surgical Stress

The magnitude of the endocrine and metabolic changes occurring during, and following, surgical trauma is considerable and has been described by Moore (1959). Increased secretion of both adrenal medullary and adrenal corticoid hormones was noted after gastrectomy with concurrent alteration in electrolyte balance, and loss of nitrogen. These alterations in metabolism last about four or five days after operation. Because changes of such variety and magnitude occur it would seem highly desirable to examine methods of minimising stress in surgical patients.

Stress and Disease

Stress has also been implicated in the aetiology of many diseases, and the biochemical changes previously described suggest the mechanisms by which these diseases arise. However, a formula presented by Lagerlöf (1967),

Disease = psychic stressor x constitution x other factors,

shows the difficulty in estimating the importance of stress in an individual where there are three unknown variables.

Several authors have discussed the role of stress in causing disease (Selye, 1958; Raab, 1971; Levi, 1971), and respiratory disease, renal, cardiac, gastrointestinal, collagen and other disorders have all been suggested as end-results of stress in some individuals.

1.3 Psychophysiology

Having discussed the purely biochemical changes occurring during stress, an examination may now be made of the way in which social and psychological factors can influence this state.

Limbic System

As early as 1911 Canon and de la Paz showed that emotional states influenced endocrine function, in this case adreno-medullary activity. Moreover, in 1936 Selye suggested that psychological, as well as physical, stimuli influenced the activity of the pituitary-adrenal cortical axis. Since then the considerable amount of research in this field argues against conlcuding that any endocrine system functions independently of psychological stimuli (Mason, 1964).

It has now been established that the area of the nervous system particularly involved in the control of emotional states, and the relaying of the effects of these to the endocrine system is the limbic system of the brain. The limbic system consists of a rim of cortical tissue surrounding the hilum of the cerebral cortex, and some associated deep structures, namely, the amygdala, hippocampus and septal nuclei (Ganong, 1977). There are many nervous connections between the limbic system and the hypothalamus, which then regulates endocrine activity, but few nervous pathways between the cerebral cortex and the limbic system. Nevertheless these must be the pathways by which social and emotional events, perceived by the cerebral cortex, influence the endocrine balance of the body.

Social Environment

Mason and Brady (1964) have suggested that the central nervous system controls the tonicity of the neuroendocrine system. Moreover, the amount of interaction and involvement with the physical and social environment influences the central nervous system. Therefore, the level of hormonal activity is an index of the degree of involvement with the surroundings.

Welch (1964) developed this theme and proposed that every environment exerts its own level of environmental stimulation. This level of stimulation is largely determined by the amount of social interaction, which increases with the number of people present.

Psychoendocrinology

There is evidence that neuroendocrine responses are altered by psychological factors (Roessler and Greenfield, 1962; Simon et al, 1961). However, the endocrine changes which occur are not associated with a specific emotional state, but are relatively undifferentiated. The interpretation of endocrine changes defines the emotion experienced (Schachter and Singer, 1962).

Most psychoendocrinological research has examined the effect of emotional states on the activity of the adrenal medulla and cortex. Several investigations have demonstrated that the adrenal medulla is activated in a variety of situations which may be associated with anxiety (Bogdonoff et al, 1960; Tolson et al, 1965). A U-shaped relationship

18

between emotional arousal and some aspects of performance, including learning, has been described. At low levels of activation the subject is hyporesponsive and exhibits unorganized behaviour. On the other hand, at high levels of arousal he is hyperresponsive and behaves in a disorganized manner. At moderate levels of activation there exists a positive relationship between plasma catecholamine levels and performance (Frankenhaeuser and Järpe, 1963).

Similarly, almost any emotional situation, such as examinations, participation in competitive sports, emotional disturbances, etc., will cause increased corticosteroid secretion. There is a positive relationship between anxiety and plasma adrenocorticosteroid levels (Fiorica and Muehl, 1962). Franksson and Gemzell (1955) demonstrated an increase in the plasma concentration of these hormones during the pre-operative period and suggested that this was due to "psychic tension". A later study (Bursten and Russ, 1965) confirmed these findings and, in addition, found a positive correlation between the length of time the patient had to wait for surgery and the magnitude of the rise in steroid secretion. Pleasant stimuli also cause an increase in stress (Fröberg *et al*, 1971). Although most attention has been paid to glucocorticoid secretion, increases in aldosterone excretion have also been reported under academic examination, and other anxiety provoking, conditions (Venning *et al*, 1957).

The opposite response, diminishing adrenocortical activity, also appears to be regulated by the central nervous system. Handlon *et al* (1962) were able to show that watching Disney nature films (conducive to tranquility) lowered plasma 17-hydroxycorticosteroid levels in their subjects.

1.4 Psychological Stress

It has been clearly demonstrated that anxiety can result in an increased corticosteroid secretion, and some of the literature about anxiety, emotions and psychological stress will be examined. Unfortunately, the distinction between the meanings of these terms is often blurred. Selye (1956) restricted his concept of stress to the changes in the physiological functioning of the body, but stated that these changes could result from psychological states. However, other writers (Janis, 1958; Lazarus, 1971) asserted that psychological stress differs from physiological stress and the two are not necessarily related, although similar metabolic changes might result.

The importance of factors within the individual in defining psychological stress is clearly recognized (Engel, 1962; Lazarus, 1966). Lazarus and Averill (1972) described anxiety as "an emotion based on the appraisal of threat" and stated that anxiety results when a person is unable to fully comprehend the world about him. Information received by the sense organs is necessary for comprehension, but the perception of this information is the crucial factor. Frankenhaeuser (1967) suggested that perception could be modified by the expectations of the subject. She also demonstrated that the subject's expectations could be altered by verbal instructions given before or during an experiment.

Although factors within the individual are important in determining the impact of a situation some groups of psychological stressors have been identified. Lazarus (1966) described six varieties of psychologically stressful stimuli:

1. Uncertainty about physical survival;
2. Uncertainty about maintaining one's identity;
3. Inability to control the immediate environment;
4. Pain and privation;
5. Loss of loved ones;
6. Disruption of community life.

Most of these stressors may be experienced by patients admitted to hospital for surgical operations and several authors have studied the causes of anxiety and fear experienced by patients, Kornfeld (1972) stated that "hospitals are frightening places for most people". He further pointed out that many procedures are inflicted upon patients which are unfamiliar and provoke anxiety, although they are commonplace to the staff involved. Fear of pain and of the unknown are often expressed by people awaiting surgery (Levine, 1970; Carnevali, 1966; Graham and Conley, 1971).

As has already been indicated the assessment by the individual is of prime importance in determining the degree of stress experienced in any circumstance. Lazarus (1971) stated that in psychological stress the "reaction depends on how the person interprets or appraises (consciously or unconsciously) the significance of a harmful, threatening or challenging event...". Certain characteristics of a situation are associated with the appraisal of anxiety (Lazarus and Averill, 1972). If a situation cannot be interpreted, then it cannot be dealt with, and the individual experiences helplessness. Helplessness is also associated with the inability to anticipate events: "Anticipation allows for preparation and, hence, the possibility of control". In addition, uncertainty results in a sense of helplessness. Further, Mandler (1972) suggested that helplessness is an important component of anxiety.

After the stimulus and appraisal the response occurs and Lazarus (1966) described four main classes of stress reaction. Disturbed affects such as fear or anxiety, anger, depression and guilt are mentioned as stress responses, and have also been described by other workers. Janis (1958) discussed anxiety as a stress reaction to the threat of surgery and also reported the occurrence of anger in some patients when they were exposed to unexpectedly stressful situations after operation. Secondly, motor responses such as tremor, increased muscle tension, speech disturbances, etc., and fight or flight responses may occur. Cognitive

20

functioning is altered, and may be improved or impaired as a response to stress, usually being impaired at greater degrees of stress. Thus, very anxious patients may have great difficulty in understanding the information given. Finally, physiological functioning—both hormonal and autonomic—is altered in stress and these changes are sometimes used as objective measures of stress.

The importance of cognitive factors in the appraisal of threat has been emphasised and the role of helplessness in the experience of anxiety has been discussed. The importance of prediction and control as means of reducing helplessness and thus minimising anxiety is evident. Janis (1958) found that patients wish to know the things that directly involve them and the sensations they are likely to experience. He went on to state that the patient might have adverse emotional reactions upon encountering the unexpected. In addition, he found that the sick felt less helpless and more in control when they found some way of taking an active role in their own recovery. He recommended giving them precise and detailed information, but recognised that there are often considerable difficulties in implementing this proposal. He considered that subjects receiving accurate information about surgery did the "work of worrying" in advance and thus demonstrated reduced emotional responses post-operatively. Work by Vernon and Bigelow (1974) supported some aspects of Janis' work but they could not find evidence that the consequences of preparation were related to "anticipatory fear".

Bird (1955) also emphasised the importance of communication in the pre-operative period, but also stated that the patient's anxiety interfered with comprehension, and, therefore, repetition was essential. Meyers (1964) studied the effect of different types of communication on the patient's reaction to stress. A new procedure was devised as a mildly stressful stimulus for the patients in the study. It involved swabbing the skin on the patient's forearm, covering the area with gauze and then lifting a corner of the gauze at 15-second intervals in order to examine the skin. While this procedure was being performed the researcher communicated with the patient in one or other of three different ways. Thus, the first group of patients was given a factual explanation of the actions being performed. The second group was given a "distracting" commentary, and the third received no verbal communication whatsoever during the procedure. Patients who received pertinent information had more accurate recall and reported less psychological stress than the other subjects. She concluded that "patients need to have the means provided to cognitively structure, that is, to give meaning to, the events which happen to them". Furthermore, she suggests that "the communication approach will negate or at least minimise some of the stress inherent in hospitalisation".

It has been demonstrated that giving subjects a description of the sensations to be experienced during a procedure reduced distress to a greater extent than a description of the procedure to be performed

(Johnson, 1976). It was suggested that the emotional response to a threatening event is effected by incongruency between expectations and experience. Volicer and Bohannon (1975) found that the aspects of hospitalisation perceived as very stressful by patients are related to a lack of communication of information, or a lack of communication in a meaningful way, on the part of hospital staff.

CHAPTER 2

Literature Review—
Clinical Aspects

The previous chapter included a discussion of the theoretical background to this study. However, it is also necessary to ascertain the current state of research in related areas, and in this chapter relevant clinical studies are examined.

2.1 Pain

Communication, which enables the patient to comprehend his circumstances more fully and thus reduces anxiety, is important in a consideration of pain. Pain can be both a stimulus and a response to stress. It has already been described as a psychological stressor, and there is considerable evidence to show that anxiety increases the pain experienced. Blaylock (1968) reviewed the psychological and cultural components of the reaction to pain and he described the physical stimulus and the emotional response to it as being the experience of pain. Schumacher *et al* (1940) suggested that the ability of the nervous system to feel a sensation is similar in most people, but the amount of suffering may vary.

Beecher (1957) described primary and secondary components of the pain experience. The primary component is the sensation of pain itself, while the secondary component is the suffering, reactive aspect and the emotional response to pain. In 1956 Beecher compared the pain experienced by soldiers wounded in battle and by civilian surgical patients. The soldiers experienced less discomfort. He concluded that the main difference between these groups was in the level of anxiety and the patients' attitude towards their wounds. The soldiers had just escaped from unpleasant circumstances associated with a continual fear of death. Other authors have also emphasised the role of fear and anxiety in the perception of pain (Mullen and Van Schoick, 1958; Livingston, 1944). A study by Drew *et al* (1968) demonstrated clearly the part of anxiety in the manifestation of pain as indicated by the amounts of post-operative drugs received. Patients undergoing a relatively painless, but very threatening, procedure received more drugs after operation than general surgical patients.

Malmo and Shagass (1949) proposed that anticipation largely determines the amount of suffering experienced. They found that a physical stimulus caused more distress in subjects who were anxious or afraid of pain. Murray (1971) has reiterated this. He suggested that anticipation, and resulting anxiety, were basic ingredients in the reaction component of the pain experience, and that other factors, including the meaning ascribed to sensations and past experience, also contribute to the individual's response to pain. When anxiety about pain is reduced, then the subjective experience of pain is minimised. Johnson (1976) used this concept of the two component parts of the pain experience to examine the possibility of modifying the reactive element. It was hypothesised that the "intensity of the reactive component of the pain experienced is a function of the congruency between expected and experienced physical sensations". She found that subjects given a complete or partial description of sensations to be experienced reported a lesser degree of distress than other subjects.

Moss and Meyer (1966) carried out an experimental study to evaluate the effect of modifying the patient's perceptions of a painful stimulus. With each patient in the experimental group a nurse discussed various aspects of the pain and the methods by which it could be relieved; the patient then decided on the course of treatment to be adopted. The experimental group of patients obtained relief of pain, while the distress of the control group was not alleviated. The results were interpreted to mean that "the nurse has succeeded in altering the experimental group's perception of the stimuli associated with pain by changing their attitude toward the stimuli".

A number of studies have examined the effect of an "interpersonal nursing approach", which aims to relieve psychological stress, on various parameters. In this style of nursing the attention is directed towards patients as individuals, their immediate needs and perceptions of their illness and its treatment. Bochnak et al (1962) found that exploring the meaning of the complaint with the patient significantly reduced the amount of analgesics required. Furthermore, the patient's pain was relieved more quickly and thoroughly when drugs were given. These findings were substantiated by McBride (1967). In addition, she found that a drop in pulse rate and blood pressure occurred when the anxiety, as well as the stimulus to pain, was treated. In contrast, the patients in the control group, given the appropriate treatment but no directed inter-personal communication, showed a rise in pulse rate and blood pressure.

2.2 Pain and Anxiety in Surgical Patients

Anxiety and pain experienced by surgical patients have been studied by several investigators. Luna (1971) examined the effect of a "nurse-patient interaction process" (i.e., an interpersonal nursing approach) on patients admitted for emergency appendicectomy. Each patient was helped to mobilize his ability to cope in advance by provision of adequate information and psychological support from the nurse. The experimental subjects were able to handle their suffering more effectively

24

than the control patients and they reported less pain post-operatively.

Egbert *et al* (1964) also discussed with patients before operation the pain which is likely to be experienced post-operatively and the measures which would be available to control it. The amount of analgesics needed post-operatively diminished and the patients were discharged from hospital more rapidly. However, the subjects were also taught how to relax their abdominal muscles and it is not easy to differentiate between the effects of the psychological preparation and the physical relaxation.

Hayward's (1975) experimental study examined some relationships between pre-operative information and post-operative pain and anxiety in surgical patients. He demonstrated a positive relationship between pre-operative anxiety and post-operative pain. Hayward's work is the only British nursing research dealing with this subject currently available and the present study uses some of his findings and measures of post-operative welfare.

Wolfer and Davis (1970) carried out a descriptive study of the pre-operative emotional condition of surgical patients and their post-operative welfare. Their findings differed from those of Hayward: they found no substantial relationship between the patient's pre-operative level of fear and anxiety and any aspect of their post-operative recovery. However, they developed various self-report ratings of emotional state, pain, and various aspects of physical condition. Some of these are discussed later.

2.3 Pre-operative Preparation

The present study is not primarily concerned with pain, although this is an important measure of the patient's condition. Therefore, it was important to examine other more general studies of hospital patients. A number of investigations have been carried out to examine the effect of purposeful pre-operative preparation, and various measures have been used to evaluate the results. Some investigations have concentrated entirely on attempting to influence the psychological state of the patient. However, the majority of researchers have combined the psychological and physiological aspects of preparation, although the emphasis has varied in different studies.

Work by Healy (1968), Mezzanotte (1970) and Levine (1970) indicates the value of telling patients about their prospective treatment and care, as well as teaching exercises. However, the lack of comparable control groups of patients, as of statistical analysis, diminishes the value of these studies.

A few workers have concentrated on the physical aspects of pre-operative preparation. Aiken (1972) evaluated the effects of teaching systematic relaxation to patients for open-heart surgery and found that the incidence of post-operative complications fell. On the other hand, Lindeman and Van Aernam (1971) have studied the effect of a planned programme for the teaching of deep-breathing, coughing and bed-exercises, as against the unco-ordinated instruction already taking place. Lindeman (1972) evaluated the results of group, as opposed to individual, teaching of the same topics. In both studies, the dependent variables used were tests of ventilatory function, length of hospital stay and total analgesics required. The length of learning time was also measured in the second experiment. It was concluded that systematic teaching was superior to unplanned instruction, and that group tuition was as effective as individual teaching and saved the nurse's time. Unfortunately, in the first of these investigations the control patients were admitted to hospital at a different time of the year from the experimental patients, and there was a significant difference in the ventilatory function in the two groups before operation. Because of this the differences between the pre-operative and post-operative measures were calculated, and the results for the two groups compared. However, it is possible that the size of the difference was a function of the pre-operative state of the respiratory system. Thus their conclusions cannot be accepted unreservedly.

In contrast, other researchers have concentrated on the psychological aspects of nursing care, but using physical measures of effectiveness. Dumas and Leonard (1963) investigated "the effect of nursing on the incidence of post-operative vomiting". The experimental treatment was "directed towards helping the patient attain a suitable psychological state for surgery". The incidence of vomiting in these patients while in the recovery room was reduced.

Johnson (1966) and Schmitt and Wooldridge (1973) have carried out experimental projects to investigate the possible effects of improved psychological care before operation. Both studies found that as a result patients were discharged from hospital more rapidly. Schmitt and Wooldridge also reported that less anaesthesia and analgesia were required, urinary retention became less frequent, and that patients remembered more about the actual day of their operation. These authors have demonstrated that psychological preparation improves post-operative condition. However, Lindeman and Stetzer (1973) found that a pre-operative visit by an operating room nurse was ineffectual in altering the patient's post-operative behaviour, although patients undergoing minor surgery had a reduced level of post-operative anxiety.

Schmitt and Wooldridge (1973) also found that the experimental patients had a smaller increase in pulse and blood pressure after operation than the patients in the control group. These differences, and other differences between the groups, were attributed to a reduction in stress following the specific psychological preparation for operation.

2.4 Investigations of Stress

Although Dumas (1966) proposed that stress could be used as a basis for nursing practice, few nursing research studies have examined the way

26

in which the nurse alters physiological stress in her patients. Technically, corticosteroid hormones are not easy to measure either in blood or urine. Therefore, the investigations that have been reported have all used other, less direct, indicators of stress.

Some studies have, for instance, examined substances which are altered by the hormones secreted from the adrenal cortex. Pride (1968) investigated the effect on potassium excretion in the urine of an interpersonal nursing approach, designed to relieve psychological stress. Her findings suggested that this measure was sensitive enough for use, for it differentiated between groups of patients receiving different styles of nursing. However, potassium excretion is greatly influenced by potassium intake and, unless the diet is carefully controlled, this measurement may not be reliable.

More recent workers have studied the relationship between the sodium: potassium ratio in the urine and psychological stress. Gentry *et al* (1973) demonstrated that very anxious patients admitted to hospital have increased sodium retention and potassium excretion, resulting in a decreased sodium : potassium ratio. Foster (1974) has also used sodium : potassium ratio as a measure of stress in patients. Three consecutive 12-hour urine specimens were collected from the patients studied and the sodium : potassium ratio and vanillylmandelic acid were measured. During the second of these 12-hour periods the experimental patients were subjected to an interpersonal approach. The sodium : potassium ratio dropped during the second collection in all the patients, and the author concluded that this change was probably due to stress from hospitalization. In fact, it is more likely that this variation was caused by the circadian rhythm in corticosteroid secretion (Conroy and Mills, 1970). However, the third specimens collected differentiated between the control and experimental groups of patients. Foster concluded, therefore, that sodium : potassium ratio is a valid indicator of the body's response to stress. It is interesting that this ratio did not correlate with the amount of vanillylmandelic acid (an excretion product of catecholamines) in the urine. This measure needs to be examined further as the amounts of electrolytes excreted are influenced greatly by the quantities ingested.

A similar study to evaluate the effect of an interpersonal approach to patients involved the measurement of non-esterified fatty acids and eosinophils (Chapman, 1970). These substances did not show any significant difference in the different groups of patients used. However, the amounts of analgesics required and the length of stay in hospital were reduced in subjects receiving the experimental nursing approach.

Other workers have looked at bodily processes influenced by the sympathetic nervous system and catecholamines released from the adrenal medulla. Thus, Mertz (1962) examined the results of an interpersonal approach to patients, in this instance, following emergency admission. She measured pulse and blood pressure and found that both

27

of them dropped in patients whose psychological stress was diminished. On the other hand, similar patients, who had not received this type of attention, showed a rise in both measurements.

Munday (1973) used the Palmar Sweat Index (calculated from the number of open sweat gland pores in the fingertips) and the pulse rate as measures of reaction to stress. However, the uncontrolled variables in this study means that the usefulness of the measurements cannot be evaluated.

Minckley (1974), in a study of the effect of early definite or late indefinite scheduling for operation, also measured palmar sweating, but examined the volume of sweat produced, as an indicator of sympathetic nervous activity. It was found that the time of scheduling for operation made little difference to the patient's response. However, she was unable to account for the fluctuation of palmar sweat values. She also measured fingertip blood volume. She states that these measures "are reliable in their appearance in relation to the syndrome response to mental stress" but that the tools available are not yet adequately refined. She suggests that further research is needed to find better ways of using these physiological responses.

2.5   Teaching in Nursing

From the examination of the literature, it is evident that psychological preparation for operation and the teaching of exercises to be performed after operation have a positive influence on the patient's post-operative condition. In terms of Neuman's model of nursing (1974) the intervention used in these studies is at the primary level, that is, endeavouring to "strengthen the flexible line of defence". In these studies patients were given information regarding their circumstances and about what was likely to happen to them; they were told about the sensations likely to be experienced; they were helped to talk about their feelings concerning hospitalization, etc.; they were taught exercises to perform after operation. The literature about pain and anxiety indicates that psychological stress in these patients may have been reduced and physiological changes of stress may also have been minimised. If one of the objectives of nursing is to minimise the stress experienced by patients, then it seems that one important function of the nurse is the teaching of patients.

Many writers have discussed teaching as a part of nursing. Peplau (1952) described nursing as an "educative process". Similarly Henderson (1966) implied that teaching was one of the nurse's functions when she said that nursing helps an individual to perform those activities related to health that he would "perform unaided if he had the necessary strength, will or knowledge". Redman (1972) suggests that it may be "most useful to the nursing practitioner to view all interaction with the patient as contributing to the broad process and objectives of teaching-learning". She also stated that "it would seem essential for every nurse to obtain some degree of proficiency (in teaching skills)".

Teaching can be considered as activities designed to help another person learn. Pohl (1973) says that an individual's learning "will depend upon the nature of his physical, mental and emotional development and upon his past and present experiences". This reinforces the emphasis on the patient as a unique individual, discussed earlier, which is of prime importance in Neuman's model of nursing.

2.6   Summary of Literature Review

The first part of this review of the literature has explained the theoretical background for this study. The evidence discussed indicates that preparation before operation may help the patient to understand and anticipate occurrences, and take an active part in his own recovery, thus relieving anxiety. It has been demonstrated that anxiety is associated with alterations in physiological function, including an increase in the secretion of corticosteroid hormones, which results in a number of biochemical changes in the body. Therefore, it is possible that the pre-operative preparation can reduce the degree of biochemical change after operation, and aid the patient's recovery.

The second section of the review concentrates on the relevant clinical research. The importance of communication in relieving psychological stress is emphasized and the role of the nurse as a teacher of her patients is discussed. Theoretical concepts about pain are considered in greater detail by Hayward (1975) but here some of the work which illustrates the importance of communication in relieving anxiety and pain is mentioned. In addition, studies examining the effect of pre-operative preparation on post-operative pain, and on other measures of recovery and welfare, are described.

The model of nursing underlying this study is one based on the concept of stress (Neuman, 1974) and, therefore, all of the nursing research studies examining stress are discussed. However, no published work has studied the effect of pre-operative preparation on post-operative stress and it was, therefore, decided to carry out an experimental study of this.

CHAPTER 3

Selection of Dependent Variables

3.1 Introduction

Following the examination of the literature it was decided to carry out an experimental study to examine the effect of some aspects of pre-operative preparation on post-operative stress and recovery. The first consideration was the selection of the dependent variables to be used to indicate the effect of the pre-operative preparation on the patients in the study.

In this chapter the selection of these measures is discussed and the difficulties which occurred and resulting modifications are described. A pilot study was carried out some time before beginning the main study and one of the main reasons for this preliminary work was to evaluate a number of proposed dependent variables. In this section the relevant findings from the pilot study will be introduced. The pilot study is described in full in Boore (1976).

3.2 Recovery and Welfare

In terms of Neuman's (1974) model of nursing, the pre-operative preparation was intended to strengthen the flexible line of defence of the recipients of this preparation.

If the flexible line of defence is strengthened, then the impact of stressors is reduced and the reaction should also be lessened. Biochemical measures of stress are needed to examine directly the degree of physiological stress experienced by the patient. However, the stress present would be expected to alter other physiological and psychological variables within the patient. Wolfer (1973) has reviewed the "Definition and Assessment of Surgical Patients' Welfare and Recovery". He distinguishes between recovery and welfare as follows: "'Recovery' can be viewed as the process of restoration and/or attainment of normal physiological and anatomical functioning". In contrast, "patient welfare" is defined as "the complex, multidimensional, and changing affective and cognitive state of an individual as he undergoes hospitalization and surgery". In the present study both concepts are relevant.

Many variables have already been mentioned as having been used to measure the recovery of the patient. These include changes in bodily functioning such as systemic complications, vomiting, infection, changes in vital signs, etc. In addition, the speed with which the patient achieves ambulation and full mobility, the amount of analgesics and sedatives required, and the number of post-operative days in hospital have all been used to evaluate the patient's recovery. On the other hand, only a few suitable scales have been developed to measure the patient's general psychological state, or "welfare".

Minckley (1974) used seventeen criteria to obtain a daily recovery score including the ability to perform respiratory activities, bed exercises, compliance with expectations in carrying out activities of daily living (e.g., defaecation, sleep, diet, etc.), level of mobility, incidence of complications. In this study the patients were all undergoing the same operation—a corrective hip operation—and the criteria were decided upon from the expectations of behaviour on each post-operative day. The total recovery score each day was divided by the expected score for the same post-operative day, and thus, if the patient's progress was satisfactory the score was 1·000. A score lower than this indicated that the patient was experiencing difficulty in recovery, while a higher score signified that the patient was progressing faster than usual. She suggests that a similar method could be used to measure recovery in patients enduring some other surgical procedures. Four other physiological variables were measured, pulse, blood pressure, finger pulse wave height (indicating fingertip blood volume) and palmar sweat volume. The patient's emotional state (welfare) was measured with a Mood Word Checklist derived by Malmstrom (1972) from other larger lists. Some of the methods used for measuring recovery and welfare might have been made use of in the present study had they been published a little earlier.

However, other methods were used in this study and the selection of measures used will now be discussed.

3.3 Biochemical Measures of Stress

It was decided to examine two indicators of stress in the patients in the study. The indicators chosen were 17-hydroxycorticosteroid excretion and sodium : potassium ratio in the urine.

17-hydroxycorticosteroid Excretion

Quantitatively cortisol is the most important of the 17-hydroxycorticosteroid hormones excreted by the adrenal cortex, and its production is increased during stress. The metabolism of cortisol in the endoplasmic reticulum of the liver cells results in a range of metabolites. Most of the metabolites are conjugated with glucuronic acid in the liver, and approximately 90% of the hormone and metabolites are excreted in the urine.

The measurement of plasma cortisol was considered but for several reasons this idea was discarded. In order to measure plasma cortisol

31

venepuncture is necessary and the daily repetition of this might itself act as a stressor in some patients, and thus alter the blood levels of the substance to be measured. Although having to collect urine specimens daily may also act as a stressor in some individuals, it was thought that this was less likely to affect the results critically. In addition, repeated venepunctures were felt to be ethically unjustifiable as relevant data could be obtained painlessly. However, the main contra-indication for measuring plasma cortisol was that the hormone level in the blood would have been sampled once only. On the other hand, urine levels of the excretion products give an indication of blood levels over a period of time. This was considered to be more appropriate to this study.

It would have been most useful to measure the amount of 17-hydroxy-corticosteroids excreted in 24 hours. However, 24-hour urine collections are often incomplete and to involve the nursing staff in the extra work might have led to considerable antagonism, and could possibly have jeopardised the whole project. Therefore, the decision was taken to use three-hour samples which were collected each day by the research assistants. However, this also has disadvantages. The major problem is that patients may not always completely empty the bladder when passing urine. The time of formation of the urine thus collected cannot accurately be known. Because there is a circadian rhythm in ACTH production, and consequently in corticosteroid secretion and excretion (Conroy and Mills, 1970), it was necessary to obtain the specimens at approximately the same time each day. The urinary excretion of 17-hydroxycorticosteroids reaches maximum values at about twelve mid-day (Bartter et al, 1962) and, therefore, a collection encompassing this period was considered to be satisfactory.

It was considered necessary to confirm that the corticosteroid levels in the three-hour urine samples bore a consistant relationship to the corticosteroid excretion during the remainder of the 24-hour period. Eight patients, not otherwise involved in the research project, were asked to save all their urine for 24 hours from 6.00 a.m. one day until 6.00 a.m. the following morning. During this time a three-hour urine sample was collected, as for the patients taking part in the experimental study. Excretion of 17-hydroxycorticosteroid hormones and sodium : potassium ratio were measured in all urine specimens. Patients involved were four men and four women in the age range of patients in the study. Because the patients had to be responsible for their own 24-hour urine specimen they were not asked to collect this until between the third and tenth day after a variety of operations. It was found that the amount of hormone excreted per gram of creatinine was higher in all the three-hour samples than in the 24-hour samples and the differences ranged from 0·68 to 2·21 mg/g creatinine. These results indicate that it is satisfactory to examine the hormone excretion in the three-hour urine sample in the study.

The method of analysis used was that described in Varley et al (1976) and the results were expressed initially as mg/100 ml. The concentration of creatinine in the urine was obtained by use of the Auto Analyser and the 17-hydroxycorticosteroid excretion levels were then expressed as mg/g creatinine. This allowed the inaccuracies in measuring urine specimens on the wards to be discounted.

In the main study corticosteroid hormone levels could only be measured in four urine samples from each patient, because the time required to perform the analysis was considerable. The greatest difference between the control and experimental patients in the pilot study was found on post-operative days one, two and three. However, urine specimens were most frequently unobtainable on the first post-operative day, and, therefore, it was decided that 17-hydroxycorticosteroid excretion would be measured pre-operatively and on days two, three and four post-operatively.

Sodium : Potassium Ratio

It was decided to examine the ratio of sodium to potassium in the three-hour urine specimens for several reasons. ACTH, released in stressful conditions, has a supportive role in the regulation of aldosterone production (Davis, 1967), and aldosterone causes sodium retention and potassium excretion. In addition, cortisol and corticosterone, which are also secreted in increased amounts during stress, enhance the excretion of potassium induced by aldosterone (Ross, 1959). Also glucocorticoids alone appear to cause the release of potassium from cells and may stimulate potassium loss in the urine and sodium reabsorption (Hall et al, 1974; Bondy and Ronenberg, 1974). All of these changes will reduce the sodium : potassium ratio in the urine. However, the quantity of sodium and potassium in the diet considerably influences the amount excreted in the urine, and it was not possible to control the amounts ingested. Nevertheless, it was considered worthwhile to use this measure because it was quick and easy to carry out the estimations and thus all specimens could be examined.

Sodium and potassium levels in the urine were measured using an Instrumentation Laboratory 343 Flame Photometer. Results were shown in digital form within thirty seconds, and the ratio was then calculated.

It was decided that the urinary sodium : potassium ratio would be measured pre-operatively and then on each post-operative day until discharge.

Urine Specimens

It was decided that three-hour urine specimens would be satisfactory for the biochemical measurements involved in this study. However, some difficulties were experienced in obtaining these even though the researchers were responsible for collecting the required specimens. For the duration of the pilot study it was arranged that specimens would be collected from 12 noon to 3.00 p.m. Nevertheless, patients often passed urine between 11.00 a.m. and 12 noon (before lunch) and between 2.00 p.m. and 2.30 p.m. (before visiting time) and on occasion, particularly in the early days post-operatively, forgot that specimens were required. The ward staff were often not aware which patients were being studied and thus discarded specimens. Some patients, mainly those who had undergone gastric surgery, were unable to pass urine at the required time on the first day post-operatively. On the third post-operative day, several specimens were lost because glycerine suppositories had been administered to patients during the period of urine collection.

To counteract these problems it was decided to make several minor changes in the main investigation. The times of urine collection both pre- and post-operatively, was brought forward to begin between 11.00 a.m. and 11.30 a.m. and end between 2.00 p.m. and 2.30 p.m., thus coinciding with the times at which the patients usually voided. In addition, all nurses beginning work on the wards used for this research received a letter explaining the project and asking for their co-operation. They were asked to avoid discarding specimens of urine and to wait until collections were completed before inserting suppositories. In order to help the ward staff identify the patients involved in the study a card, asking that urine should be saved, was fixed to the patients' beds between 11.00 a.m. and 2.00 p.m. each day.

3.4 Objective Measures of Recovery

Temperature

It has recently been found that, following routine herniorrhaphy, it may take four to five days for the raised body temperature to return to the patient's normal (Folkard, 1974). It was thought, therefore, that this might be a useful measure of the patient's post-operative progress.

Mercury and glass clinical thermometers have many limitations. The time required to obtain the maximum reading can be as long as eleven minutes and the variability in the accuracy of commercially available clinical thermometers has been shown to be considerable (Nichols and Verhonick, 1967). Moreover, the reading obtained after three minutes varies from $0.2°F$ to $1.6°F$ below that obtained after eight minutes (Nichols and Kucha, 1972). It is generally considered that electronic clinical thermometers are more accurate and record faster and, in view of the above mentioned limitations of the usual thermometers, an electronic clinical thermometer was used in the main study although this was not available during the pilot study.

Because there is a circadian rhythm in body temperature (Conroy and Mills, 1970), the recording must be carried out at approximately the

34

same time each day. In addition, there is a post-ovulatory rise in body temperature in women, although random assignment of subjects to experimental or control group allows this to be discounted.

Analgesic Consumption

The recording of analgesic consumption was chosen as a measure for use in this study because of previously published work indicating that nursing activities can alleviate pain (McBride, 1967; Moss and Meyer, 1966) and may reduce post-operative analgesic consumption (Healy, 1968; Hayward, 1975).

However, factors other than the severity of pain which the patient experienced may influence the quantity of drugs administered. In the present study patients in the experimental group were given specific information about requesting analgesics, and this could have led to increased consumption. However, Hayward gave similar instructions but still found that the experimental group received less analgesia than the control group of patients.

In addition, the importance of age and sex as factors influencing analgesic requirements has not yet been determined. Andersen (1973) found that age and sex had no discernible influence on the demand for analgesics, but Lindeman (1972) found that older subjects required fewer drugs post-operatively. As discussed by Hayward, a third major influence is the ward policy about post-operative administration of drugs. This is a process which is almost entirely controlled by the nursing staff, and there may be considerable differences in practice between different wards. In this study the experimental design, in which the composition of the groups was matched for sex (and therefore ward) and age distribution, allowed these last two factors to be discounted.

At the beginning of the pilot study it was intended to express the amount of analgesics administered as "units of morphia", which is the amount of analgesic equivalent to 10 mg of morphia in activity. However, the dose of analgesics prescribed varied according to the weight of the patient and it seemed more appropriate, therefore, to examine the number of doses of analgesic administered.

Incidence of Complications

The previous discussion concerning the metabolic effects of glucocorticoids indicated the importance of examining the incidence of post-operative complications among the patients in this study. Many other reports, discussed below, confirm the importance of examining this incidence as an indicator of patient recovery.

It has often been assumed that the teaching of breathing exercises reduces respiratory complications in surgical patients (Morton, 1973; Collart and Brenneman, 1971). This assumption was supported by Lindeman and Van Aernam (1971) who demonstrated that teaching patients deep-breathing and coughing improved post-operative lung function and reduced the length of stay in hospital. The finding that upper respiratory infections are significantly more common in students who had recently suffered distressing changes in their lives (Jacobs *et al*, 1970) suggests that stress may be a causative factor in post-operative respiratory infections.

It has been shown that 90% of emboli arise from thrombi in the veins of the legs, pelvis and abdomen, and suggested that stasis of blood in the lower limbs is the main cause (Hodgson and Good, 1964). As early as 1856 Virchow described three factors which promote thrombus formation, namely, changes in the rate of blood flow, changes in the vessel wall and changes in the coagulability of blood. However, measures such as leg exercises and early ambulation to improve blood flow, though often recommended, do little to prevent deep vein thrombosis when the process begins during operation (Fitzmaurice and Sasahara, 1974). On the other hand, glucocorticoids have been shown to increase the "stickiness" of platelets inducing intravascular platelet clumping (Haft and Fani, 1973) and there is evidence to suggest that sympatho-adrenal stimulation plays a significant role in the hypercoagulability that accompanies surgery (Britton *et al*, 1974). Therefore, the present author proposes that minimising stress may inhibit the formation of deep vein thrombi.

Loiseau *et al* (1971) found that, in a particular surgical unit, the patient's endogenous flora played an important role in the aetiology of wound infections. In addition, Buescher (1964) suggested that an alteration of normal hormone balance (as in stress) can initiate the manifestation of disease from latent and sub-clinical infections. Taken together, the results of these studies suggest that the incidence of wound infections may be influenced by the pre-operative preparation given to the patients in this investigation.

Nausea and Vomiting

It has been shown that the incidence of post-operative vomiting can be reduced by the use of an interpersonal nursing approach in the pre-operative period (Dumas and Leonard, 1963). In this study, the nurse helped the patient attain a suitable psychological state for surgery by exploring with him his perception of the cause of distress and an appropriate method of relief, which was then implemented. The experimental patients, who received this interpersonal nursing approach, were found to have a significantly lower incidence of post-operative vomiting than the control patients who only received routine care.

Recently Hayward (1975) attempted to use the incidence of post-operative vomiting and complaints of nausea as indicators of post-operative recovery. However, he was unsuccessful in this, due to inadequate recording by the hospital staff.

In this context reference may be made to a study by Andersen (1973).

36

Although the literature suggests that narcotics cause nausea, this study of 405 patients indicated that post-operative nausea was caused, not by narcotics, but by the inadequate relief of pain.

During the conduct of the pilot study it was found to be impossible to obtain accurate information regarding complaints of nausea and the incidence of vomiting. Although it had been agreed that this information would be recorded, it was sometimes found that the patient's verbal report and the written record did not agree. This measure was, therefore, abandoned.

3.5   Subjective Measures of Welfare

The objective measures described previously do not in themselves give a complete picture of the welfare of the individual. Therefore, it was considered necessary to attempt to obtain some assessment of the physical and mental condition of each patient. It was considered that the patient's own perception of his condition was indicative of his welfare and recovery, and, therefore, it was decided to ask the subjects to evaluate their own physical and mental state and pain experienced. In addition, it was considered that professional judgement was important and, thus, the nursing and medical staff were also asked to assess each patient's progress.

Physical State

Aydelotte's study on the "Relation between Nursing Activity and Patient Welfare" (Aydelotte and Tener, 1960) suggested that one way to evaluate patient welfare was by measuring the amount of time spent in various activities. However, many observers were used to collect the information in her study and this was impossible in the present project. Therefore, a self-report measure was used to discover the proportion of time during the day which patients spent in bed, at the bedside or in the dayroom (or elsewhere). Throughout the day the patients were asked to complete a simple graph showing the approximate lengths of time spent in these places.

During the pilot study it was found that some patients were documenting their changes in mobility for the day all at one time, instead of recording these changes graphically when they occurred, or shortly afterwards. This gave rise to serious doubts about the reliability of these graphs and, therefore, their use was discontinued within two weeks of beginning the work.

Additionally, a patient Subjective Scale was used in order to obtain an impression of the patient's condition. This was based on the tools developed by Hayward (1975). He asked patients about the pain experienced, whether it was local or general, their morale, nausea, sleep, appetite, and measures giving comfort. In the present study the areas of welfare examined were pain, morale, sleep, appetite and ability to help themselves. However, whereas in Hayward's study observers had assessed the patient's condition on each point, in the present investigation the patients were asked to do this themselves.

Shortly after beginning the pilot study the subjective scale was expanded, and based on the Recovery Inventory devised by Wolfer and Davis (1970). The patients were then questioned about nine aspects of their physical state, viz. sleep, appetite, strength and energy, stomach condition, bowel condition, urination, self-assistance, movement, and interest in surroundings. Wolfer and Davis had used a six-point scale ranging from very poor to excellent. When this measure was considered for use in the pilot study it was thought unnecessary to include excellent on the scale, and the remaining five-point scale would then be comparable to the scale being used to gain an impression of mental state (discussed later). Changes were later made in this.

Mental State

Considerable difficulty was experienced with the assessment of this aspect of patient welfare, and no completely satisfactory measure was found.

A Moods and Feelings Inventory devised by Wolfer and Davis (1970) was examined. This is a short self-report measure of fear and anxiety in hospitalised patients. The inventory consists of 20 adjectives describing both positive and negative feelings. Ten of the words form a fear-anxiety scale and interspersed with these are another 10 adjectives, four of which are used as an index of "positive affect". The emphasis in this scale is on the examination of the fear-anxiety aspects of pre-operative mood. Thus, it was felt to be unsuitable for use in the present study in which a more comprehensive barometer of mood was required, mainly for post-operative use.

It was decided, therefore, to use the Mood Adjective Check List in this study. This list of 45 adjectives' had been previously used in psychological research (Nowlis, 1966), and it allows examination of 12 different dimensions of mood. This instrument is very versatile because it is designed in such a way that each dimension of mood can be examined in isolation.

During the pilot study it was found that the Mood Adjective Check List was also not suitable for use. Since it was originally devised in the United States many of the words were not understood or were ambiguous when used in this country. The few patients who tried it out found it was too long, particularly during the first few days post-operatively. Its use was, therefore, discontinued shortly after the beginning of the pilot study.

No other completely suitable test of mental state was found. Therefore, during the pilot study the patients were simply asked to assess themselves as to their "morale" or "general mood" on a five point scale similar to that used by Hayward (1975). However, following the pilot study, further changes were made and are described next.

Physical and Mental State

The items used by Wolfer and Davis (1970) in their Recovery Inventory are intended to be indicators of the patient's physical condition. The first eight items, sleep, strength and energy, gastric state, state of bowels, appetite, urination, ability to help themselves, and ease in movement, are all physical attributes. However, the ninth (and final) item in this inventory is "interest in surroundings" and it was felt that this was more related to the patient's psychological welfare than to the physical condition. Therefore, following the pilot study correlations were calculated between the summed score on the first eight items, and the score obtained on "interest in surroundings" for each post-operative day. Similarly, correlations were calculated between the score obtained for "interest in surroundings" and that obtained for "general mood". This last mentioned item was being used as an indicator of psychological condition. On most of the post-operative days the correlations were greatest between "interest in surroundings" and "general mood". Therefore, the scores obtained on these two items were combined to give a numerical value for Mental State.

The aggregate of the numbers assigned to the other eight items comprised the Physical State score.

Furthermore, during the pilot study it was found that on some of the individual items many subjects were reaching the maximum score of five at an early stage in their post-operative recovery. In order to increase the sensitivity of these measures, in the main study each item was scored on a six-point scale, as originally used by Wolfer and Davis (1970).

Shortly after the beginning of these preliminary studies it was found that on the first post-operative day some patients had difficulty comprehending and answering the questions, which were all printed on one page. Thus, it was decided to assess the difficulty experienced when each aspect of condition was printed, in large type, on a card with the scale underneath. The series of cards was displayed one at a time. The patients indicated, either verbally or by pointing, the point on the scale which they felt was descriptive of their state at the time. The observer immediately scored this on the patient's record sheet. This method was found to be satisfactory and was used for the remainder of the study.

Pain

The amount of pain experienced was assessed by the use of a "pain thermometer", as used by Hayward, on which the patient was asked to indicate the amount of pain being suffered at present. The scale ranged from "no pain at all" at the bottom, through "a little pain", "quite a lot of pain", "very bad pain", to "as much pain as I can bear", at the top. This was scored from one to five.

At the beginning of the pilot study the patients were only asked about pain daily, when the other subjective scales were being completed. It quickly became apparent that this was unsatisfactory. If an analgesic had recently been administered the score obtained was unrepresentative of the patient's suffering. Accordingly, it was decided to assess the pain experienced twice daily, when the patient was first seen each day and three to three-and-a-half hours later, when last seen. The scores were summated. This was the procedure carried out during the rest of the study.

Nursing and Medical Assessment

It was assumed that qualified doctors and nurses have a "mental picture" of their expectations of a patient following a particular operation. On the basis of this assumption it was considered that they should be able to assess a patient's condition as "as well as expected", "slightly better", or "slightly worse than expected", or "better" or "worse than expected" at any particular moment. Therefore, during the pilot study the ward sister or charge nurse and the registrar caring for the patient were asked to evaluate each patient's condition on this scale on the second and sixth post-operative days and the day of discharge.

However, a number of problems arose. Although it was intended that the medical registrar and the ward sister or charge nurse would assess each patient's condition on three separate occasions, this did not occur. A medical assessment of condition was obtained for only half of the patients, and only on one occasion. Nevertheless, the ward sister or charge nurse carried out their evaluations readily. Two assessments were obtained for every patient, and three for those who remained in hospital for longer than eight days post-operatively.

In addition, it was found that at the beginning of the pilot study the nursing staff nearly always described the patient as "as well as expected". There may be two explanations for this. Firstly, although it was explained that the patient's condition at that particular moment was to be assessed, the nurses were reluctant to commit themselves to an opinion, when the patient's condition might later alter. In addition, it is possible that they had a psychological "set" because the phrase "as well as expected" is frequently used when giving information to relatives about a patient's condition. Although discussing this problem with the nursing staff improved their use of this scale, certain changes were made,

Using the scale developed by Hayward (1975), it was decided to ask the ward sister or charge nurse and the registrar to assess the patient's post-operative progress as follows: "unusually well", "better than usual", "about average", "not as well as usual", or "progressing very slowly/not well at all". This evaluation was carried out by each of them just before the patient's discharge from hospital.

For an experimental study the selection of reliable, sensitive criterion measures is important. The time, effort and expense of this type of research cannot be justified unless satisfactory dependent variables are available. In this study it is recognized that the subjective measures were not, on their own, of a standard to merit carrying out an experimental study. However, the other measures used were satisfactory and it seemed reasonable also to include the subjective measures described above.

CHAPTER 4

Methods

4.1 The Pilot Study

The importance of the pilot study in the selection and refinement of dependent variables has already been demonstrated. The second main reason for carrying out a pilot study was to assess the feasibility of the proposed methods.

Initially it was intended to examine the effect on post-operative stress and recovery of psychological preparation and, separately, the teaching of deep breathing and leg exercises. The proposed method was to involve five comparable groups of patients, each participating in a different pre-operative regimen. A study of the record of previous admissions and the conduct of the pilot study made this appear feasible. However, industrial problems within the National Health Service then resulted in a considerable reduction in the number of suitable patients admitted to hospital. Therefore, the main study only included two groups of patients, the experimental and the control groups.

The other change made as a result of the pilot study was in the selection of patients included in the study.

For the purposes of this study it was decided to confine the sample to patients with non-malignant disease admitted for routine surgery. The ward records for the previous 12 months were examined and surgical conditions for inclusion in the project were selected. These were conditions in which the numbers previously admitted suggested the certainty of being able to obtain an adequate total, as well as the probability of achieving equality between the five groups. Patients to be included in this investigation were aged between 18 and 65 and were to undergo cholecystectomy, gastric surgery, repair of inguinal or femoral hernia, or varicose vein surgery.

Following the pilot study it was decided to limit the patients studied to those undergoing cholecystectomy or hernia repair. The reasons for this decision were as follows:

1. The numbers of patients admitted for gastric and varicose vein surgery were found to be relatively few;
2. Extrapolation from the numbers of patients admitted for cholecystectomy and herniorrhaphy during the period of the pilot study and during the previous 12 months suggested that there would be more than adequate numbers to carry out the main study;

3. Patients with varicose veins were discharged within two or three days of surgery;
4. Most of the difficulties in obtaining urine specimens arose in the early post-operative days following gastric surgery.

No further changes were initiated as a result of the pilot study and the remainder of this report is concerned with the methods and results of the main study.

4.2 Hypotheses

The hypotheses tested in this study were:
1. The pre-operative giving of information about prospective treatment and care, and the teaching of exercises to be performed post-operatively, will minimise the rise in biochemical indicators of stress;
2. A relationship will be demonstrated between the measurements of biochemical indicators of stress and some other indicators of patient welfare.

4.3 Background to Study

Research Environment

It was decided to carry out the research project in a non-teaching District General Hospital in the provinces. The particular hospital was chosen because little research had previously been carried out there, and also, as a District General Hospital, it seemed likely that less specialised surgery would be undertaken. New building was still taking place, but at that moment the hospital contained 778 beds. The population of the catchment area was approximately 200,000, about half of whom were working class and half lower and upper middle class. The two general surgical wards, one for males and one for females, were L-shaped and the 32 beds in each ward were arranged in single and four-bedded rooms, with adequate toilet facilities close by. The male ward was directly above the female, and stairs at the corner of the L allowed work to proceed on both wards concurrently.

Staff

Following informal discussion with the acting chief nursing officer and the two consultant general surgeons involved, formal permission to carry out the project was obtained from the District Management Team. Further detailed discussion took place with the senior nurses and medical staff in order to outline the aims and proposed methods of the study. However, the more junior nurses and doctors who would be involved in the study were given less detailed information in order to minimise the risk of any alteration in their routine practice. They were told that patients would be interviewed pre-operatively and then their condition evaluated post-operatively. It was emphasised that patients, not nurses, were being studied and that research assistants would be collecting post-operative urine samples and carrying out the other assessments. The ward sisters/charge nurses and doctors were asked for their co-operation in assessing the patient's post-operative progress.

Further information on some aspects of the project was requested and, finally, all those involved agreed that the investigation should proceed.

There were two surgical teams each consisting of a consultant, a registrar and a houseman, with a senior house officer shared between them. Both teams undertook the treatment of patients with similar disorders on the two wards involved and operating sessions were held every day of the working week.

Research Assistants

Two part-time research assistants were employed to carry out the post-operative work of the project. It was decided that they must be State Registered Nurses because they would be accepted more readily by the hospital staff and by the patients. However, the ethos of nursing predisposes members of the profession to giving sympathy and encouragement to the sick. This might alter the patient's psychological state and, thus, modify the degree of stress experienced and the amount of corticosteroid hormones secreted. Therefore, it was necessary to emphasise the importance of exhibiting interested but dispassionate behaviour towards the patients being studied. One of the research assistants, who had previously helped in another research project, found this fairly easy. The other had some difficulty in withholding the sympathy and encouragement that she felt the patients needed. However, she learnt to display the new behaviour required in this situation.

4.4 Sample

The sample studied was male and female patients between 18 and 65 years of age admitted for cholecystectomy or unilateral herniorrhaphy. However, towards the end of the study two patients undergoing planned appendicectomy were also included. Suitable patients were selected before admission by examination of the admission lists and the patient's notes. As far as possible all patients fulfilling these criteria were included in the inquiry with the exception of:
1. those with other concurrent disease;
2. those with a history of psychiatric illness;
3. patients receiving corticosteroid therapy;
4. those at present taking diuretic drugs;
5. members of the nursing and medical professions.

44

Initially, subjects were paired on the basis of three criteria, namely, sex, operation, and consultant under whose care the patient was admitted. This last factor was considered important because the medical preparation and treatment sometimes varied between the surgical teams, and the analgesics prescribed post-operatively also differed. The first patient admitted was allocated randomly to either the experimental or control group, and the next similar patient was assigned to the other group. However, towards the end of the study a frequency matching procedure was used (Billewicz, 1964). In frequency matching the identity of each pair of patients is not preserved but allocation of individuals to the control or experimental group is manipulated so that the distribution of significant characteristics is the same in each group. The experiment is then regarded as having been performed on comparable groups, rather than on matched individuals.

Eventually each group contained 40 patients and the two groups were exactly matched for sex, operation and consultant (Table 1). Age, social class, previous operation, smoking habits and stage in menstrual cycle (when appropriate) were also recorded. The distribution of these characteristics is shown in Table 2.

TABLE 1.

Distribution of Patients Within Groups Demonstrating
Characteristics Used in their Assignment

Sex	Male	19
	Female	21
Operation performed	Herniorrhaphy	14
	Cholecystectomy	15
	Cholecystectomy and exploration of common bile duct	10
	Appendicectomy	1
Surgeon	A	20
	B	20
Total Number of Patients in Each Group		40

4.5 Pre-operative Regimen

The researcher carried out the pre-operative programme as described below.

The patients were admitted during the morning and their permission obtained to include them in the study. A three-hour urine specimen was collected. Thus, between 11.00 a.m. and 11.15 a.m. each patient was asked to pass urine so as to empty the bladder. All urine subsequently

TABLE 2.

Distribution of Patient Characteristics Not Used
for Assigning Patients to Groups

		Experimental	Control
Social Class	1	—	1
	2	8	5
	3	28	27
	4	3	5
	5	1	2
Age	18–25 years	3	5
	26–35 years	6	4
	36–45 years	5	8
	46–55 years	13	12
	56–65 years	13	11
Previous	Yes	23	19
Operations	No	17	21
Smoking Habits	None	20	18
	Less than 10 cigarettes daily	4	6
	More than 10 cigarettes daily	13	14
	Cigars or pipe	3	2
Time of last	Not applicable	28	28
Menstrual Period	Less than 10 days ago	6	6
	11–13 days ago	—	—
	14–16 days ago	—	3
	17–19 days ago	2	1
	More than 20 days ago	4	2

passed up to and including a final specimen obtained between 2.00 p.m. and 2.15 p.m. was collected. After thorough mixing, an aliquot was stored in the deep freeze until the biochemical estimations could conveniently be performed.

Between 11.00 a.m. and 12 noon the patient was again visited and the body temperature recorded using the Sensitrex Electronic Clinical Thermometer.

Later in the afternoon the patient was interviewed. It is known that a state of excessive anxiety may interfere with learning (Speilberger, 1966), and, therefore, the interview was conducted as informally as possible, with the aim of reducing anxiety. The patient was told about the investigation in more detail. Thus, he or she would be visited every day post-operatively by one of the two research assistants, both qualified nurses, who would collect a three-hour urine specimen and take the patient's temperature. In addition the subject would be asked to assess his or her own physical and psychological condition. The measures to be used by the patient were demonstrated at this interview and the results on these indicators recorded.

The data collection sheets designed for use in this study are shown in Appendix I, Figures 1 and 2.

Finally, the preparation appropriate to the group to which the patient had been assigned was presented as follows:

Experimental Group

The information given to this group of patients was similar to that used by Hayward (1975) which he defined as information which can appropriately be given by a State Registered Nurse. This was based on his preliminary work which showed that many patients expressed anxiety about the topics included. The specific information given related to the pre-operative preparation on the ward, including pre-operative starvation and pre-medication, etc., transfer to the theatre, the induction of anaesthesia, the recovery room, and the post-operative circumstances including the presence of drainage tubes or intra-venous infusions, etc. The problem of pain and the availability of analgesics, and the importance of early ambulation were discussed.

In addition, the patients were taught a number of post-operative exercises similar to those described by Mezzanotte (1970). The importance of these in maintaining efficient lung and circulatory function was emphasised.

The patients were taught, by demonstration and practice, how to inspire and expire fully, how to cough following inspiration and how to reduce pain by supporting the operation wound when coughing. Simple foot, ankle and leg exercises were similarly taught. They also practised relaxing their abdominal muscles. The patients were encouraged to practise these exercises several times before going to theatre, and advised to perform them every one or two hours post-operatively, when awake, until fully ambulant again.

The information to be imparted was selected and to this extent the interview was carefully planned. However, the patients in the study varied considerably in background and ability to absorb this information. The teaching, therefore, was adapted to suit the individual patient. This variation was in the use of different words, according to the understanding demonstrated, and in the quality of explanation given. In addition, part of the interview was unstructured as each patient was encouraged to talk about anxieties related to the forthcoming operation. When possible, reassurance was given by offering specific information, and sometimes just talking about the operation appeared to relieve anxiety.

47

Control Group

Members of this group were used to control the possibility that extra attention paid to individuals and groups might affect their performance, (The Hawthorne effect). The patient and researcher talked about various topics unrelated to the hospital. If the patient asked specific questions about his or her care, they were answered briefly and without encouraging discussion.

The pre-operative interview with each patient in the study lasted about 35 minutes. Each subject was asked not to discuss the interview with other patients or with members of staff.

4.6 Post-operative Assessments

Patients were not visited by anyone connected with the project on the day of operation, but each day subsequently, until discharged from hospital, or until the 14th post-operative day, they were seen by one of the research assistants who carried out the post-operative work. The two assistants were not informed of the specific preparation received by each patient.

The routine was as follows:

On each post-operative day one of the research assistants visited each patient. The three-hour urine sample was collected between 11.00 a.m. and 2.00 p.m. At 11.00 a.m. and 2.00 p.m. the patient was asked to indicate how much pain was being experienced at these times. Between 11.00 a.m. and 12 noon the patient's temperature was recorded and each patient was asked to assess his or her own condition on the subjective scales. Information about analgesics administered and post-operative complications was then obtained from the records. The doctor's and nurse's assessment forms were completed by them before, or just after, the patient was discharged from hospital.

Biochemical Indicators of Stress

The excretion of 17-hydroxycorticosteroids was measured in the urine samples obtained pre-operatively and on days two, three and four post-operatively. The sodium : potassium ratio was measured in all urine specimens obtained.

Objective Measures

Temperature: The patient's oral temperature was recorded daily using the electronic thermometer; each patient had his own disposable probe.

Analgesic Consumption: A record was kept of the number of administered doses of analgesics regulated by the Controlled Drugs Act. The amount of analgesics administered from the time of arrival in the recovery room was recorded. This information was obtained by

48

examining the patient's drug record "Kardex" and the nursing notes (in which drugs administered in the recovery room were recorded). When there was doubt about the accuracy of the recording, the Controlled Drugs Register, in which the administration of drugs regulated by the Controlled Drugs Act is recorded, was also examined.

Incidence of Complications: Information about the incidence of post-operative complications was obtained from the patient's medical notes and nursing notes. The occurrence of a complication was recorded when some treatment was initiated.

Subjective Scales

Mental and Physical State: Ten cards, each representing one aspect of physical or mental condition, were presented to patients, and they were then asked to assess their own state on each item. A six-point scale was used for each item ranging from "very poor" to "excellent". The first eight items were aspects of physical condition and the scores obtained were summated (possible total of 48) and recorded as an indicator of physical state (See Appendix II, Figure 1).

These items were: sleep, strength and energy, presence or absence of gastric symptoms, state of bowels, appetite, urination, ability to help themselves, and ease in movement.

The last two items ("interest in surroundings" and "general mood") were used in the same way to give a Mental State Score (possible score 12) (see Appendix II, Figure 2).

Pain: Each day at 11.00 a.m. and 2.00 p.m. patients were asked to indicate, using the Pain Thermometer, how much pain they had (see Appendix II, Figure 3). This consisted of a five-point scale and the scores obtained at 11.00 a.m. and 2.00 p.m. were summated and, therefore, a maximum score of 10 (indicating "no pain") could be obtained.

Medical and Nursing Assessments: As near as possible to the day of the patient's discharge from hospital the ward sister or charge nurse and the surgical registrar responsible for the patient were asked to evaluate the subject's post-operative progress. This assessment form also used a five-point scale (see Appendix II, Figure 4).

All post-operative data collected were recorded on a Results Recording Form (see Appendix I, Figure 2) in numerical form and then transferred direct to computer cards to await analysis.

CHAPTER 5
Results

5.1 Introduction

The results obtained from the total number of patients (40 in each group) were examined, but it was also decided to scrutinise two subdivisions of this total. Those patients who had undergone cholecystectomy (25 subjects in both the experimental and control group) comprised one section, and the second subdivision contained those individuals who had had a hernia repair or an appendicectomy (15 patients in each group).

The results from the experimental and control groups were compared for each of the dependent variables used. Some of the data fulfilled the criteria for the use of parametric statistical tests, and Student's t-test was used to examine the steroid hormone excretion, temperature and analgesic consumption. The non-parametric Mann-Whitney U test was used for the sodium : potassium ratio and all the subjective measures of welfare. The Fisher Exact Probability test was used to examine the difference in incidence of complications between experimental and control groups of patients. Finally, correlations were performed between the various measures of stress and recovery to find whether any relationship could be demonstrated. Unless otherwise stated the probability used was the two-tailed probability of obtaining a particular value and the level taken as statistically significant was 0·05.

Most of the calculations performed were carried out by using the Statistical Package for the Social Sciences (Nie *et al*, 1975) on the Regional Computer Centre Joint System ICL 1906A/CDC 7600. The Mann-Whitney U Tests were carried out on the same computer system using an already available programme. Fisher Exact Probability Tests were performed using the Faculty of Medicine Statistics Package on the Cyber 72 Interactive Computer.

5.2 Biochemical Measures of Stress

17-hydroxycorticosteroid excretion

Figure 2 shows the results obtained from the total number of patients and Figure 3 demonstrates the findings from the two subdivisions.

50

Figure 2. 17-hydroxycorticosteroid excretion (mean ± s.e.) against days in hospital—all patients.

Experimental group ———
Control group   - - -

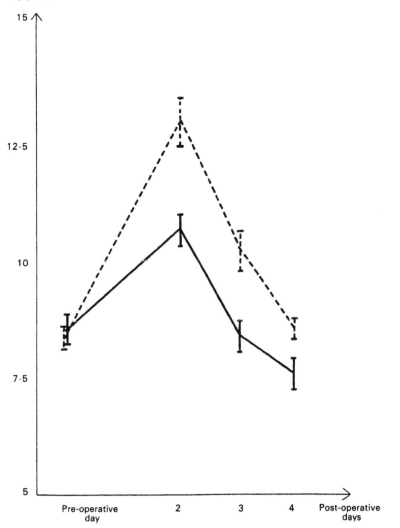

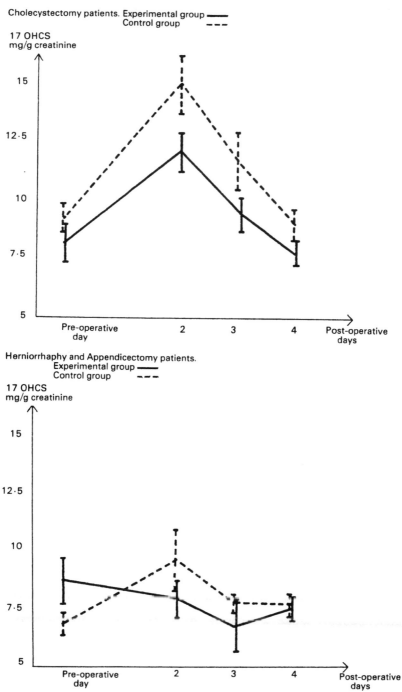

Figure 3. 17-hydroxycorticosteroid excretion (mean ± s.e.) for different groups of patients.

Cholecystectomy patients. Experimental group ———
                        Control group ‑ ‑ ‑

17 OHCS
mg/g creatinine

15

12·5

10

7·5

5

Pre-operative   2   3   4   Post-operative
day   days

Herniorrhaphy and Appendicectomy patients.
         Experimental group ———
         Control group ‑ ‑ ‑

17 OHCS
mg/g creatinine

15

12·5

10

7·5

5

Pre-operative   2   3   4   Post-operative
day   days

TABLE 3.

17-hydroxycorticosteroid excretion (mg/g creatinine) in three-hour urine samples

		Experimental group Mean	s.e.	n	Control group Mean	s.e.	n	t	P 2-tailed	1-tailed
All patients	Preop.	8·481	0·632	40	8·354	0·472	40	0·16	0·873	
	Day 2	10·757	0·707	36	13·006	1·015	36	−1·82		0·037
	Day 3	8·436	0·682	36	10·336	0·860	39	−1·73		0·044
	Day 4	7·660	0·375	39	8·609	0·455	38	−1·61		0·056
Cholecystectomy patients	Preop.	8·306	0·829	25	9·277	0·624	25	−0·94	0·354	
	Day 2	12·255	0·874	23	15·111	1·258	22	−1·86		0·035
	Day 3	9·510	0·779	22	11·714	1·240	25	−1·50		0·070
	Day 4	7·749	0·511	25	9·071	0·638	24	−1·62		0·056
Herniorrhaphy and appendi-cectomy patients	Preop.	8·773	0·997	15	6·815	0·520	15	1·74	0·096	
	Day 2	8·108	0·801	13	9·697	1·315	14	−1·03		0·157
	Day 3	6·746	1·149	14	7·876	0·473	14	−0·91		0·188
	Day 4	7·501	0·531	14	7·817	0·539	14	−0·42		0·340

TABLE 4.

Differences in 17-hydroxycorticosteroid excretion (mg/g creatinine) from pre-operative sample

(i.e. post-operative excretion minus pre-operative excretion)

		Experimental group			Control group				P
		Mean	s.e.	n	Mean	s.e.	n	t	(one-tailed)
All patients	Day 2	2·106	0·692	36	4·622	0·918	36	−2·19	0·015
	3	0·353	0·632	36	2·008	0·927	39	−1·47	0·071
	4	−0·865	0·532	39	0·210	0·605	38	−1·34	0·091
Cholecystectomy	Day 2	3·657	0·774	23	5·932	1·263	22	−1·54	0·065
patients	3	1·879	0·713	22	2·437	1·401	25	−0·36	0·362
	4	−0·557	0·746	25	0·035	0·882	24	−0·51	0·308
Herniorrhaphy	Day 2	−0·639	0·967	13	2·564	1·116	14	−2·17	0·019
and	3	−2·044	0·869	14	1·242	0·680	14	−2·98	0·003
appendicectomy	4	−1·417	0·655	14	0·918	0·643	14	−2·54	0·008

54

Table 3 presents the same information and includes the value calculated by the Student's t-test and the probability of obtaining such a value. The two-tailed probability is given for the pre-operative day, but for the three post-operative days the one-tailed probability is used. It was originally hypothesized that the pre-operative preparation given would reduce steroid secretion in the experimental patients, i.e., the direction of change was predicted, and thus the use of the one-tailed probability is appropriate (Siegel, 1956).

The results obtained from the total sample showed that the steroid levels in the urine were lower in the experimental than in the control group on each of the post-operative days when measured (i.e., second, third and fourth days after operation). On the second and third days the difference found was significant. A statistically significant difference between the experimental and control group was also found in the cholecystectomy patients on the second day after the operation.

Although the difference between the experimental and the control group was in the predicted direction on the three post-operative days the t values obtained for the herniorrhaphy patients were not significant. However, an examination of the mean values obtained showed that the steroid levels measured before operation were considerably lower in the control group than in the experimental group. In addition, the mean values of 17-hydroxycorticosteroids in the urine of the control group after operation were markedly higher than before surgery, while in the experimental group the hormone levels measured were lower after operation than they were beforehand. Therefore, it was decided to look at the difference in steroid excretion between the pre-operative measure and the value obtained on each of the second, third and fourth post-operative days. The pre-operative level was subtracted from the post-operative excretion level for each post-operative day, the mean and standard error were calculated and t-tests were performed for the total sample and for the two subdivisions. These results and the one-tailed probability of obtaining such results are shown in Table 4. Again, the differences found were all in the predicted direction, the rise in the excretion of these hormones was always less in the experimental patients than in the control subjects, to the extent that a fall in the quantities excreted was seen in some instances. Considering the results obtained from the total group, the probability of obtaining the value of t for the second post-operative day was less than 0·02, although no other significant results were obtained. There was no significant difference between the groups of cholecystectomy patients. However, an examination of the results from the herniorrhaphy patients revealed a statistically significant difference between the experimental and the control group on each day after operation. The values of t obtained had a probability (P) of less than 0·02 on the second post-operative day; P was < 0·005 on the third day and P < 0·01 on the fourth day post-operatively.

Sodium : Potassium Ratio

The results for the whole group are shown in Figure 4 and in Appendix III (Table 1). In this Table the median, as well as the mean is included. This information has been given because a ratio of two values often results in a skewed distribution and this information was needed in

Figure 4. Sodium:potassium ratio (Na:K) (mean ± s.e.) in three-hour urine samples against days in hospital—all patients.

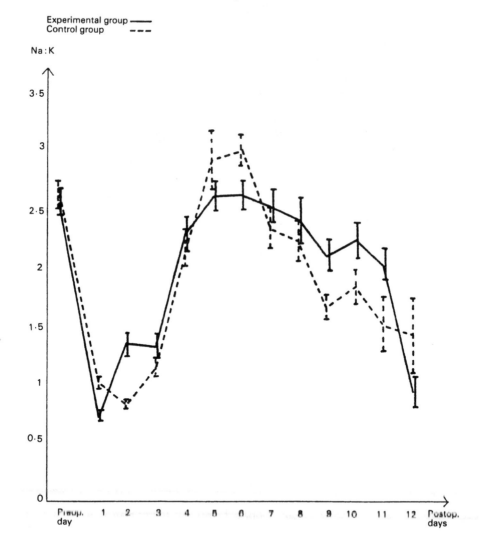

order to choose the most appropriate statistical test. One of the conditions for the correct use of the t-test is that the observations must be normally distributed. The differences between the mean and median show that this is not so for this measure. In almost all cases the median is smaller than the mean indicating that the distribution of results is skewed to the right. It was necessary, therefore, to use a non-parametric test of significance, and the Mann-Whitney U test was chosen as the most appropriate. No statistically significant differences between the experimental and control groups were found either for the total sample, or for either of the sub-samples.

Figure 4 demonstrates the considerable variation in sodium: potassium ratio during the period in hospital for the whole group of patients. Similar results were obtained from the cholecystectomy and herniorrhaphy groups separately. The pre-operative ratio was about 2·5 and this was followed by a marked drop to low levels over the first few days after operation as sodium was retained in the body, and potassium lost in the urine. On the fourth day after operation the ratio began to rise and then, for a few days, maintained levels higher than before operation as the balance of sodium and potassium in the body was corrected.

5.3 Objective Measures

Temperature

Figure 5 shows the results obtained for the whole group of patients and these are also shown in tabular form in Appendix III (Table 2). In both experimental and control groups, and in the total sample as well as the two subsections, the results were very similar. A rise in temperature was found after operation with a gradual return to the pre-operative level by the fourth post-operative day. In no group was the mean temperature above 36·8°C on any day. A significant difference was found between the two groups in the total sample on the third post-operative day when the control group had a lower temperature than the experimental group. However, the actual difference in temperature was less than 0·2°C.

Analgesic Consumption

There was no significant difference between the number of doses of analgesics administered to either group for the whole sample, or for either of the two subsamples.

Incidence of Complications

A complete list of the complications that occurred among the patients in this study is shown in Table 5. Table 6 gives the incidence of the main complications in the two subsamples. Where the numbers involved

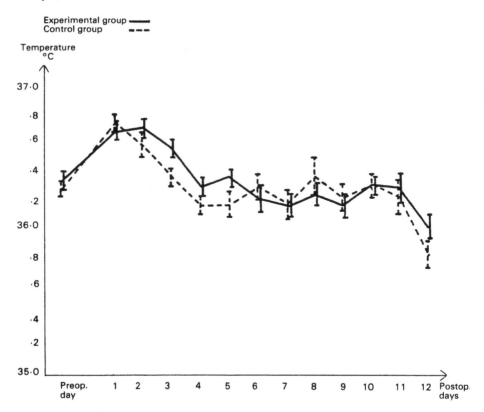

Figure 5. Body temperature (mean ± s.e.) against days in hospital—all patients.

Experimental group ▬▬
Control group ▬ ▬ ▬

suggested the necessity the significance of the results obtained was tested by the Fisher Exact Probability Test. This test was used because the smallest number in a cell was less than five and the chi-square test became inappropriate. The one-tailed probability of obtaining such results is also given in the Tables. One-tailed probability was used because the direction of the difference between the groups can be predicted on theoretical grounds.

The incidence of wound and respiratory infections was greater in the control than in the experimental group, and the overall incidence of complications was also higher in the control group. In looking at the total sample, the difference in the incidence of wound infections in the two groups was significant. In addition, the difference in the number of patients affected in the different groups among the cholecystectomy patients was significant.

TABLE 5.

Incidence of complications in total sample

	Experimental group	Control group	P (one-tailed)
	n = 40	n = 40	
Wound infection	2	8	0·044
Respiratory infection	2	5	0·22
Urinary infection	2	2	
Urine retention	2	1	
TOTAL	8	16	
Number of patients affected	8	15	0·069

Miscellaneous events (not included in statistical analysis)

Rash	1	1	
Diarrhoea	1	1	
Oral thrush	1	—	
I.V. site inflamed	—	1	
Migraine	1	—	
Fibrositis	—	1	

5.4   Subjective Measures

The Mann-Whitney U Test was used to test the significance of the difference between the groups in these subjective measures. It was necessary to use a non-parametric statistical test because one of the conditions for use of parametric tests is that "the variables involved must have been measured in at least an interval scale" (Siegel, 1956). In an interval scale the distances between consecutive points on the scale are known and are constant. In the subjective measures used this condition was not met.

Physical State

The results for the whole group are in Appendix III (Table 3) and are illustrated in Figure 6. No significant differences between the experimental and control groups were found.

Figure 6 and the corresponding graph of the Mental State Scores (Figure 7) are similar. For both attributes the experimental group had slightly lower scores before operation than the control group of patients. The drop in the mean score obtained for the physical state on the first post-operative day was followed by a steady rise back to the pre-

TABLE 6.

Incidence of main complications in the two subsamples

	Experimental group	Control group	P (one-tailed)
	n = 25	n = 25	
Cholecystectomy patients			
Wound infection	2	7	0·069
Respiratory infection	1	4	0·174
Urinary infection	1	2	
Urine retention	1	1	
TOTAL	5	14	
Number of patients affected	5	13	0·019
	n = 15	n = 15	
Herniorrhaphy patients			
Wound infection	—	1	
Respiratory infection	1	1	
Urinary infection	1	—	
Urine retention	1	—	
TOTAL	3	2	
Number of patients affected	3	2	

operative level by the fifth day after surgery. The scores obtained by the experimental group continued to rise while the control group mean scores appeared steady at about the pre-operative value.

Mental State

Figure 7 shows the results obtained from the whole group of patients and the same results are in Appendix III (Table 4). Again, there were no significant differences between the experimental and control groups of patients.

As expected, there was a considerable drop in mean score obtained on the first post-operative day, followed by a steady increase. As shown in

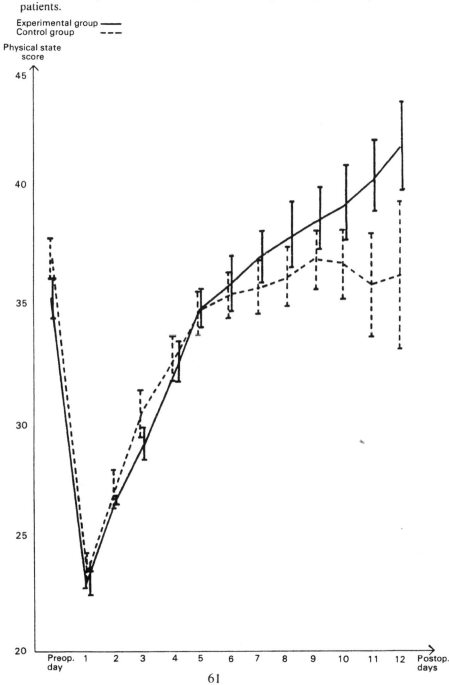

Figure 6. Physical state score (mean ± s.e.) against days in hospital—all patients.

Experimental group ——
Control group - - -

Physical state score

Figure 7. Mental state score (mean ± s.e.) against days in hospital—all patients.

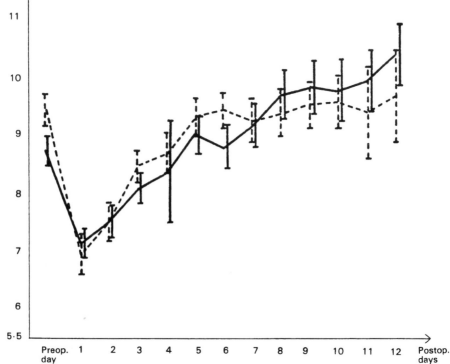

the Figures, the control group of patients appeared to stabilise at about the score obtained before operation. On the other hand, the experimental group showed a steady improvement throughout their hospital stay. The mean scores from the patients in the herniorrhaphy subsample were lower in the experimental group than in the control group.

Pain Score

The mean scores obtained from this measure are shown in Figure 8 and in Appendix III (Table 5). A high score on this scale indicates a low

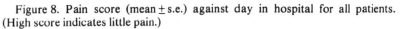

Figure 8. Pain score (mean ± s.e.) against day in hospital for all patients. (High score indicates little pain.)

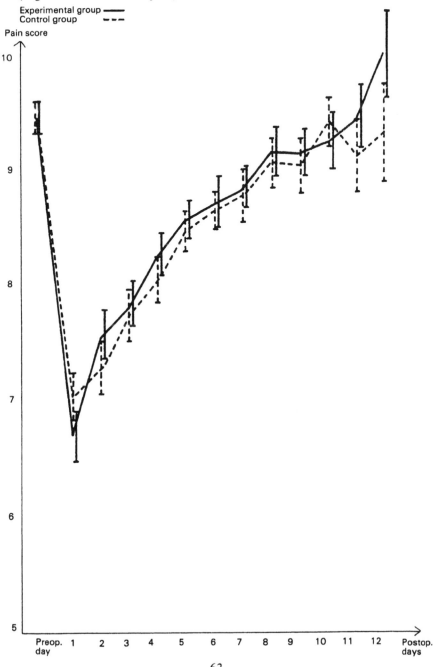

Experimental group ——
Control group – – –

Pain score

level of pain reported, i.e., the patient's condition is improving. There was very little difference to be seen between experimental and control groups and no significant results were obtained. The experimental group of herniorrhaphy patients had a lower score after operation than the control group.

Nursing and Medical Assessment

The results obtained on these measures are shown in Appendix III (Table 6). In both assessments the experimental group had a slightly higher mean score than the control group, but the differences were so small that no test of significance has been performed.

5.5 Relationship between Steroid Excretion and Other Variables

It was decided to examine the relationship between 17-hydroxycorticosteroid excretion and some of the other measures used in the study, viz. sodium : potassium ratio, temperature, incidence of complications and scores on physical state, mental state and pain scale.

The theoretical relationship between stress and infection led to the decision to examine only this group of complications. The patients' results were grouped according to whether or not they had developed an infection during their post-operative progress. The steroid excretion levels of the two groups were then compared on the pre-operative day and on each of the three post-operative days by means of the t-test (Table 7). On the second and third days after operation the steroid levels in the patients who developed infections were higher than in the other patients, but the difference was not significant.

TABLE 7.

Comparison of 17-hydroxycorticosteroid excretion in patients who developed infection and those who did not

| | Infected patients | | | Healthy patients | | | | |
	Mean	s.e.	n	Mean	s.e.	n	t	P
Pre-operative Day	8·220	0·566	21	8·403	0·474	59	−0·248	0·800
Post-operative Day 2	12·359	0·845	18	11·712	0·791	54	0·559	0·584
Day 3	10·397	1·285	20	9·070	0·607	55	0·933	0·644
Day 4	7·995	0·537	20	8·175	0·357	57	−0·278	0·778

The relationship between steroid excretion and each of several other variables (i.e., sodium:potassium ratio, mental state, physical state, and pain) was examined by calculating Spearman Correlation Coefficients (a non-parametric test) on the pre-operative day and on days two, three and four after operation. Pearson Product-Moment Correlation Coefficients (for parametric data) were calculated between steroid excretion and temperature on the same days. In addition, the results obtained for these four days were combined and the correlations again calculated. These values are shown in Table 8.

Before operation a significant correlation ($P < 0.05$) between steroid excretion and body temperature was found, and a similar correlation occurred when the results for the four days were combined. However, on the three post-operative days no significant relationship appeared and on two of those days the sign of the correlation coefficient calculated was changed. No significant relationship was demonstrated between 17-hydroxycorticosteroid excretion and mental state or pain. On the other

TABLE 8.

Relationship between steroid excretion and other variables

17-hydroxycorti-costeroid excretion correlated with:	Spearman correlation coefficient (rho)				Pearson correlation coefficient (r)
	Physical state	Mental state	Pain	Sodium: potassium ratio	Temperature
Pre-operative day n = 80					
Correlation	−0·042	0·043	−0·032	0·083	0·203
P	0·712	0·704	0·778	0·462	0·036
Day 2 n = 72					
Correlation	−0·215	−0·107	−0·039	−0·292	0·022
P	0·070	0·372	0·745	0·013	0·428
Day 3 n = 75					
Correlation	−0·275	−0·150	−0·076	—0·206	−0·163
P	0·018	0·198	0·515	0·077	0·081
Day 4 n = 77					
Correlation	0·030	0·113	−0·010	−0·284	−0·089
P	0·797	0·329	0·933	0·013	0·220
Combined results for the 4 days n = 304					
Correlation	−0·220	−0·100	−0·032	−0·260	0·100
P	0·001	0·081	0·581	0·001	0·042

65

hand, a negative correlation (P < 0·02) between steroid levels and physical state score occurred on the third post-operative day. In addition, the combined results gave a negative correlation (P = 0·001) between the same measures. Similarly, a significantly negative correlation (P < 0·02) was found between 17-hydroxycorticosteroid excretion and sodium : potassium ratio on the second and fourth days after operation, and the combined results also produced a negative correlation (P = 0·001).

The possibility that steroid excretion on the days shortly after operation influenced the value of other measures later in the post-operative course of the patients was considered. It was decided to calculate correlation coefficients between steroid hormone levels on the second and third days after operation with the values obtained for the sodium : potassium ratio, physical state, mental state and pain on the fifth to tenth post-operative days. No significant correlations were found.

CHAPTER 6

Discussion

In this discussion the word "group" is used only to refer to either the experimental or the control groups of patients. The results from the total sample (40 patients in each of the experimental and control groups) and from the two subsidiary samples are discussed here. The first subdivision comprises those patients admitted for cholecystectomy (25 patients in each group) and the second includes those patients who had undergone herniorrhaphy or appendicectomy (15 patients in each group).

6.1 Biochemical Results

The first hypothesis states that "the pre-operative giving of information about prospective treatment and care, and the teaching of exercises to be performed post-operatively, will minimise the rise in biochemical indicators of stress". The results obtained in this experimental study allow this hypothesis to be accepted. It is not known whether the experimental subjects performed the exercises after operation. Nevertheless, it was found that the patients who received the specific preparation, i.e., who were given the appropriate information and who were taught the exercises, had a lower mean level of 17-hydroxycorticosteroid hormones in their urine after operation than the control group of patients, who did not receive this planned instruction. The difference between the two groups is significant for the results from the total sample.

In the review of the literature it is mentioned that a rise in glucocorticosteroid secretion is a normal response to operation (Moore, 1959), but the present work indicates that the magnitude of this rise can be modified. It appears that, for a relatively minor operation such as a herniorrhaphy or appendicectomy, the rise can be prevented, or reduced to the extent that excretion is again at pre-operative levels by the second day after operation. It is probable that anxiety caused by admission to hospital promotes an increase in steroid hormone secretion, and the continued fall in 17-hydroxycorticosteroid excretion after operation, in the experimental group of herniorrhaphy patients, demonstrates a return to the patients' normal level of hormone secretion.

A patient experiencing admission to hospital for an operation is exposed to the effect of two main types of stressor, physiological and psychological, and the influence of each varies in different operations.

This is illustrated by the results from the two subdivisions. Those patients who had undergone cholecystectomy had higher levels of 17-hydroxycorticosteroid excretion after operation than those who had undergone herniorrhaphy or appendicectomy. A moderately serious operation, such as a cholecystectomy, acts as a relatively severe physiological stressor. In the patients undergoing this operation the difference between experimental and control groups in the change in steroid excretion is not significant, although the rise in the experimental group was still less than in the control group of patients. The effect of surgery is so great that the reduction in stress due to the minimisation of anxiety is masked. In other words, the steroid secretion due to anxiety probably forms only a small proportion of the total 17-hydroxycorticosteroid secretion in these patients. On the other hand, the effect of anxiety reduction is clearly demonstrated by the results from the herniorrhaphy patients, in whom the diminution in the rise of steroid excretion in the experimental, as compared to the control, group is highly significant. The interpretation placed upon these findings is that the operation itself is a less severe stressor and, therefore, the amount of 17-hydroxycorticosteroid hormones secreted as a result of psychological stress is a much larger proportion of the total steroid hormone secretion in these patients.

Among the cholecystectomy patients the results obtained from one subject in the control group are of particular interest. Almost all individuals undergoing this operation excreted greater amounts of 17-hydroxycorticosteroid hormones after surgery than they had done beforehand. However, in this particular patient steroid levels in the urine were lower after operation, she made very poor progress post-operatively, and had to remain in hospital for many weeks. She was the only patient for whom the assessment of post-operative progress by both the surgical registrar and the ward sister was "very slowly/not well at all". As previously described in the literature reviewed an increase in steroid hormone secretion is essential for adaptation, and adaptation to surgery did not appear to occur satisfactorily in this patient. A recent paper discusses occult adrenal insufficiency in surgical patients (Hubay et al, 1975) and describes several patients in whom this was found after surgery. One of the suggested causes is unrecognised Addison's disease, when the condition may only manifest itself following trauma, surgery, infection, etc. This particular patient had a pigmented skin, one of the early signs of Addison's disease, and it is possible that she was unable to respond to surgery by a normal increase in steroid hormone secretion.

The sodium : potassium ratio in the three-hour urine specimens does not discriminate between the experimental and control groups of patients in this study, although it has been used successfully in investigations of psychological stress in patients who have not undergone surgery. This ratio has been shown to correlate with the level of anxiety experienced in patients admitted to a coronary care unit (Gentry et al, 1973). In addition, Foster (1974) has demonstrated that the sodium : potassium ratio in the urine is amenable to modification by nursing intervention designed to relieve psychological stress. In her study the change in the ratio differentiated between those who received the experimental nursing approach and the control group of patients. The results from the present work, compared to these earlier studies, suggest that the influence of anxiety on this measurement of stress is masked by the greater effect of the operative procedure. In addition, the sodium : potassium ratio in the urine is influenced by other factors, i.e., mineralocorticoid secretion and the intake of these minerals in the diet. Some of these extraneous influences cannot be controlled in a research project and they are likely to reduce the sensitivity of this measurement as an indicator of stress.

The estimation of 17-hydroxycorticosteroid hormones in blood is a direct measure of stress in an individual, and the assay of the excretion products of these hormones in the urine, is, therefore, a more accurate method of evaluating stress than the measurement of the sodium : potassium ratio. However, in the present study a statistically significant negative correlation was found between the sodium : potassium ratio and the steroid hormone excretion in the urine, showing that this ratio is indeed a valid indicator of stress. The cheapness, ease and reliability of the measurement of sodium and potassium suggests that the continued use and evaluation of the sodium : potassium ratio as a measure of stress may be valuable. It may be particularly useful for monitoring the progress of individuals, rather than of groups, in a similar way to Foster's (1974) examination of the direction of change of the ratio in the urine of the individual patients in her groups. On the other hand, it is possible that this ratio will not be sensitive enough for use when patients are experiencing surgery, or are exposed to other such physiological stressors which cannot be modified. In these circumstances the effect on the sodium : potassium ratio of nursing care designed to minimise stress in the patients may be masked.

6.2 Objective Measurements

The measurement of body temperature did not differentiate clearly between the experimental and control groups of patients and did not correlate highly with steroid excretion. However, the rise in temperature demonstrated by the patients after operation, and the return to normal levels over the first four post-operative days, are similar to the findings reported by Folkard (1974). Body temperature is maintained at normal levels by the balance between heat production and heat loss and this balance is regulated by the hypothalamus. It appears that the "thermostat" is reset at a higher temperature at operation and then takes a few days to return to its previous setting. The time required for the return to normal is similar to the time taken, in the present study, for steroid levels to return to their pre-operative values. Steroid hormone secretion is also controlled from the hypothalamus, and it is possible that the nervous stimulation involved in coping with the effects of surgery may spread to other parts of the hypothalamus and affect the temperature regulating centre. However, it would then be expected that the experimental group of herniorrhaphy patients, who did not show a rise in steroid excretion after operation, would also not demonstrate the same rise in temperature as the other patients. Nevertheless, a similar rise in temperature was found in these patients. Therefore, it would appear more likely that this is a direct effect on the temperature regulating centre of the hypothalamus independent of stimulation of the area controlling steroid secretion.

There was practically no difference in the amount of analgesia administered to the patients in the experimental and the control groups in the present work. This finding is of interest because several similar studies have shown that patients who received special preparation before operation required less analgesia after surgery than patients in control groups (Egbert et al, 1964; Schmitt and Wooldridge, 1973; Hayward, 1975). There may be several interacting factors influencing the administration of analgesic drugs to patients and, therefore, the finding in the present study is not easy to explain. In the current research the preparation of the experimental patients included an emphasis on the importance of obtaining adequate amounts of analgesia, in order to facilitate easy movement and satisfactory breathing and coughing. This may have encouraged the experimental patients to request analgesia at a lower level of discomfort than the control patients, although, as discussed later, the patients in the two groups reported similar amounts of pain. In addition, it is possible that trained nurses, responsible for the administration of analgesics regulated by the Controlled Drugs Act, have developed expectations of the amount of analgesia required by patients undergoing specific operations, and administer drugs according to the operation, instead of following an evaluation of the individual patient's needs. It would be valuable to examine more closely the factors involved in reaching the decision to administer analgesic drugs to surgical patients.

The incidence of complications in the different groups was also examined in order to evaluate the effect of pre-operative preparation. It was found that the incidence of complications was greater in the control group of patients, and that the majority of complications occurred among those who had undergone cholecystectomy. Thus, although the change in steroid excretion does not show a significant difference between the experimental and control groups of cholecystectomy patients, the difference in the number of individuals suffering from complications is significant. The most common complications were respiratory and wound infections which suggests that the patient's normal immune response was depressed and, thus, already present bacteria were able to multiply. As discussed earlier, Buescher (1964) suggested that changes in hormone balance may allow latent and sub-clinical infection to become manifest, and it has been found that stress increased the incidence of respiratory infections in students (Jacobs *et al*, 1970). The findings of the present study support the proposition that stress reduces the immune response and aggravates the risk of developing overt infection. However, it appears that the preparation given to the experimental patients lessens this risk significantly by minimising anxiety, resulting in a lower level of steroid secretion. On the other hand, although the patients who developed an infection after operation had a higher mean level of urinary 17-hydroxycorticosteroid excretion on the second and third days post-operatively than those who did not develop an infection, the difference is not significant. In addition, the change in steroid excretion in the experimental and control groups of cholecystectomy patients is not significantly different. It seems likely that the relatively small reduction in steroid hormone secretion among the experimental patients undergoing cholecystectomy was nevertheless great enough to reduce the incidence of overt infection.

6.3 Subjective Scales

None of the subjective measures used (physical state score, mental state score, pain, and doctor's and nurse's assessment) distinguished between the experimental and control groups. However, the physical state score gave a high negative correlation with 17-hydroxycorticosteroid excretion in the urine. Thus, it seems probable that steroid secretion does influence physical state, but that the physical state scale used in the present work was not sensitive enough to demonstrate the difference between the experimental and control groups. Hayward (1975) found that, in one of the two hospitals used for his research, the experimental patients obtained significantly higher scores after operation than the control group on some aspects of physical condition, i.e., sleep, appetite, lack of nausea. It appears necessary to try to develop an indicator of patient condition that considers a number of aspects of physiological well-being, and is more sensitive than that used in the present study. The approach used by Minckley (1974) may be helpful, particularly for research with patients in whom progress can be predicted with some degree of accuracy. A grid of the expected behaviours on succeeding days after a hip replacement operation was devised and the patients' observed behaviour was then compared with this grid. Similar grids could perhaps be developed for the assessment of progress after some other operations, and the usefulness evaluated.

Hayward also found that, in one of the two hospitals, patients who received the pre-operative preparation had a higher "morale" score after operation than the control patients. In the present study no difference between the groups was demonstrated on the mental state scale, which included Hayward's "morale" question. Difficulty was experienced in finding an appropriate method for evaluating the patients' general psychological state after operation, and the attempt was not entirely satisfactory. The development of a satisfactory tool for measuring this would be valuable.

As discussed in the section on pain in the review of the literature, the experience of pain has been described as consisting of two elements, the physical sensation and the reaction to that sensation. Many research studies have attempted to modify the reactive element in pain and to investigate the effect of this change on the experience reported. Several researchers have demonstrated that nursing intervention can diminish the amount of pain experienced by patients (Bochnak et al, 1962; Moss and Meyer, 1966; McBride, 1967) and that pre-operative preparation can reduce the pain suffered after operation (Luna, 1971; Hayward, 1975). However, in the present study, there was no difference between the experimental and control groups in the intensity of pain reported. In a similar study, Johnson (1966) also found that preparation for operation did not affect the pain experienced or the amount of analgesia required after operation. These findings are not easy to explain, but two factors may be involved. Johnson (1966) produced evidence to support the hypothesis that the emotional response to a threatening event is affected by incongruency between expectations and experience. In addition, Blaylock (1968) has discussed the differences between cultural groups in the reaction to pain, partly determined by the meaning attributed, and the expected response, to pain. It is possible that the cultural background of the patients influenced their reporting of the pain experienced. It is also possible that, in the present work, the population from which the sample was drawn have reasonable expectations of the pain likely to be suffered after operation, and the experience was similar to the expectations. In these circumstances the preparation given to the experimental patients would not influence the reactive component of pain, and there would be no demonstrable difference between the two groups.

The lack of differentiation between the two groups by the medical and nursing assessments of the patients' post-operative progress may indicate that the scale used was not sensitive enough to discriminate between the experimental and control groups. The scores given by both doctors and nurses tended to cluster around the mid-point on the scale, but the doctors were less inclined to give a patient a low score than were the nursing staff. This may indicate that the nurses, who have more contact with the patients, are able to appraise the patients' condition more realistically than the medical staff. On the other hand, it is possible that surgeons feel that the success of their work is demonstrated by the satisfactory recovery from surgery of their patients. If so, then this could perhaps influence their assessment of patients' post-operative progress.

6.4   The Second Hypothesis

The second hypothesis states that "a relationship will be demonstrated between the measurement of biochemical indicators of stress and some other indicators of patient welfare". It was found that 17-hydroxycorticosteroid excretion was significantly higher in the control group of patients, and that the incidence of infection was also significantly raised. As discussed earlier, theoretically these two findings are related, but no direct relationship can be demonstrated statistically. The high negative correlation between steroid excretion and physical state score allows the second hypothesis to be accepted, although the measure of physical state used was not sensitive enough to differentiate between the experimental and control groups of patients.

6.5   Theoretical Background

The theoretical background to this research, discussed in the literature review, suggests the most satisfactory explanation for the findings described, namely that the control group of patients had a higher level of steroid hormone excretion and a higher incidence of complications than the experimental group. It is proposed that the explanation for these findings is that the pre-operative preparation reduced anxiety experienced by the experimental patients, and it did this in two ways. Firstly, the information given to the patients before operation allowed them to interpret and understand their surroundings and circumstances, and helped them to anticipate the events usually occurring during the post-operative period. This ability to understand and to anticipate minimises the feeling of helplessness (Lazarus and Averill, 1972), and helplessness being an important component of anxiety (Mandler, 1972), thus, reduces anxiety. Secondly, the learning of exercises, and the performance of these exercises after operation, is likely to give the patient a feeling of involvement in his or her own post-operative progress. Janis (1958) reported that surgical patients felt more in control, and less helpless, when they had some way of contributing to their own recovery. Therefore, the teaching of exercises, by lessening helplessness, should also reduce anxiety. It is also possible that the breathing exercises directly improved respiratory function. However, it is more probable that the differences found between the experimental and control groups were the result of a decrease in anxiety among the experimental patients. The research findings discussed in the section on psychoendocrinology in the literature review, and the positive correlation between anxiety and plasma adrenocorticosteroid levels (Fiorica and Muehl, 1962), reinforce the suggestion that the lower level of 17-hydroxycorticosteroid excretion in the experimental patients was caused by the minimisation of anxiety.

6.6 The Neuman Model

As represented in the Neuman Model applied to nursing (Neuman, 1974) the nurse is involved in the recognition of stressors or potential stressors, of strengths and weaknesses in the patient, and of the reaction to, and recovery following, stress. Emphasis is placed on understanding all the circumstances and the interrelationships between the different aspects considered. Following the recognition of all these factors and assessment of their relative importance, the appropriate intervention, which may be primary, secondary or tertiary, is carried out. The intervention chosen, and the method of implementation selected, is influenced by many factors within the organisation, the nurse and the patient. Conditions such as level of staffing, availability of equipment, and the organisational hierarchy, will influence the way in which a particular nurse is able to carry out the assessment of needs and the implementation of nursing care. The values held by the individual nurse and by the groups to which she belongs, personality factors, and the educational preparation she has received will all modify both the recognition of stressors and the assessment and implementation of the appropriate action. The patient's personality and previous experience will influence his own view of problems and actions considered helpful.

Although the importance of considering all aspects is emphasised by Neuman, it is not possible when carrying out a study such as the present project to evaluate and examine all the relevant variables within the situation. However, it is considered reasonable to examine a specific aspect of care in the light of Neuman's Model, and hope that eventually the findings of many studies may be integrated into a coherent whole.

In the care of surgical patients certain common stressors can be identified which, on theoretical grounds, should affect the majority of these patients. The major physiological stressors are the operation itself and the physiological changes occurring as a result. The damaged tissue causes pain but, although this has a physiological basis, the psychological response to it determines the degree of suffering. Patients in the experimental group in this study were given information about pain, analgesics and relaxation of abdominal muscles to help them cope with this stressor. In addition, a potential physiological stressor is the development of a respiratory infection, and the aim of teaching breathing exercises is to prevent this occurrence. However, with surgical patients the group of stressors most amenable to nursing intervention are the psychological stressors, broadly defined as anxiety. Some important groups of psychological stressors have been identified (Engel, 1962; Lazarus, 1966), and specific factors which cause anxiety in hospital patients have also been described (Levine, 1970; Kornfeld, 1972; Hayward, 1975). In the present study this knowledge was used in developing the schedule of information to be presented to surgical patients before operation. The pre-operative preparation given to the experimental groups was at the level of primary intervention, described by Neuman, with the aim of strengthening the flexible line of defence. This was achieved by giving information to help the patient identify his circumstances and so diminish feelings of helplessness and anxiety. Some studies (Meyers, 1964; Johnson, 1976) have considered the effect of different types of communication on the emotional state of the patient. The present research demonstrates that giving accurate information to surgical patients can lessen the stress experienced several days later.

The Betty Neuman Model: a total person approach to viewing patient problems (Neuman, 1974) has been used as the theoretical framework for the current work. It is suggested that this model may be useful as a conceptual framework for nursing practice and research and merits further, more general, discussion. The designers of this model suggested that it could encompass many of the other proposed models of nursing. Similarly, some previous nursing research, which has been discussed earlier in the present study, can be viewed in terms of Neuman's model, although not originally described in this way. Some investigators have identified stressors, i.e., factors which cause anxiety in hospital patients, and some other researchers have examined methods of modifying the effect of these stressors. In those studies which have evaluated the effect of pre-operative preparation, the degree of stress experienced by the patients has been lessened by primary intervention to strengthen the flexible line of defence and, therefore, minimise the impact of stressors.

Other investigations have examined certain aspects of secondary intervention, as described by Neuman, in which the nurse helps to relieve stress already present. Peplau (1952) emphasised the importance of psychological care in nursing, and many researchers have studied ways in which the nurse can modify the psychological state of the patient and, thus, reduce stress. That pain can be relieved in this manner has been reported (Bochnak *et al*, 1962; Moss and Meyer, 1966; McBride, 1967) and a few studies have demonstrated the relationship between the psychological state and the physiological functioning of an individual. An approach to care in which attention is directed towards the patient as an individual with feelings to be expressed, which is thought to help the patient accept his situation and to relieve psychological stress, has been examined. Pride (1968) and Foster (1974) have both shown that such an "interpersonal approach" to patient care caused changes in biochemical indicators of stress, demonstrating that stress had in fact been reduced.

Although a few researchers have investigated the effect of nursing care on physiological evidence of stress in patients, further work is needed in this area, and it is also necessary to examine critically the indicators of stress employed. The present research project used the most direct measure of stress that was feasible but, for practical reasons, most published nursing studies of stress have examined indirect measurements of stress (sodium : potassium ratio, potassium excretion, eosinophil count, palmar sweat index) or have looked at the effect of nursing intervention on the sympathetic nervous system and the adrenal medulla. Such measures will be useful in some circumstances but require further evaluation.

In theory, Neuman's model appears generally applicable to nursing, and the findings of the present study support this view. However, further evidence of its validity is necessary before it can be accepted for universal use. It would be valuable to examine the short and long-term effects of different types of nursing intervention, primary, secondary and tertiary.

6.7 Recommendations

This research project has demonstrated that giving information about prospective treatment and care, and teaching exercises to be performed post-operatively, reduces stress in surgical patients after operation. This was indicated by a lower excretion of 17-hydroxycorticosteroid hormones in the experimental group of patients. Moreover, the incidence of infection was decreased in these patients. These findings support the results of other work, all of which demonstrate the importance of pre-operative preparation of patients. In addition, the link between the psychological state and the physiological state of an individual is emphasised.

It has already been suggested that further research is carried out to examine the usefulness of Neuman's model for nursing practice, and to assess its value in the development of a conceptual framework for nursing. The remaining recommendations arise from the results of the present study, but also from the findings of other research.

The present work was founded on the theory of stress, as described by Selye (1956), and it is suggested that all nurses should have some knowledge of this concept. At present, many nurses have not met with the word as used in this study. Fundamental to an understanding of stress and its application to nursing is an appreciation of the numerous types of stressors, and the interrelationship between the various factors in a given situation. The recognition of the interrelationship is essential, but it is also necessary to be able to isolate specific factors which may cause stress and learn how to minimise this. In this research considerable emphasis has been placed on the influence of the psychological state of the patient on the level of stress measured. It is known that anxiety increases 17-hydroxycorticosteroid secretion and, therefore, nurses need to develop the ability to recognise differing manifestations of anxiety, and the capacity to help patients by relieving psychological stress. In this context, it is possible to assist the development of an awareness of one's own feelings and the feelings of others, and a sensitivity to non-verbal cues. These attributes are of value in assessing psychological needs and in giving the appropriate care, and the development of these qualities should, perhaps, be included in basic nurse training. However, this then has implications for the planning of curricula for the preparation of nurse educators.

The present study has specifically examined the effect of pre-operative preparation of surgical patients and, with other studies, has clearly demonstrated the importance of this teaching. Therefore, it is the responsibility of the nursing practitioner to ensure that such instruction is included in the pre-operative care of surgical patients. Some aspects, e.g., breathing exercises, may be taught by the physiotherapist, although this is often only for those patients with respiratory problems, but the co-ordination of the teaching, and the reinforcement of the learning, remains the responsibility of the nurse. Undoubtedly, the amount of time required will be a source of difficulty, but it has been shown (Mezzanotte, 1970; Lindeman, 1972) that group instruction can be of equal, or superior, value to individual preparation, and this may aid in the incorporation of such teaching into the ward routine. However, in order to be able to carry out such preparation effectively it is necessary to develop skills in communication and teaching, and this should also be included in basic nurse training.

These suggestions are obviously relevant to nursing practitioners and educators, but also have implications for nursing administrators, who are able to facilitate the improvement of care given to patients. Many trained nurses may need to gain, or improve, skills in teaching and communication to enable them to give better care to their patients. In addition, the opportunity to maintain a high level of professional knowledge, which is continually advancing and changing, is required.

The aim of this study was to increase knowledge about the effect of nursing care on patients, with the hope of improving the care given, and it is felt that some addition to nursing science has been made. However, the dissemination and implementation of research findings is essential if such work is to be a contribution to high quality patient care.

APPENDIX I

Figure 1. Patient data sheet

Name   Study no.

1	2	3

Group no. 1–5

2

Card no.

5	6

Sex. Male 1
       Female 2

7

Date of admission

Date of operation   Operation Hernia   1
                          Cholecystectomy 2
                          Cholecystectomy
                          with exploration
                              C.B.D.   3

8

Surgeon   A   –   1
                            B   –   2

9

Occupation   Social class 1 – 5

10

Age.   18–25   1
         26–35   2
         36–45   3
         46–55   4
         56–65   5

11

Previous operations Yes   1
                          No   2

12

Smoking.   No   1
            Under 10/day 2
            Over 10   3
            Cigars or pipe 4

13

L.M.P.   Not applicable   0
          < 10 days ago   1
          11–13 ,, ,,   2
          14–16 ,, ,,   3
          17–19 ,, ,,   4
          20>   ,,   5

14

78

Figure 2. Experimental results recording form

Name _____ ward _____ operation _____

Complications
None	0
D.V.T.	1
Pulmonary Emb.	2
Respiratory inf.	3
Wound inf.	4
Burst Abdomen	5
Urinary Inf.	6
Urine retention	7
Haemorrhage	8
Other (specify)	9

Study No.				Grp. Card No. and day no.		Temperature			Physical state		Mental state		Pain		Na:K ratio				17-OHCS				Anal-gesics		Drs.Nur. assessment		Compli-cations
1	2	3	4	5	6	7	8	9	10	11	12	13	14	15	16	17	18	19	20	21	22	23	24	25	26	27	28
				0	0														0	0	0		0	0	0		0
				0	1																	0					
				0	2																				0		
				0	3																						
				0	4														0	0	0	0					
				0	5														0	0	0	0					
				0	6														0	0	0	0					
				0	7														0	0	0	0					
				0	8														0	0	0	0					
				0	9														0	0	0	0					
				1	0														0	0	0	0					
				1	1														0	0	0	0					
				1	2														0	0	0	0					
				1	3														0	0	0	0					
				1	4														0			0					

APPENDIX II

Figure 1. Physical condition scale

For each aspect of physical condition shown below the patient will be asked to assess his or her own state. Each item, with the scale printed below, is displayed in large print on a card, and the patient indicates the appropriate position on the scale.

1. Sleep
2. Appetite
3. Strength and energy
4. Stomach condition
5. State of bowels
6. Passing urine
7. Self-assistance
8. Ease in movement

	Very Poor	Poor	Fair	Good	Very Good	Excellent
Scored	1	2	3	4	5	6

Figure 2. Mental state scale

In the same way as for the Physical Condition Scale the patient is asked to assess their state on two items

1. Interest in surroundings
2. General mood

	Very poor	Poor	Fair	Good	Very good	Excellent
Scored	1	2	3	4	5	6

Figure 3. Assessment of pain

The patient is asked to evaluate the amount of pain suffered on the following scale. (From Hayward, 1975.)

Description		Scored
No pain at all		5
A little pain		4
Quite a lot of pain		3
A very bad pain		2
As much pain as I could possibly bear		1

Before the patient is discharged from hospital the Ward Sister or Charge Nurse and the Registrar will be asked to independently complete one of these forms each.

Patient's Name . . . .

Please could you indicate which of the following statements you think best describes the post-operative progress of this patient.

		Scored
Unusually well		5
Better than usual		4
About average		3
Not as well as usual		2
Very slowly/not well at all		1

Form completed by . . . .

82

APPENDIX III

TABLE 1.
Sodium : potassium ratio in 3-hour urine specimens—all patients

	Experimental group				Control group					
	Mean	s.e.	Median	n	Mean	s.e.	Median	n	U	Significant
Pre-operative day	2·508	0·199	2·485	40	2·649	0·231	2·195	40	781·5	No
Post-operative day 1	0·718	0·073	0·705	24	1·025	0·109	0·850	19	153·0	,,
2	1·352	0·216	0·935	36	0·835	0·081	0·865	36	537·5	,,
3	1·313	0·199	0·860	36	1·156	0·158	0·850	39	663·5	,,
4	2·322	0·294	2·020	39	2·180	0·313	1·655	38	683·5	,,
5	2·610	0·257	2·415	38	2·949	0·561	2·003	37	664·0	,,
6	2·655	0·256	2·480	35	3·026	0·288	2·760	34	512·5	,,
7	2·567	0·277	2·460	23	2·353	0·346	1·750	26	249·5	,,
8	2·442	0·400	1·900	21	2·260	0·366	1·875	22	220·0	,,
9	2·120	0·279	1·770	21	1·697	0·213	1·705	20	178·0	,,
10	2·280	0·300	2·215	14	1·856	0·312	1·585	14	80·0	,,
11	2·048	0·290	1·890	13	1·522	0·483	1·285	6	29·0	,,
12	0·956	0·263	1·070	5	1·448	0·661	1·180	5	10·0	,,
13	1·677	0·223	1·64	3	0·820	0·526	0·570	3	—	
14	1·570	—	1·570	1	1·100	0·020	1·100	2	—	

83

TABLE 2.
Variation in body temperature in all patients

	Experimental group			Control group			t	P
	Mean	s.e.	n	Mean	s.e.	n		
Pre-operative day	36·34	0·06	40	36·28	0·06	040	0·76	0·452
Post-operative day 1	36·68	0·06	40	36·74	0·06	40	-0·70	0·483
2	36·72	0·07	40	36·58	0·09	40	1·26	0·210
3	36·57	0·07	40	36·38	0·06	40	2·11	0·038
4	36·31	0·07	39	36·18	0·07	38	1·42	0·159
5	36·37	0·06	39	36·18	0·09	38	1·76	0·083
6	36·23	0·09	37	36·31	0·09	37	-0·58	0·561
7	36·17	0·08	30	36·18	0·12	28	-0·09	0·932
8	36·25	0·08	24	36·39	0·13	25	-0·88	0·386
9	36·19	0·08	22	36·21	0·09	21	-0·23	0·822
10	36·32	0·06	17	36·33	0·09	19	-0·08	0·939
11	36·30	0·10	14	36·24	0·12	10	0·38	0·705
12	36·02	0·08	8	35·80	0·09	6	1·88	0·087
13	36·00	0·00	3	35·93	0·07	3	1·00	0·423
14	36·20	—	1	35·97	0·09	3	2·65	0·118

TABLE 3.

Physical state scores—all patients

		Experimental group			Control group			U	Significant
		Mean	s.e.	n	Mean	s.e.	n		
Pre-operative day		35·22	0·87	40	37·05	0·90	40	662·0	No
Post-operative day	1	22·97	0·52	38	23·36	0·75	39	700·5	,,
	2	26·48	0·07	40	27·10	0·85	40	759·5	,,
	3	28·95	0·73	40	30·58	1·02	40	687·0	,,
	4	31·74	0·87	39	32·55	0·94	38	683·5	,,
	5	34·72	0·89	39	34·97	0·96	38	699·5	,,
	6	35·84	1·20	37	35·49	1·00	37	652·0	,,
	7	37·03	1·09	30	35·79	1·16	28	373·5	,,
	8	37·71	1·42	24	36·21	1·31	24	246·0	,,
	9	38·68	1·35	22	37·14	1·29	21	192·0	,,
	10	39·24	1·64	17	36·90	1·48	19	133·5	,,
	11	40·29	1·56	14	35·90	2·22	10	45·0	,,
	12	41·88	1·91	8	36·33	3·18	6	10·5	,,
	13	40·00	2·52	3	31·33	1·45	3	—	
	14	40·00	—	1	33·00	2·00	3	—	

85

TABLE 4.

Mental state score—all patients

	Experimental group			Control group			U	Significant
	Mean	s.e.	n	Mean	s.e.	n		
Pre-operative day	8·78	0·26	40	9·42	0·27	40	638·5	No
Post-operative day 1	7·16	0·26	38	6·95	0·35	39	722·0	,,
2	7·52	0·27	40	7·52	0·33	40	798·0	,,
3	8·02	0·25	40	8·48	0·28	40	704·0	,,
4	8·33	0·87	39	8·68	0·34	38	710·5	,,
5	9·00	0·32	39	9·32	0·31	38	670·5	,,
6	8·78	0·37	37	9·40	0·31	37	582·5	,,
7	9·17	0·38	30	9·21	0·37	28	419·5	,,
8	9·71	0·42	24	9·38	0·40	24	254·5	,,
9	9·82	0·45	22	9·52	0·39	21	201·5	,,
10	9·76	0·52	17	9·58	0·44	19	150·5	,,
11	9·93	0·52	14	9·40	0·78	10	62·5	,,
12	10·38	0·53	8	9·67	0·80	6	18·0	,,
13	10·33	0·88	3	8·00	0·00	3	—	
14	9·00	—	1	8·00	1·16	3	—	

TABLE 5.

Pain score—all patients. (High score indicates less pain)

		Experimental group			Control group				
		Mean	s.e.	n	Mean	s.e.	n	U	Significant
Pre-operative day		9·45	0·14	40	9·45	0·14	40	800·0	No
Post-operative day	1	6·71	0·21	38	7·05	0·20	39	634·5	,,
	2	7·55	0·21	40	7·28	0·22	40	701·5	,,
	3	7·80	0·20	40	7·75	0·22	40	799·0	,,
	4	8·26	0·17	39	8·05	0·19	38	669·5	,,
	5	8·56	0·16	39	8·47	0·18	38	716·0	,,
	6	8·70	0·22	37	8·65	0·16	37	623·5	,,
	7	8·83	0·17	30	8·79	0·23	28	415·0	,,
	8	9·17	0·21	24	9·08	0·23	24	275·0	,,
	9	9·14	0·20	22	9·05	0·24	21	227·0	,,
	10	9·24	0·24	17	9·42	0·21	19	142·0	,,
	11	9·43	0·27	14	9·10	0·31	10	56·5	,,
	12	10·00	0·38	8	9·33	0·42	6	17·0	,,
	13	8·67	1·33	3	9·00	0·58	3	—	,,
	14	10·00	—	1	9·33	0·67	3	—	,,

TABLE 6.
Results obtained on doctor's and nurse's assessment

Doctor's assessment		Experimental group	Control group
Score	1	—	1
	2	4	4
	3	16	15
	4	18	18
	5	2	2
Mean		3·450	3·400
s.e.		0·118	0·133
n		40	40

Nurse's assessment		Experimental group	Control group
Score	1	—	2
	2	7	5
	3	22	21
	4	10	12
	5	1	—
Mean		3·125	3·075
s.e.		0·114	0·126
n		40	40

Glossary

ADRENOCORTICOTROPHIC HORMONE (ACTH). Hormone secreted from the anterior pituitary gland. Stimulates the formation and release of corticosteroid hormones from the adrenal cortex. Its main action is to stimulate the release of glucocorticoid hormones but it also facilitates the release of mineralocorticoid hormones.

ALIQUOT. A small part of a larger sample.

CATACHOLAMINES. Substances produced by the adrenal medulla and the nerve endings of the sympathetic nervous system, i.e., adrenaline and noradrenaline.

CORTICOSTEROID HORMONES. A group of hormones produced by the adrenal cortex. They all have a similar structure, based on the steroid nucleus, but with minor structural variations which determine their different actions in the body. The three types of steroid hormones produced by the adrenal cortex are:

Glucocorticoids—with many different metabolic effects—(see page 16).

Mineralocorticoids—which affect fluid and electrolyte balance.

Sex hormones.

CREATININE. A substance excreted from the body as a result of muscle metabolism. The amount of creatinine excreted from the body remains remarkably constant from day to day and, when expressed in terms of body size, is similar in different individuals of the same age and sex. Therefore, the excretion of other substances can be related to the amount of creatinine excreted.

EOSINOPHILS. A type of white blood cell which stains with an acid dye. Glucocorticoids decrease the numbers circulating in the blood by causing them to remain in the lungs and spleen.

17-HYDROXYCORTICOSTEROID HORMONES. Hormones which have a hydroxyl (-OH) group on carbon atom number 17 of the steroid nucleus. The major glucocorticoid hormone released in stress (cortisol) is one of these hormones.

HYPOTHALAMUS. Part of the brain just above the pituitary gland. Controls many of the physiological activities of the body, including endocrine function. Releases Corticotrophin Releasing Factor which is carried in the blood to the anterior pituitary gland where it stimulates the release of Adrenocorticotrophic hormone.

INTERPERSONAL NURSING APPROACH or NURSE-PATIENT INTERACTION PROCESS. An approach to the process of nursing care which aims to relieve psychological stress and anxiety. The emphasis is on treating the patient as an individual with his or her own fears, perceptions and needs, and helping him/her to meet those needs.

LIMBIC SYSTEM. This is made up of a number of parts of the brain including some tissue of the cerebral cortex, the amygdala, hippocampus and septal nuclei. It is concerned with the control of emotional states, and relaying the effects of emotional states to the rest of the body through the hypothalamus.

METABOLISM. The sum of all biochemical reactions taking place in the body. Can be divided into:
Anabolism—in which complex substances are built up, and
Catabolism—in which substances are broken down into smaller molecules.

NON-ESTERIFIED FATTY ACIDS or FREE FATTY ACIDS. These are released from the breakdown of triglycerides, in neutral fat in adipose tissue. Triglycerides are formed from one molecule of glycerol and three molecules of fatty acids and their breakdown is increased by glucocorticoids.

PALMAR SWEAT INDEX. A measure of the activity of sweat glands. Using a special technique the number of active sweat glands in a specific area of the finger is counted, and the alteration in activity can then be noted.

STRESS. The non-specifically induced changes within a biological system which result in specific physiological changes. These changes involve altered hormone secretion, particularly an increase in ACTH and, therefore, corticosteroid hormone secretion, and increased activity of the sympathetic nervous system and adrenal medulla.

STRESSORS. Factors which cause the changes which occur in stress. They may be internal or external to the body. Physiological changes such as hypoglycaemia or disease, environmental factors, for example, heat, cold or over-crowding, or psychological states such as anxiety, can all act as stressors.

VANILLYLMANDELIC ACID. Produced in the body from the breakdown of catacholamines, and excreted in the urine.

References

AIKEN, L. H. (1972) Systematic relaxation to reduce pre-operative stress. *Can Nurse,* **68,** 38–42.

ANDERSEN, R. (1973) Post-operative pain and nausea. *Tidsskr Nor Laegeforen,* (Engl Abstract). **93,** 1368–1369.

AYDELOTTE, M. K. and TENER, M. E. (1960) *An Investigation of the relation between nursing activity and patient welfare.* Nurse Utilisation Project Staff, State University of Iowa.

BARTTER, F. C., DELEA, C. S. and HALBERG, F. (1962) Map of blood and urinary changes related to circadian variations in adrenal cortical function in normal subjects. *Ann NY Acad Sci,* **98,** 969–983.

BEECHER, H. K. (1956) Limiting factors in experimental pain. *J Chronic Dis,* **4,** 11–21.

BEECHER, H. K. (1957) The measurement of pain. *Pharmacol Rev,* **9,** 59–209.

BILLEWICZ, W. Z. (1964) Matched samples in medical investigation. *Br J Prev Soc Med,* **18,** 167–173.

BIRD, B. (1955) Psychological aspects of pre-operative and post-operative care. *Am J Nurs,* **55,** 685–687.

BLAYLOCK, J. (1968) Psychological and cultural influences on the reaction to pain: A review of the literature. *Nurs Forum,* **7,** 271–272.

BOCHNAK, M. A., RHYMES, J. and LEONARD, R. C. (1962) Comparison of two types of nursing activity on the relief of pain. In: *Innovations in nurse-patient relationships: automatic or reasoned nurse actions.* (ANA Clinical Papers No. 6) 5–11. New York, American Nurses' Association.

BOGDONOFF, M. D., ESTES, E. H., HARLAN, W. R., TROUT, D. L. and KIRSHNER, N. (1960) Metabolic and cardiovascular changes during a state of acute nervous system arousal. *J Clin Endocrinol Metab,* **20,** 1333–1340.

BONDY, P. K. and RONENBERG, L. E. (eds.) (1974) *Duncan's diseases of metabolism—endocrinology.* 7th ed. Philadelphia, W. B. Saunders Co.

BOORE, J. R. P. (1976) *An investigation into the effect of some aspects of pre-operative preparation of patients on post-operative stress and recovery,* Unpublished PhD. Thesis, University of Manchester.

BRITTON, B. J., HAWKEY, C., WOOD, W. G. and PEELE, M. (1974) Stress—a significant factor in venous thrombosis. *Br J Surg,* **61,** 814–820.

BUESCHER, E. L. (1964) Psychophysiological factors in susceptibility and response: a survey. In: *Symposium on medical aspects of stress in the military climate.* Walter Reed Army Institute of Research, Walter Reed Army Medical Center, Washington D.C.

BURSTEN, B. and RUSS, J. J. (1965) Pre-operative psychological state and corticosteroid levels of surgical patients. *Psychosom Med,* **27,** 309–316.

CANNON, W. B. and de la PAZ, D. (1911) Emotional stimulation of adrenal secretion. *Am J Physiol,* **28,** 64–70.

CARNEVALI, D. L. (1966) Pre-operative anxiety. *Am J Nurs,* **66,** 1536–1538.

CHAPMAN, J. S. (1970) ·Effects of different nursing approaches on psychological and physiological responses. *Nurs Research Reports 5.* American Nurses Foundation.

COLLART, M. E. and BRENNEMAN, J. K. (1971) Preventing post-operative atelectasis. *Am J Nurs,* **71,** 1982–1987.

CONROY, R. T. W. L. and MILLS, J. N. (1970) *Human Circadian Rhythms.* London, J. and A. Churchill.

COSGRIFF, S. W. (1951) Thromboembolic complications associated with ACTH and cortisone therapy. *JAMA,* **147,** 924–926.

DAVIS, J. O. (1967) The regulation of aldosterone secretion. In: Eisenstein, A. B. (ed.) *The adrenal cortex,* Boston, Little, Brown & Company.

DREW, F. L., MORIARTY, R. W. and SHAPIRO, A. P. (1968) An approach to the measurement of the pain and anxiety responses of surgical patients. *Psychosom Med,* **30,** 826–836.

DUMAS, R. G. (1966) Utilisation of a concept of stress as a basis for nursing practice. *In: ANA Clinical Sessions,* 193–212. (San Francisco) New York, Appleton Century Crofts.

DUMAS, R. G. and LEONARD, R. C. (1963) Effect of nursing on the incidence of post-operative vomiting. *Nurs Res,* **12,** (Winter) 12–15.

EGBERT, L. D., BATTIT, C. E., WELCH, C. E. and BARTLETT, M. K. (1964) Reduction of post-operative pain by encouragement and instruction of patients. *N Engl J Med,* **270,** 825–827.

ENGEL, G. L. (1962) *Psychological development in health and disease.* Philadelphia, Saunders.

FIORICA, V. and MUEHL, S. (1962) The relationship between plasma levels of 17-OHCS and a psychological measure of manifest anxiety. *Psychosom Med,* **24,** 596–599.

FITZMAURICE, J. B. and SASAHARA, A. A. (1974) Current concepts of pulmonary embolism: implications for nursing practice. *Heart and Lung: The Journal of Cricital Care,* **3,** 209–218.

FOLKARD, S. (1974) *Personal communication.*

FOSTER, S. B. (1974) An adrenal measure for evaluating nursing effectiveness. *Nurs Res,* **23,** 118–124.

FRANKENHAEUSER, M. (1967) Some aspects of research in physiological psychology. In: Levi, L., (ed.) *Emotional stress, physiological and psychological reactions—medical, industrial and military implications.* Basel, Karger.

FRANKENHAEUSER, M. and JÄRPE, G. (1963) Psychophysiological changes during infusions of adrenaline in various doses. *Psychopharmacologia,* **4,** 424–432.

FRANKSSON, C. and GEMZELL, C. A. (1955) Adrenocortical activity in the pre-operative period. *J Clin Endocrinol Metab,* **15,** 1069–1072.

FRÖBERG, J., KARLSON, C., LEVI, L. and LIDBERG, L. (1971) Physiological and biochemical stress reactions induced by psychosocial stimuli. In: Levi, L. (ed.) *Society, stress and disease. Vol 1. The psychosocial environment and psychosomatic disease.* London, Oxford University Press.

GANONG, W. F. (1977) *Review of medical physiology* (8th ed.) Los Altos, Lange Medical Publications.

GENTRY, W. D., MUSANTE, G. J. and HANEY, T. (1973) Anxiety and urinary sodium/potassium as stress indicators on admissions to a coronary care unit. *Heart and Lung: The Journal of Critical Care,* **2,** 875–877.

GRAHAM, L. E. and CONLEY, E. M. (1971) Evaluation of anxiety and fear in adult surgical patients. *Nurs Res,* **20,** 113–122.

HAFT, J. I. and FANI, K. (1973) Intravascular platelet aggregation in the heart induced by stress. *Circulation,* **47,** 353–358.

HALL, R., ANDERSON, J., SMART, G. A. and BESSER, M. (1974) *Fundamentals of clinical endocrinology.* London, Pitman Medical.

HANDLON, J. H., WADESON, R. W., FISHMAN, J. R., SACHER, E. J., HAMBURG, D. A. and MASON, J. W. (1962) Psychological factors lowering plasma 17-Hydroxycorticosteroid concentration. *Psychosom Med,* **24,** 535–542.

HAYWARD, J. (1975) *Information—a prescription against pain.* (The study of nursing care: series 2) London, Royal College of Nursing.

HEALY, K. (1968) Does pre-operative instruction make a difference? *Am J Nurs,* **68,** 62–67.

HENDERSON, V. (1966) *The nature of nursing.* New York, Macmillan.

HODGSON, C. H. and GOOD, C. A. (1964) Pulmonary embolism and infarction. *Med Clin North Am,* **48,** 977–992.

HUBAY, C. A., WECKESSER, E. C. and LEVY, R. P. (1975) Occult adrenal insufficiency in surgical patients. *Ann Surg,* **81,** 325–332.

JACOBS, M. A., SPILKEN, A. Z., NORMAN, M. M. and ANDERSON, L. S. (1970) Life stress and respiratory illness. *Psychosom Med,* **32,** 233–242.

JANIS, I. L. (1958) *Psychological stress, psychoanalytic and behavioural studies of surgical patients.* New York, John Wiley & Sons.

JOHNSON, J. E. (1966) Influence of purposeful nurse-patient interaction on the patient's post-operative course. *In: Exploring progress in medical-surgical nursing practice.* No. 2, 16–22. (A series of papers presented at the 1965 Regional Clinical Conference sponsored by the American Nurses' Association in Washington and Chicago) New York, American Nurses' Association.

JOHNSON, J. E. (1976) Stress reduction through sensation information. *In:* Sarason, I. G. and Spielberger, C. D. (eds.) *Stress and Anxiety* **2,** New York. Halstad Press.

KORNFELD, D. S. (1972) The hospital environment: its impact on the patient. In: Lipowski, Z. J. (ed.) *Advances in psychosomatic medicine. Psychosocial aspects of physical illness.* **8,** 252–270.

LAGERLÖF, H. (1967) Psychophysiological reactions during emotional stress: medical implications. In: Levi, L. (ed.) *Emotional stress, physiological and psychological reactions—medical, industrial and military implications.* Basel, Karger.

LAZARUS, R. S. (1966) *Psychological stress and the coping process.* New York, McGraw-Hill.

LAZARUS, R. S. (1971) The concepts of stress and disease. In: Levi, L. (ed.) *Society, stress and disease. 1. The psychological environment and psychosomatic disease.* London, Oxford University Press.

LAZARUS, R. S. and AVERILL, J. R. (1972) Emotion and cognition: with special reference to anxiety. In: Spielberger, C. D. (ed.) *Anxiety: current trends in theory and research.* New York, Academic Press.

LEVI, L. (ed.) (1971) *Society, stress and disease. Vol 1. The psychosocial environment and psychosomatic disease.* London, Oxford Unversity Press.

LEVINE, D. C. (1970) Fears, facts and fantasies about pre- and post-operative care. *Nurs Outlook,* **18,** 26–28.

LINDEMAN, C. A. (1972) Nursing intervention with the presurgical patient —effectiveness and efficiency of group and individual pre-operative teaching —phase 2. *Nurs Res,* **21,** 196–209.

LINDEMAN, C. A. and STETZER, S. L. (1973) Effect of pre-operative visits by operating room nurses. *Nurs Res,* **22,** 4–16.

LINDEMAN, C. A. and VAN AERNAM, B. (1971) Nursing intervention with the presurgical patient—the effects of structured and unstructured pre-operative teaching. *Nurs Res,* **20,** 319–332.

LIVINGSTON, W. K. (1944) *Pain mechanisms.* New York, MacMillan Co.

LOISEAU, M. M. L., HEMMER, C., BOISIVON, A. and GERBAL, R. (1971) Source of surgical wound infection. (Contribution a l'etude de l'origine de l'infection en milieu chirurgical) *Pathol Biol,* **19,** 847–855.

LUNA, H. Q. (1971) The effects of varied types of nursing approach on pain behaviour after surgery. *ANPHI Pap,* **6,** 7–31.

MALMO, R. and SHAGASS, C. (1949) Physiologic studies to reaction to stress in anxiety and early schizophrenia. *Psychosom Med,* **20,** 9–24.

MALMSTROM, E. J. (1972) *Composite mood adjective check list.* (mimeographed). Los Angeles, University of California.

MANDLER, G. (1972) Helplessness: theory and research in anxiety. In: Spielberger, C. D. (ed.) *Anxiety, current trends in theory and research.* **2.** New York, Academic Press.

MASON, J. W. (1964) Psychoendocrine approaches in stress research. In: *Symposium on medical aspects of stress in the military climate.* 378–379 Washington DC, Walter Reed Army Institute of Research.

MASON, J. W. and BRADY, J. V. (1964) The sensitivity of psychoendocrine systems to social and physical environment. In: Liederman, H. and Shapiro, D. (eds.) *Psychobiological approaches to social behaviour.* Palo Alto, Stanford University Press.

McBRIDE, M. A. B. (1967) Nursing approach, pain and relief: an exploratory experiment. *Nurs Res,* **16,** 337–341.

MERTZ, H. (1962) Nurse actions that reduce stress in patients. (Clinical papers no. 1) In: *Emergency intervention by the nurse.* 10–14. New York, American Nurses' Association.

MEYERS, M. E. (1964) Effects of types of communication on patients' reaction to stress. *Nurs Res,* **13,** 126–131.

MEZZANOTTE, E. J. (1970) Group instruction in preparation for surgery. *Am J Nurs,* **70,** 89–91.

MINCKLEY, B. B. (1974) Physiologic and psychologic responses of elective surgical patients: early definite or late indefinite scheduling of surgical procedure. *Nurs Res,* **23,** 392–401.

MOORE, F. D. (1959) *Metabolic care of the surgical patient.* Philadelphia, Saunders.

MORTON, A. (1973) Respiratory preparation for abdominal surgery. *Med J Aust,* **1,** 1300–1303.

MOSS, F. T. and MEYER, B. (1966) Effects of nursing interaction upon pain relief in patients. *Nurs Res,* **15,** 303–306.

MULLAN, J. and VAN SCHOICK, M. (1958) Intractible pain. *Am J Nurs,* **58,** 228–230.

MUNDAY, A. (1973) *Physiological measures of anxiety in hospital patients.* (The study of nursing care, series 2) London, Royal College of Nursing.

MURRAY, J. B. (1971) Psychology of the pain experience. *J Psychol,* **78,** 193–206.

NEUMAN, B. M. (1974) The Betty Neuman health-care systems model: a total person approach to patient problems. In: Riehl, J. P. and Roy, C. *Conceptual models for nursing practice.* New York, Appleton Century Crofts.

NICHOLS, G. A. and KUCHA, D. H. (1972) Taking adult temperatures: oral measurements. *Am J Nurs,* **72,** 1091–1093.

NICHOLS, G. A. and VERHONICK, P. J. (1967) Time and temperature. *Am J Nurs,* **67,** 2304–2306.

NIE, N. H., HULL, C. H., JENKINS, J. G., STEINBRENNER, K. and BENT, D. H. (1975) *Statistical package for the social sciences.* (2nd ed.) New York, McGraw-Hill.

NOWLIS, V. (1966) Research with the mood adjective check list. In: Tomkins, S. and Izard, C. (eds.) *Alert, cognition and personality.* London, Tavistock.

PEPLAU, H. (1952) *Interpersonal relations in nursing.* New York, Putnams.

POHL, M. L. (1973) *Teaching function of the nursing practitioner.* 2nd ed. Dubuque, William C. Brown Co.

PRIDE, L. F. (1968) An adrenal stress index as a criterion measure for nursing. *Nurs Res,* **17,** 292–303.

RAAB, W. (1971) Cardiotoxic biochemical effects of emotional-environmental stressors—fundamentals of psychocardiology. In: Levi, L. (ed.) *Society, stress and disease. Vol. I. The psychosocial environment and psychosomatic disease.* London, Oxford University Press.

REDMAN, B. K. (1972) *Process of patient teaching in nursing.* (2nd ed.) St. Louis, C. V. Mosby Co.

ROESSLER, R. and GREENFIELD, N. S. (eds.) (1962) *Physiological correlates of psychological disorder.* Madison, University of Wisconsin Press.

ROSS, E. J. (1959) *Aldosterone in clinical and experimental medicine.* Oxford, Blackwell Scientific Publications.

SCHACHTER, S. and SINGER, J. E. (1962) Cognitive, social and physiological determinants of emotional state. *Psychol Rev,* **69,** 379–399.

SCHMITT, F. E. and WOOLDRIDGE, J. (1973) Psychological preparation of surgical patients. *Nurs Res,* **22,** 108–116.

SCHUMACHER, G. A., GOODELL, H., HARDY, J. D. and WOLFF, H. G. (1940) Uniformity of the pain threshold in man. *Science,* **92,** 110–112.

SELYE, H. (1936) Thymus and adrenals in the response of the organism to injuries and intoxications. *Br J Exp Pathol,* **17,** 234–248.

SELYE, H. (1956) *The stress of life.* New York, McGraw-Hill Book Co.

SELYE, H. (1958) *The chemical prevention of cardiac necroses.* New York, Ronald Press.

SIEGEL, S. (1956) *Nonparametric statistics for the behavioural sciences.* Tokyo, McGraw-Hill Kogakusha Ltd.

SIMON, A., HERBERT, C. C. and STRAUS, R. (eds.) (1961) *The physiology of emotions.* Springfield, C. C. Thomas.

SPIELBERGER, C. D. (1966) *Anxiety and behaviour.* New York and London, Academic Press.

TOLSON, W. W., MASON, J. W., SACHAR, E. J., HAMBURG, D. A., HANDLON, J. H. and FISHMAN, J. R. (1965) Urinary catecholamine responses associated with hospital admission in normal human subjects. *J Psychosom Res,* **8,** 365–372.

VARLEY, H., GOWENLOCK, A. H. and BELL, M. (1976) *Practical clinical biochemistry. Vol 2. Hormones, vitamins, drugs and poisons.* 5th ed., London, Heinemann Medical.

VENNING, E. H., DYRENFURTH, I. and BECK, J. C. (1957) Effect of anxiety upon aldosterone excretion in man. *J Clin Endocrinol Metab,* **17,** 1005–1008.

VERNON, D. T. A. and BIGELOW, D. A. (1974) Effect of information about a potentially stressful situation on responses to stress impact. *J Pers Soc Psychol,* **29,** 50–59.

VIRCHOW, R. (1856) Weitere untersuchungen uber die verstopfung der lungenarterie und ihre folgen. In: *Gesammelte abhandlungen zur wissenschaftlichen medicin* 227 (from Traube's Beitr. Z experiment) Pathologie u. Physiologie, **2,** 21, 1846).

VOLICER, B. J. and BOHANNON, M. W. (1975) A hospital stress rating scale. *Nurs Res,* **24,** 352–359.

WELCH, B. L. (1964) Psychophysiological response to the mean level of environmental stimulation: a theory of environmental integration. In: *Symposium on medical aspects of stress in the military climate.* Walter Reed Army Institute of Research, Walter Reed Army Medical Center, Washington DC.

WOLFER, J. A. (1973) Definition and assessment of surgical patients welfare and recovery: selected review of the literature. *Nurs Res,* **22,** 394–401.

WOLFER, J. A. and DAVIS, C. E. (1970) Assessment of surgical patients pre-operative emotional condition and post-operative welfare. *Nurs Res,* **19,** 402–414.